ENDING
GOVERNMENT
BAILOUTS

As We Know Them

ENDING GOVERNMENT BAILOUTS

As We Know Them

EDITED BY
Kenneth E. Scott
George P. Shultz
John B. Taylor

AUTHORS
Nicholas F. Brady
Darrell Duffie
Joseph Grundfest
Richard Herring
Thomas M. Hoenig
Thomas Jackson
William F. Kroener III
Charles S. Morris
Kenneth E. Scott
George P. Shultz
Kenneth Spong
Johannes Stroebel
Kimberly Anne Summe
John B. Taylor
Paul Volcker

HOOVER INSTITUTION PRESS
STANFORD UNIVERSITY
STANFORD, CALIFORNIA

The Hoover Institution on War, Revolution and Peace, founded
at Stanford University in 1919 by Herbert Hoover, who went on
to become the thirty-first president of the United States, is an
interdisciplinary research center for advanced study on domestic and
international affairs. The views expressed in its publications are entirely
those of the authors and do not necessarily reflect the views of the staff,
officers, or Board of Overseers of the Hoover Institution.

www.hoover.org

Hoover Institution Press Publication No. 588
Copyright © 2009 by the Board of Trustees of the
    Leland Stanford Junior University
First printing, 2010
16 15 14 13 12 11 10   9 8 7 6 5 4 3 2 1

Manufactured in the United States of America

The paper used in this publication meets the minimum requirements
of the American National Standard for Information Sciences—
Permanence of Paper for Printed Library Materials,
ANSI Z39.48–1992. ⊚

Cataloging-in-Publication Data is available from Library of Congress
ISBN 978-0-8179-1124-9 (cloth: alk. paper)
ISBN 978-0-8179-1123-2 (e-book versions)

CONTENTS

v

PART III WHAT FINANCIAL FIRMS CAN DO

PART IV BANKRUPTCY VERSUS RESOLUTION AUTHORITY

PREFACE

Last spring, around the time Congress began considering and modifying the financial reforms proposed by the U.S. Treasury, our Working Group on Economic Policy at the Hoover Institution decided to establish a "Resolution Project" to focus on alternative ways to deal with failing financial institutions. We were motivated by the growing backlash around the country about the bailouts and our own concerns that the bailout mentality was a grave danger to the country. The Resolution Project included Andrew Crockett, Darrell Duffie, Richard Herring, Thomas Jackson, William Kroener, Kenneth Scott, George Shultz, Kimberly Summe, and John Taylor. Ken Scott became the chairman of the Project and recruited the participants, organized the meetings, and provided overall leadership.

The first meeting of the Resolution Project was held in August, and soon we found ourselves diving into the weeds of qualified financial contracts, convertible contingent debt, the third party repo market, and the U.S. Bankruptcy Code. We had no choice other than to get into these details if we were going to understand, let alone solve, the bailout problem. But we also had to be able to pull back from the weeds, and so George Shultz wrote down some broad ideas organized around the theme "Make Failure Tolerable." From this theme we then decided to broaden our scope and aim the work of the Resolution Project toward a conference where we would invite others to speak on related topics or to comment and critique. The conference was held in December 2009, and the papers presented there became the chapters in this volume. We were delighted that experienced senior policy makers such as Nick Brady, Paul Volcker, Tom Hoenig, and Gary Stern agreed to contribute and that many distinguished attorneys and economists were able to participate and add to the commentary.

The chapters are organized into four parts. Part I starts with George Shultz presenting the ideas and questions that underlie the theme of the book. It then moves on to remarks by former Federal Reserve chairman Paul Volcker and former secretary of the Treasury Nicholas Brady. All three express their concerns about the dangers of bailouts and call for, among other reforms, tightening the limits on the activities of banks with access to the Fed's discount window as a way to reduce the likelihood of bailouts.

Part II then examines the nature of systemic risk, starting with a review by John Taylor of the academic and policy literature and then delving into the experience with the Lehman Brothers bankruptcy by Kimberly Summe. A common theme of both the literature review and the practical experience with Lehman is that the direct connection between financial firms appears to be a smaller problem than commonly believed. The evidence shows that direct connections between banks in the interbank loan market would not lead to significant cascading and that none of the derivative counterparties to Lehman filed bankruptcy.

Part III considers reforms that financial firms can implement, whether or not induced or required by government regulatory agencies. Darrell Duffie shows how firms' issuance of debt that is convertible into equity at the time of crisis can automatically increase capital ratios just when such an increase is needed. He also considers mandatory rights offerings with the same purpose. Richard Herring's proposal is that financial firms develop wind-down plans and file these with their regulators and supervisors for approval. To deal with international complexities, supervisors in different countries could then develop a set of principles for wind-down plans based on firms' submissions. In the third chapter in Part III, Joe Grundfest raises some practical implementation questions about wind-down problems and offers some suggestions about how to deal with these problems.

Part IV explores in detail the two main alternatives to government bailouts in the case of a failing financial firm: bankruptcy versus resolution authority. Bill Kroener leads off with a review of the pros and cons of expanding the FDIC resolution authority, drawing on his experience at the FDIC. Tom Hoenig, in a chapter coauthored with Chuck Morris and Ken Spong, then lays out an explicit example of how a resolution authority could operate subject to a well-understood and consistent set of rules and procedures. Tom Jackson offers a new proposal for bankruptcy for failing financial firms, which he calls Chapter 11F. He shows how various objections to the bankruptcy process can be dealt with in practice. Following these proposals, Ken Scott reviews and evaluates them from the perspective of a number of essential elements that a good resolution process must address.

Following the chapters, Johannes Stroebel provides a summary of the commentary on the chapters by formal discussants and the audience at the conference. The commentary ranges from constructive critiques to strong endorsements to ideas for future research.

While the chapters in this book cover an enormous range of topics, several conclusions or recommendations can be gleaned from them as well as from the commentary. The concluding summary by George Shultz and John Taylor endeavors to do so. Finally, a brief overview of what went wrong is provided in an appendix by Ken Scott. It shows that it is indeed possible to explain the causes of the crisis in understandable terms and clarifies why resolving the bailout problem is essential to preventing future crises.

KENNETH E. SCOTT, GEORGE P. SHULTZ,
AND JOHN B. TAYLOR

Acknowledgments

The conference which led to this book was the third policy conference sponsored by the Working Group on Economic Policy at the Hoover Institution. The first was held in July 2008 and the second in March 2009. We gratefully acknowledge the following individuals and foundations, as well as those wishing to remain anonymous, for their significant support of the Working Group and this book:

Lynde and Harry Bradley Foundation
Preston and Carolyn Butcher
Stephen and Sarah Page Herrick
William E. Simon Foundation

We wish to thank John Cogan, Darrell Duffie, Joseph Grundfest, and other members of the Working Group for brainstorming as we put the conference together. Many of the chapters were written as part of the "Resolution Project" which is also sponsored by the Working Group.

We want to thank the dedicated staff of the Hoover Institution who helped with the conference, especially Marie-Christine Slakey and Christy Hamilton, and those who helped produce the book, especially Michael Bass, Marshall Blanchard, Linda Kulman, Stephen Langlois, Jennifer

Presley, Aline Magee, Julie Ruggiero, and Eryn Witcher. The acknowledgments by authors of the chapters in the book are referenced in the notes to the chapters.

KENNETH E. SCOTT, GEORGE P. SHULTZ,
AND JOHN B. TAYLOR

PART I

THE DANGER OF BAILOUTS AND KEY PRINCIPLES OF REFORM

1

Make Failure Tolerable

Geoge P. Shultz

These are tough times for the U.S. economy and for many others around the world. Tense moments in the last half of 2008 produced unprecedented actions that, according to recently published detailed accounts, were taken without the benefit of reflective strategy, on a case-by-case basis, and in an environment of panic. The result, especially in the United States, has been massive bailouts of faltering organizations with consequent commitment of huge amounts of taxpayer dollars and heavy involvement of the federal government through ownership in customarily private sector activities: selecting boards of directors and chief executives, regulating pay, and otherwise influencing corporate behavior. The American people are clearly upset about these bailouts. In the view of many, the people who created the problem should pay a penalty instead of being bailed out by the taxpayers. Who would disagree with that sentiment?

Difficult times are still with us and clearly lie ahead. Unemployment is high, the Fed has unleashed every trick in its bag (and even some that no one realized were in its bag) to stimulate the economy, government spending seems out of control, tax rates are rising with the clear prospect of more to come and with their well-documented disincentive effects, and protectionist actions are all too evident. Remember, the 1930s were characterized by the heavy tax of virulent protectionism and an increase in the top marginal income tax rate from 25 percent in 1932 to 80 percent by 1936.

WHAT TO DO?

The way to proceed is to set a strategy designed to produce growth based on the vigor of the private sector with inflation under control. One essential pillar of that strategy must deal with the current bailout mentality. The right question is, How do we make failure tolerable? If clear and credible measures can be put into place that convince everybody that failure will be allowed, then the expectations of bailouts will recede and perhaps even disappear. We would also get rid of the risk-inducing behavior that even implicit government guarantees bring about. "Heads, I win; tails, you lose" will always lead to excessive risk. And we would get rid of the unfair competitive advantage given to the "too big to fail" group by the implicit government guarantee behind their borrowing and other activities. At the same time, by being clear about what will happen and that failure can occur without risk to the system, we avoid the creation of a panic environment.

Here are a few ideas that can help make failure tolerable.

1. The first is to make a careful assessment of just what systemic risk means and how it comes about. In recent times, the words "systemic risk" have taken on the impact of a yell of "Fire!" in a crowded theater. Careful analysis is essential. My own experience with labor disputes thought to be national emergencies and a few other so-called failure situations tells me that the problem can be overestimated or can be reasonably contained. So, what are the size dimensions of the problem? Remember, markets can handle lots of size. What are the kinds of interconnections that cause trouble? Are certain kinds of activities so risky that they need to be reined in somehow? To what degree does excessive leverage create problems? Can capital requirements be structured in such a way that any risk is borne in important ways by the person deciding to take the risk? Are some activities too risky to permit financial organizations to use them for their own accounts?

2. How might intervention deal directly with the issues posed by a failure rather than by using a bailout to prevent the failure in the first place? Such action depends on the earlier analysis of what creates the risk. Then these questions arise: How can these risks be dealt with directly? What can be learned from other areas, such as the handling of major labor disputes, about how to handle systemic risk?

3. The phrase "too big to fail" implies some sort of restriction on size that would place an unnatural limit on reach and capacity. Actually, the difficulties of managing very large, disparate, and complex organizations tend to limit size. Competitors tend to cut them down. That is the

history of conglomerates in the United States. Nevertheless, financial institutions present special problems because, by their nature, their activities can affect large sectors of the economy.

4. So, an escalating schedule could be required of necessary capital ratios geared to size and matched with escalating limits on leverage. The presumption here is that size happens because it brings advantages. Since size implies a certain risk to society, some additional costs would also be appropriate. Therefore, increased capital and leverage requirements are justified. Alternatively, or simultaneously, well-defined and compelling specific capital ratios and leverage limits could be related to the riskiness of the activity undertaken.

5. Understood and transparently used methods of delinking parts of large organizations could be developed so that if one goes haywire, the others can remain in business. Are you old enough to remember Christmas tree lights from long ago? When one light failed, they all went out. And the longer the string, the harder it was to find the guilty bulb and therefore the more time-consuming was the remedial action. Derivatives and securitization, so to speak, made the vulnerable string of lights even longer, increasing vulnerability and making the system more difficult to fix. The Christmas-tree-lights problem caused manufacturers to come up with a delinking system so that, these days, when one light goes out, the others stay on. If the manufacturers of Christmas tree lights are smart enough to do this, why shouldn't we be smart enough to work out delinking arrangements in the financial and corporate spheres? Obviously, limited-recourse suborganizations would have to be clearly advertised as such, so that those who play with whatever fire exists will know they could get burned.

6. Then there are organizations that grow because they are heavily subsidized. This is a deliberate process designed by government to encourage some form of activity such as homeownership. The widespread American instinct that homeownership is a good thing, that owners take care of their properties better than renters, and that people prefer to live in a nest they have created according to their own style of life are great virtues and arguably deserve some subsidy. The question is how to structure the subsidy. Tax deductions for interest payments on mortgages are one model. They are widely used and present no problem of abuse. The gross misfortunes generated by Fannie and Freddie, with their guarantees that represent large and somewhat invisible exposure, suggest that this broad approach is the wrong one. Keep the subsidy focused on the individual who has some real skin in the game, and cause lenders to keep at least some reasonable amount of their skin in the game.

7. Bankruptcy proceedings need to be examined carefully. Are different processes needed for different kinds of organizations? Do we need a system especially adapted to the financial services industry? To what degree do problems arise from slowness of application? If quicker resolution would be helpful, can some greater degree of automaticity or presumption be built into these processes? Of course, the key part of a bankruptcy reorganization proceeding is that the organization continues to function while the proceedings take place. This fact deals automatically with some of the risk factors. And the proceedings take place within an understood rule of law.

8. There has been considerable discussion of the contribution to the problem by certain financial instruments.

Warren Buffett says derivatives are weapons of financial mass destruction. Securitization has been identified by many as a cause of problems because this process separates the originator of a risk from the consequences. And while risk may be spread, risk is also obscured in this process. Should something be done about these instruments? And what about other risky activities such as taking positions in private equity, hedge funds, or other trading activities? Should organizations like banks, with their access to credit from the Fed, be prohibited from trading in these kinds of presumed assets? Or, if they or other financial organizations do trade in such assets, they do so in the form of a mutual fund and not on their own account. Such a requirement would remove the risk from the financial organization. The holders of the mutual funds would bear the risks and would be entitled to the gains.

9. Recent problems got their start from a Fed-induced long period of exceptionally easy credit and a government-produced push for homeownership on terms (no down payment, no questions asked) that together produced excessive risk taking and mortgage originations. Can we expect government to act in a way consistent with prudent practice in the private sector, most especially the financial services industry?

I am attracted to Andrew Crockett's standards in his "Reforming the Global Financial Architecture":

> There are four key prerequisites of an acceptable . . . regime . . . that permits the orderly winding down of a failing institution: (i) imposing losses on stakeholders that are predictable and consistent with

avoidance of moral hazard; (ii) avoiding unnecessary damage to "innocent bystanders," especially when that would provoke a loss of confidence in otherwise sound financial institutions; (iii) minimizing taxpayer costs; and (iv) sharing equitably across affected countries any residual fiscal burden.[1]

This conference is designed to help answer the kinds of questions I've listed earlier. The mission must be set out with clarity and urgency. The financial system is the central problem. The goal must be to remove the word *bailout* from our vocabulary. With that accomplished, one needed pillar for the strategy of growth without inflation will be in place.

NOTE

1. Andrew Crockett, "Reforming the Global Financial Architecture," speech presented at Asia and the Global Financial Crisis Conference, Santa Barbara, CA, October 18–20, 2009.

2

Financial Reforms to End Government Bailouts as We Know Them

PAUL VOLCKER

THE POLICY WORKSHOP AND THIS resulting book have an ambitious intellectual and practical challenge: setting out ways and means for ending government bailouts as we know them.

I want to paraphrase George Shultz when I say the object is to make the world safe for failure—failure of even the largest or "systemically important" institutions. That is an ambitious goal, but I share George's feeling that the bailout mentality has been reinforced and become pervasive after the unprecedented rescues that have taken place in the past year or more, not just in the United States but in the world. The result has been at great expense to the different fiscal positions of various governments and in terms of monetary policy actions. A by-product has been an unfortunate loss of credibility for central banks.

I wonder in looking at this whole problem of the financial system whether there isn't some correlation between the number of financial engineers and the number of damaging failures in the market.

In any case, we have a large problem, and I don't think we've seen the last of it. While zero interest rates may be necessary at the moment, they lead to some dangerous possibilities in terms of breeding more speculative excesses.

Let me try to deal with the particular issues of financial reform related to "too big to fail" and moral hazard. I was reminded in rereading a bit of *The Wealth of Nations* that Adam Smith had an answer to some of these problems. He worried about failures of banks—he thought they were overly inclined to involve themselves in speculative activities. The only good remedy he could think of was to keep them small. I'm not sure that what was possible in Scotland in 1776 is possible in the United States or other advanced financial systems today. I think we probably have to look for other answers, but if in the process we can keep the biggest banks somewhat smaller, that would help.

Let me try to clear up some definitions as you think about this problem. We talk about failure; we've had one clear failure in this period: Lehman Brothers. The stockholders lost everything. And while it remains to be seen how much the creditors lost, they certainly were affected. That was a failure situation without bailout. I think it's fair to say it had some repercussions.

Then we had a number of institutions here and abroad: Bear Stearns, Countrywide, Wachovia, Washington Mutual,

Merrill Lynch—I'd include Fannie and Freddie on this list—that also failed in that they could no longer stand alone. As they merged, creditors were saved (though stockholders were wounded). They were too big to fail in terms of current attitudes but were not necessarily bailed out. It depends on what you mean by "bailed out," since those institutions no longer exist or won't exist over time. They are examples where assistance was needed to smooth a merger or to smooth liquidation, but they weren't permitted to continue.

Next we have a whole list of other troubled institutions that received large official assistance going beyond usual liquidity support by the Federal Reserve and/or the Treasury. They're still independent and operational; while some may be limping, they're still there. In most cases management is still in place, and some are doing quite magnificently in terms of compensation. That, it seems to me, fills every definition of a true bailout.

What about systemic interdependence? It's a fuzzy concept. Part of it means that the failure of some institutions, because they are so interconnected in obligations—in particular, to creditors and in terms of liabilities or assets—that their failure will cascade through the system and give rise to a wide-scale breakdown of the financial system. That was thought to be the case of AIG and, earlier, Bear Stearns.

But beyond the kind of mechanical spreading of breakdowns and failures there may be an even more important psychological point: if the creditors or the stockholders hurt in a failing institution, you may have incipient panic among other institutions that otherwise would be able to stand on their own. The psychological panic—a classic run on banks—gives rise to a problem for the whole system. This seems to me one of the most difficult areas to deal with. We can talk about being tough on institutions or letting them fail, but as was the case in the fall of 2008, the officials were obviously concerned about the psychological effects of inducing runs on, or a sense of panic in, other institutions.

After that background, let me give a little picture of how I would like to see this situation approached. There are a lot of areas in which there is substantial consensus, at least in concept (some of that broad agreement will break down in practice) as to how to protect the financial institutions, the system, and individual institutions within the system from the kind of systemic breakdown to which I refer. It begins, I think, with risk management in the major institutions themselves. Obviously they did not do as well as they should have. Whether their incentives were correct or not is a large question. And I think there will be pressure—there *should* be pressure—on those institutions to improve risk management.

In the regulatory area, capital standards get a lot of attention. I think that's appropriate. I believe there's a limit on how far capital can be increased while keeping institutions economically viable, but there's certainly room for a more effective approach in this area. There have to be some limits on leverage in important institutions. We have had accounting problems. We've had the problem of off–balance sheet assets and liabilities—with more liabilities than assets, I'm afraid. Those kinds of issues ought to be taken care of by a more effective regulatory system. And while they may not require legislation in and of themselves, there are important questions of who does the regulation that obviously are the provenance of legislation and congressional policy.

We have the whole difficult area of compensation practices to deal with. I must confess that I admired a *Wall Street Journal* article in which Henry Mintzberg, a professor at McGill business school up in Canada (maybe the location says something), was arguing that the whole idea of stock compensation and stock options is mistaken. He argues that people ought to be paid in cash salaries, depending on a judgment as to their effectiveness over time. It's a short summary of a very persuasive article, and though I don't know how many people will be persuaded, compensation practices are important.

Finally, clearance and settlement practices in the derivatives area are of some consequence. The matter has caught everybody's attention after the AIG fiasco with credit default swaps, and the administration and others have been working hard to get settlement practices that can better assure outstanding derivatives can be taken care of in a way that will not unsettle the whole system and lead to systemic problems.

That's all fine against a background that there is a limit to how far we can go on regulation without losing the essence of active, flexible, innovative private markets. Private markets are important, and we've got to keep them flowing. So how do we solve that dilemma between regulation, appropriate capital standards (appropriate meaning higher than they've been), derivatives, and reasonable compensation practices, while keeping the strength of private markets? Let me take this opportunity to put my own approach on the table, and it starts with a kind of philosophical differentiation in my mind.

On one side we have banks, and it strikes me that banks are still the center of the financial system. They have lost ground, relatively, in direct supplies of credit to other instruments over the past two or three decades, but they are still the heart of the system: they run the payments system for individuals, businesses, and governments; they run it domestically and internationally. No economy can survive without an effective payments system, and that's the job of banks. They are key providers of credit to businesses, particularly to small and medium-sized businesses, and certainly to individuals. They are the conduit for monetary policy and have a special role in the economy for that reason.

Commercial banks and commercial banking systems in the United States and elsewhere are characterized today by a fairly high degree of concentration. Given the importance of the function and the size of the institution, there obviously are systemic implications. As opposed to capital markets, continuing relationships are an inherent part of the commercial banking business: they serve consumers, they serve businesses, they serve government, and they serve nonprofit institutions.

Capital markets, which trade in securities, among other things, have a significant function in providing a certain degree of liquidity and access of large-scale buyers and sellers of securities to markets that can develop and serve their needs, but they're basically impersonal markets. They don't depend on continuing customer relationships in the same way that commercial banks do. They are important but impersonal. They are less interconnected than commercial banks by the nature of their responsibilities and therefore by and large less systemically important, although large capital market institutions obviously create a problem and have systemic implications.

My bottom line is that I would treat banks differently from nonbanks. What do I mean by that? Commercial banks have a long history—decades; centuries—in which they've been protected and supervised one way or another by governments and central banks. The protection is in recognition of the importance of stability and continuity in those areas of the market. I think that should continue in its traditional way of deposit insurance, Federal Reserve liquidity support, and close (in relative terms) regulation. There can be improvements in each of those areas, which come under the subject matter I mentioned earlier to provide protection against a general breakdown of the market.

Capital markets, in contrast, have not traditionally enjoyed the same protection, and, of course, they haven't had the same degree of regulation. I'm fine with going light on the regulation and not providing the protection, but I think this is where we really want to make the point that these institutions are not going to be too big to fail, that they will be permitted to fail, that in case of difficulty they will either fail or be merged. They should not, in my opinion, have the option of receiving official support and continuing as independent institutions.

Once one says that, the question arises, how do you deal with such institutions if they're big and failure is likely to have broader implications? This is where the question of a resolution authority comes into play. There's a general consensus, as I see it, on the need for this in the United States and elsewhere. This should be coordinated internationally—a regulatory authority or some official body that will take over a big, presumably systemically important institution on the brink of failure and will become responsible for an orderly liquidation or a merger of that institution. In other words, it would provide a kind of funeral parlor, not an emergency ward, not a recovery ward in a hospital, but something that will be dealt with in a way that does not provide any rescue, any relief for the stockholder or indeed for the bondholder, if it turns out in the end that the institution is so weak in terms of assets that it cannot meet the obligations of its bondholders as well. There may be some need for some transitional official assistance to smooth the path toward liquidation or to smooth the merger, but it should not be assistance to keep the institution alive in my view.

That would be different for the commercial banks, where the possibility of keeping significant institutions alive, presumably with the loss of stockholder funds, might be reasonable. On the other hand, I would reduce the opportunities for the large commercial banking institutions needing assistance by saying they should not get involved heavily in essentially capital market activity.

What do I mean by that? The easy examples are they shouldn't be doing hedge funds, they shouldn't be doing equity funds, and they shouldn't be doing proprietary trading either in securities or in commodities. Those are functions that are logical for the unprotected capital market but do not seem to me reasonable for the protected commercial banking sector. And of course, if they're prohibited from those activities, they will also become smaller institutions than they now are. It won't make them small—only smaller in the case of some of the very large institutions, which I think does go in the right direction.

Among other things, such activities inherently involve important conflicts of interest in those institutions. They make them more difficult to manage. They obviously have diverted management attention and understanding in the past, and I think we ought to make an effort to simplify the management of the protected sector of the economy.

So that is the broad view that I see: a distinction between commercial banks and capital markets. Just to be clear, I don't go back to the pre-Glass-Steagall distinction. Glass-Steagall essentially prohibited underwriting of corporate securities. I think underwriting is now close enough to securitization and to normal lending to large companies that I would permit banks to do underwriting. But I would draw the line on proprietary trading; I think a distinction can be made between proprietary trading and customer-related trading, which would be a much smaller volume and that that distinction ought to be enforced.

So I think that gives you some kind of basis, at least going some distance toward "ending government bailouts as we know them." I have conceded the possibility of something that might be called a bailout for a commercial bank in exceptional circumstances, but it would be a different kind of bailout than we have had, so I think it fits within the mandate of this group to end the bailouts as we know them.

Let's let commercial banks be commercial banks. Let's let capital market institutions do their thing in capital markets, essentially unprotected. Let's not have any more protection of the commercial banks than is absolutely necessary but recognize that regulation and some protection in that area is likely to continue to be needed.

3

Fifty Years in the Business: From Wall Street to the Treasury and Beyond

NICHOLAS F. BRADY

I'D LIKE TO THANK MY FRIENDS George Shultz and John Taylor for organizing this thought-provoking debate on the proper role for government to play in America's financial system. Years of experience have taught me that when George Shultz starts to worry about something, pay attention, and in that regard the conference topic that resulted in this book could not be timelier.

I have had a continuing interest in commercial and investment banking for more than five decades. As a little background, I worked at Dillon Read for thirty-four years, the last seventeen as CEO. And in 1982 I served on the

Senate Banking Committee as a U.S. senator representing the state of New Jersey. In 1988, Ronald Reagan appointed me secretary of the Treasury, a post I held for four more years under President George H. W. Bush. My experience as both a practitioner and a government regulator has given me strong convictions about what this country should do to provide an efficient yet safe system to handle its citizens' financial assets.

While I served at Treasury, we were fighting a war in Iraq and an economic recession at home. We faced a commercial banking industry choked with emerging market debt and underwater real estate loans, a bankrupt savings and loan industry, and government spending at such a high rate that the nation was headed for a bleak future. Does any of this sound familiar?

Our first task was to reconstitute the savings and loan industry and the real estate market it financed. We passed legislation to create the Resolution Trust Corporation to clear out the toxic assets of that era, taking over some 750 insolvent savings banks in the process. To do this, we had no choice but to seek funding from Congress and undergo the intense political criticism that came with it.

Next, in a major contrast to today, we set about to rein in escalating spending by the U.S. government, which was, for that time period, clearly out of control. The Budget Act of 1990 established legally binding caps on the amount that Congress could spend on discretionary items in exchange for a limited increase in taxes. President Bush knew that the Budget Act could easily contribute to a reelection defeat in 1992, but he decided that it was the right thing to do for the country. As it turned out, of course, he did lose the election, but he set the stage for the decade of economic growth that followed.

On the practitioner side, at Dillon Read I learned first-hand that running an investment bank is unlike any other business. It involves managing the flow of large sums of money, time-compressed transactions, and the high-octane calculus of derivatives and leverage. The thing that sticks with me most is how people-intensive the business is. No matter how tight you try to make the script, it's always being tested—as anyone who has watched a person on a trading desk execute a word-of-mouth contract can attest. It's the reason I feel so strongly about clearly laid-out rules.

I vividly remember that my first assignment as a new hire at Dillon Read was to read the dictionary-thick volume on markets from the Pecora Commission, which investigated the underlying causes of the 1929 stock market crash. From that reading it became apparent why Congress established securities laws to limit the businesses that commercial and investment banks could legally conduct under one roof. As a 1971 Supreme Court opinion on the matter said: Senator Glass made it clear in his deliberations before the passage of the Banking Act of 1933 "that it was 'the fixed purpose of Congress' not to see the facilities of commercial banking diverted into speculative operations by the aggressive and promotional character of the investment banking business."

That view guided Wall Street effectively for sixty-plus years, until the Gramm-Leach-Bliley Act repealed Glass-Steagall in 1999. I reluctantly supported the repeal on the basis that underwriting activities had become sufficiently refined so as to pose a much lower risk to the system. But that's not the point. Senator Glass had his eye on an important principle: don't allow the banking industry to create a combustible mix that will contaminate the nation's central banking system. The legislation was as much a philosophy as it was a law.

Of course today's combustible mix is different from what Senator Glass identified in the 1930s. Now it's banks operating hedge funds, running prop desks for their own account, taking highly leveraged principal positions in various forms, and trading derivatives. Nonetheless, we're faced with the same central problem that concerned Senator Glass: combustibility. The House has already passed banking legislation, and the White House and the Senate have put forward proposals to address the financial crisis. It may relieve you to know that I am not going to address them point by point. But I have identified eight observations that guide me as I think about the problem.

1. There's been no thorough description of what actually happened to turn the nation's financial underpinnings upside down. And in my experience, you can't fix what you can't explain. As an aside, the least convincing explanation is one floating around financial firms that attributes the events to "a perfect storm" (i.e., "It's not my fault").

I served on a number of truly bipartisan presidential commissions, including the Brady Commission on the 1987 stock market crash. While the issues varied, the purpose of each commission was to stand before the American people and explain in understandable language the complex set of circumstances that caused the problem. In each case the findings of the commission were presented to the public before laws were changed. How different it is today, with our lawmakers' rush to judgment. They're going about it exactly backward.

2. The rescue fund has reached the trillions, not billions— trillions. How could we possibly miss such a huge mistake in the making? The answer: Bankers and regulators were looking but not seeing. The industry was so focused on creating alternative forms of credit, combined with higher returns and over-the-top compensation, that people ignored—or, at best, miscalculated—the risks in front of them. Both the industry and the regulators drank the Kool-Aid, leading them to believe in the theory that the self-correcting, all-curative power of market forces would keep the financial system from imploding. Talk about a theory that was proved wrong. This leads the hit parade.

3. We've provided trillions—I can hardly believe it—of taxpayer funds to stabilize the system, and, for the moment, the financial markets have reached an uneasy equilibrium, giving us time to make the correct choices. The danger is in getting it wrong. We simply can't afford another blowup and its aftermath.

4. We need to remember the distinction between things that are critical and things that are merely important. The safety and soundness of the financial system is indisputably essential; without it, we have nothing. The long history of financial collapses and the resulting damage to our economy and our society prove this point. While efficiency, creativity, and credit availability are important, they can't be allowed to trump safety and soundness.

5. Although "too big to fail" has become the mantra of the day, I've never thought size by itself was the main issue. The larger an institution, if soundly based, the more credit it can provide. What is of primary importance is the bank's combination of activities. Does it include operations that in and of themselves, or because of their interrelationships, create a combustible mix that can threaten the system as a whole?

6. *As a corollary, banking institutions that have the right to go to the Federal Reserve shouldn't be involved in lines of business that could result in a combustible mix.* And formulas that restrain such volatile operations will only lead to endless future definitional arguments between regulators and industry participants. What we need is absolute clarity and transparency.

7. *It's delusional to think you can structure a regulatory system, no matter how sensible, based on formulas.* Either the investment bankers will outwit the regulators, or the regulators will overreact.

8. *I have never worked directly for a bank, but it is fact that the backbone of the financial system is the banks with which Americans have a personal relationship.* The average person has no interaction with the so-called shadow banks. That's why there are 220,000 people working at JPMorgan Chase and only 31,000 employees at Goldman Sachs. Banks are the one place where the American people touch the central financial system. Far-fetched as this may seem, I believe this means something. It could be a source of support for an acceptable solution.

So where does this leave us?

As tempting as it is to tinker with the present system, you can already tell that I believe there's a better way. We should strive for a simpler system financed by deposit-based institutions at its core. Under this approach, individual accounts in depository banks would continue to be protected up to $250,000, and these banks would have access to the Federal Reserve. These institutions would not be allowed to be involved in lines of business that create a combustible mix. I need only recall that this time around the systemic risk manifested itself acutely in the so-called shadow banking system, as evidenced by the bailouts of Bear Stearns and AIG, the failure of Lehman Brothers, and the shotgun marriage of Merrill Lynch and Bank of America.

The highly innovative shadow banking system, with its directive of lower transaction costs and the like, would continue to introduce new concepts and fund itself from the money markets and other sources but without federal guarantees and access to America's central bank. Institutions that currently straddle the two funding markets would have to choose which type of business to pursue and would be given a programmed yet reasonable amount of time to comply with the new law if they were to become part of the deposit-based banking system. I know this would provoke the immediate cry that the financial system would be further pinched and credit would further shrink. My answer is that any deposit-gathering system with a $250,000 guarantee from the U.S. government and access to the central monetary authorities would get all the deposits it needed to be vibrant. As a matter of interest, banking deposits have grown substantively in 2008 and 2009, as Americans have sought a safe place to put their money.

While the systemic risk for deposit-based banks would be sharply reduced, another question that arises about the banking structure I'm advocating is how we would address the same risk inherent in the shadow banking system. First, remember that by changing the law to "let banks be banks," we would have secured the largest part of the system. And according to a recent survey done by the *Financial Times*, there are only three institutions in the shadow banking system big enough to cause a systemic risk.

The next piece of architecture would be to create impenetrable firebreaks between institutions in the deposit-based system and those in the shadow banking system. This work should be central to any new legislation. I've heard from many that it's impossible, and it's true that it can't be done without trampling on somebody's dominion, but that's the nature of change. In 1989 when we created the Brady Plan to solve the debt crisis in emerging market countries, you couldn't find one out of ten financial observers who thought our solution would work. History proved the naysayers wrong. So let me note that there's a world of difference between saying that it can't be done and setting about to do it.

Many have suggested that a credible resolution structure should be created. This is a good idea. It would involve a change in the law and the selection of the proper agency to administer it. There are a number of wind-down plans that provide a useful start.

It's hard to overestimate how critical all these issues are. Congress is now working on solutions, but I'm concerned that they are looking through the wrong end of the telescope. There is too much attention being paid to maintaining the status quo without dealing with the fundamental problems that gave rise to today's critical difficulties. It seems that our political leaders are intent on instituting a national policy of "too big too fail." We can do better. I urge Congress to carefully evaluate the benefits of stabilizing the banking system

along the lines I have described and that have also been supported by a former chairman of the Federal Reserve and the
current governor of the Bank of England. We should not be
among those who are condemned to repeat the mistakes of
the past because we refused to learn from them.

In closing, let me say that at every G-7 meeting I attended—
and there were many—the United States had the lead in
world financial affairs, and others followed. The recent financial crisis dealt a blow not just to our economy but to the
world economy, and we are charged with creating it. Frankly,
this has had an effect on our standing in the world's financial
forums. This makes it all the more important to my mind to
take the time to get it right.

PART II

SYSTEMIC RISK IN THEORY AND IN PRACTICE

4

Defining Systemic Risk Operationally

JOHN B. TAYLOR

> One of the most feared events in banking is the cry of
> systemic risk. It matches the fear of a cry of "fire!" in
> a crowded theater or other gatherings. But unlike *fire*,
> the term *systemic risk* is not clearly defined.
>
> —George G. Kaufman and Kenneth E. Scott (2003)

FOR ANYONE INTERESTED IN reducing government bailouts, a clear operational definition and measure of systemic risk for financial institutions is essential. Such a definition would set boundaries or limits on bailouts. If a particular financial firm's failure did not satisfy the definition, then there would be no rationale for the government

I am grateful to Vineer Bhansali, Craig Furfine, Paul Kupiec, Jamie McAndrews, Monika Piazzesi, and Ken Scott for helpful comments.

to bail out that firm or its creditors. A clear definition of systemic risk would also suggest alternatives to a bailout in certain cases. And if the definition were widely agreed to, then firms or their creditors could not arbitrarily cry "systemic risk" as a way to get government rescue funds. As George Shultz points out, based on his experience in government, frequently "the problem can be overestimated or can be reasonably contained" (see chap. 1).

The more restrictive the definition and the more credibly it is adhered to by policy makers, the fewer bailouts we would see. Recognizing that bailouts are unavailable except in the most unlikely circumstances, firms and their creditors would have the incentive to adjust their behavior. But if, to the contrary, systemic risk is not clearly defined, then all such boundaries and incentives are blurred, systemic risk can be used to scare people and their government—just like the cry of "Fire!"—into bailouts, and the current bailout mentality continues or even grows.

Defining systemic risk operationally is essential not only for limiting bailouts but also for implementing most recent proposals for financial reform, including those described in the chapters of this book. Some of the systemic regulator proposals requires the Federal Reserve to identify firms that are systemically risky; these firms would then constitute a group called Tier I financial holding companies in the U.S. Treasury (2009) proposal. Richard Herring's wind-down proposal (this volume, chap. 7) would apply only to systemically important financial firms. Some argue that the contingent convertible debt proposals described by Darrell Duffie (chap. 6) should require a double trigger in which a regulatory declaration of systemic risk is needed as well as a drop of capital below a certain threshold at the institution in question. Thomson and Haubrick (2009) argue that we are better off placing firms in more than two bins, but a definition and measure of systemic risk is needed here too. As Kimberly Summe puts it in chapter 5, it is "imperative for policy makers to agree on" a definition of systemic risk if such proposals are to be implemented.

The purpose of this chapter is to review recent writings and research on systemic risk and assess whether the term is operational enough to be used as a guideline or criterion to determine whether the failure of a particular firm would create significant economic damage or to classify firms into a systemically important group in advance. Despite the frequent discussions in policy circles, I find that the term remains as vague and amorphous as it was six years ago when George Kaufman and Kenneth Scott published the paper in which the epigraph to this chapter appears. By way of comparison, in order to implement monetary policy, whether with the help of a Taylor rule or by some other means, one has to define and measure inflation, real GDP, and unemployment. While there are some questions and disagreements about how to define and measure these concepts operationally, they pale in comparison with questions and disagreements about how to define and measure systemic risk.

I begin with a brief overview of the concept of systemic risk as generally understood in the policy and financial economics literature, and then consider recent empirical research, case studies, and other attempts to define and measure the term more precisely. I then consider the policy implications and offer some suggestions about how to proceed.

THE CONCEPT OF SYSTEMIC RISK

Any definition of systemic risk must be based on three considerations. The first is the *risk of a large triggering event*. The second is the *risk of financial propagation* of such an event through the financial sector by contagion or chain reaction. The third is the *macroeconomic risk* that the financial disruption will severely affect the whole economy.

Triggering Events

Triggering events can come from

- the public sector, as when the central bank suddenly contracts liquidity, perhaps after a previous sharp expansion of liquidity;
- an external shock, as when a natural disaster or terrorist attack destroys the payments system; or
- the financial markets themselves, as when a large private financial firm fails.

Examples of triggering events prior to the current crisis are the default by the Russian government in 1998, which affected markets around the world; the default by the Argentine government in 2001, which had no such worldwide effect; and the 9/11 terrorist attacks, which not only physically damaged financial firms in Lower Manhattan but also affected the entire U.S. financial system.

In the current crisis, there is considerable debate about the triggering event. In my view, a series of government actions and interventions is the most plausible triggering event, including a monetary policy that kept interest rates too low for too long to an ad hoc bailout policy that led to fear and panic. One of the reasons to end bailouts is to reduce the chance that government will create such systemic events again. But others point to the failure of certain markets or private financial institutions, most commonly Lehman Brothers, as the main triggering event.

The Financial Sector Propagation Mechanism

Now consider the propagation risk from the original triggering event through the financial system. Experience suggests that it is useful to distinguish between two types of propagation risk.

The first type is where there is a *direct financial linkage* between firms that causes a failure of one institution to adversely affect other institutions in a chain reaction. The direct links can be through interbank loans (more generally interfinancial firm loans) and through derivative contracts. Interbank loans are part of the clearance and settlement system and thereby are part of the financial infrastructure. The Board of Governors of the Federal Reserve (2001) focused on the payments infrastructure when worrying about this type of risk, writing that

> Systemic risk may occur if an institution participating on a private large dollar payments network were unable or unwilling to settle its net debt position. If such a settlement failure occurred, the institution's creditors on the network might also be unable to settle their commitments. Serious repercussions could, as a result, spread to

other participants in the private network, to other depository institutions not participating in the network, and to the nonfinancial economy generally.

It is important to note that in the present crisis, no major payment, clearing or settlement system failed.

The second type of propagation risk is where there is *no direct* financial connection between the firms. In this case, a failing institution or some other triggering event causes the balance sheets of a possibly large number of other financial institutions to be significantly impacted because they all have portfolios similar to the failing institution or because they have large exposures to securities that are impacted by the triggering event. The closer the portfolios are to those of other failed firms, the greater the likelihood is of losses and failure. This type of propagation, frequently called contagion, can be interpreted as a rational, rather than as a purely irrational or psychological, response to new information. But it can be magnified if uninformed investors follow more informed investors and if the suddenness of the event causes surprise and uncertainty.

This second type of financial propagation is sometimes characterized as a "run," in which short-term creditors and/ or depositors rush to withdraw their funds from the financial institutions they view as in trouble. As they withdraw their funds, the financial firms have to sell longer-term, possibly illiquid, assets or collateral, which then creates a liquidity problem, which can become an insolvency problem. The problems are magnified if many firms sell at the same time, creating fire sales, an issue studied by Diamond and Rajan (2009) in the context of the recent crisis.

It is important to emphasize that contagion or chain reactions are not automatic, and they can be altered by changes in public policy. For example, as mentioned earlier, when Argentina defaulted on its debt in 2001, three years after the Russian default, there was no global contagion, even though the world economy was in worse shape in 2001 than in 1998. In my view, this was due to a change in policy by the major shareholders of the International Monetary Fund (IMF) that tried to clarify when a bailout would occur and when it would not.

In addition, interbank exposures can create incentives for interbank monitoring that will reduce the chain reaction effect. But if there is an expectation of a government bailout, then this will reduce the incentives to monitor and increase the likelihood of chain reaction effects. In other words, moral hazard considerations affect not only the risk at individual financial firms but also the risk of chain reactions or contagion between them. Rochet and Tirole (1996) have developed theoretical models of interbank lending in which moral hazard can play such a role.

Policy might also be able to reduce the risk in the payments infrastructure. Kahn and Roberds (1998) argue that the use of net settlement increases the probability of default in comparison with gross settlement. The trade-off is that gross settlement requires the use of more reserves. But the cost of the higher risk is borne by taxpayers and the bailouts because it increases the likelihood of damage from contagion and chain reaction. However, since interest can now be paid on bank reserves at the Fed, banks should care less about the extra reserves that are required in the gross settlement method.

The Macroeconomic Linkages

The traditional connections between such financial sector disturbances and the real economy are through changes in the supply of money, the supply of credit from banks and nonbank institutions, asset prices (including exchange rates), and interest rates.

A reduction in the supply of money is the classic connection and the one stressed by Friedman and Schwartz (1963) in their original work on the causes of the Great Depression. In that famous case, bank runs—rapid withdrawals of deposits from banks by individuals and other nonfinancial depositors—caused an increase in the ratio of cash to deposits, drastically shrunk the money supply, and thereby increased the severity of the Great Depression. Romer (1992) documents how the recovery from the Great Depression was largely due to a restoration of money.

The emphasis on the supply of credit from financial institutions has a long tradition dating back at least to the work in the 1950s and 1960s by Karl Brunner, Allan Meltzer, John Gurley, Edward Shaw, James Tobin, and continuing into the 1990s by Ben Bernanke, Mark Gertler, and Simon Gilchrist. A reduction of the availability of bank credit would make it more difficult for firms to borrow, especially for those firms that could not finance their investment in plant and equipment internally. In an international context, a reduction in the supply of credit would interfere with exporting and importing.

The interest rate (more generally the asset price) connection from the financial sector to the real economy has been more common in empirical models. This work ranges from the early large-scale econometric models to the international monetary models in the tradition of Mundell and Fleming to new Keynesian models with rational expectation. There has been much empirical modeling of the linkages over the years, and a useful symposium on the subject was sponsored by the *Journal of Economic Perspectives* in the Fall 1995 issue.

In my view, the interest rate channel has been more successful empirically than the credit channel in part because the data on credit flows are difficult to find and because different types of credit are fungible. My view is based on my research using both approaches: the interest rate view in the model in Taylor (1995) and the credit view in proprietary research I did years ago at the consulting firm of Townsend Greenspan. For the most part, interest rate connections are smoother and less abrupt than the credit connections.

There is a certain practical intuition held by many people in the financial sector that the credit linkages are more powerful than the interest rate or asset price linkages to the real sector, but there is little empirical evidence of this. For example, for many years the impact of a change in monetary policy was viewed as large because interest rate caps on deposits (Regulation Q) caused disintermediation (a reduction in bank credit) when interest rates rose and people withdrew funds from banks. However, when Regulation Q was removed, this impact of interest rates on the real economy did not change much. The experience with Carter credit controls in 1980 provided more evidence of credit effects, but this was directly government induced.

In the recent crisis, many have viewed the reduction in credit flows as more systemic than the interest rate changes because certain credit markets did freeze up, but there is still little empirical evidence supporting this view. There is no question that the real economy sharply contracted in the fourth quarter of 2008 and that the availability of credit dried up, but the cause and effect of the change in credit is very difficult to sort out. For example, Chauffour and Farole (2009) look into the supply of trade credit for exports and imports, and why it could have been vulnerable to financial disruption. But they are not able to resolve the econometric causality problem of whether a contraction of trade credit caused the worldwide collapse in exports or vice versa.

MEASURING THE EXTENT OF SYSTEMIC RISK

Let me now examine recent work trying to measure or define the financial propagation mechanism more precisely.

Data sets on direct bilateral loans from one financial institution to another are rare, unfortunately. In the case of money markets in the United States, Furfine (2003) has done some of the best work in this area. He created a data set of bilateral interconnections between banks making loans to each other in the overnight interbank federal funds market. He did this by matching send-and-receive messages in federal funds transactions. Using these data, he found that if there were a failure of the bank with the largest borrowing in this market, it would cause some failures at other banks, but the total assets of these banks are less than 1 percent of total bank assets. If the loss rate were 5 percent, then no other banks would fail. The 5 percent loss rate was what was experienced in the 1984 Continental Illinois Bank failure, according to Kaufman and Scott (2003). According to this evidence, there is very little systemic risk coming from direct interconnectedness between banks.

In another study, Furfine (2006) used his data set to estimate the interconnection between nonbanks and banks. He examined the nine banks that participated in the Long-Term Capital Management (LTCM) bailout. By looking at their borrowing in the overnight interbank market, he found that in the days leading up to the LTCM rescue, there was no evidence that other banks were restricting their lending or charging higher rates to these nine banks. In other words, there was no sense in the markets that these banks were at risk from an LTCM failure. He also found a lowering of borrowing rates for large banking organization relative to smaller ones following the LTCM rescue, which is evidence of a perceived expansion of the "too big to fail" tendency from this event.

In more recent work, Ashcraft and Duffie (2007) created another interbank data set on the federal funds market using the matching methodology of Furfine (2003). Their main objective was to model which bank is likely to lend to each other bank and at what rate, based on variables such as the reserve balances of each bank relative to their normal reserve balances at various times during the day. This largely over-the-counter (OTC) market is thus useful for understanding counterparty trading behavior in OTC markets. Clearly it would be very useful to obtain and analyze bilateral counterparty data in other OTC markets.

One objection to the numbers reported by Furfine (2003) is that they do not include second round or third round reactions of banks to changes in the market. It would therefore be useful to see whether Furfine's results hold up using the bank behavioral reactions estimated in the model of Ashcraft and Duffie (2007). These reactions could create a dynamic chain reaction effect that goes beyond the first round, which was Furfine's focus.

Unfortunately, many of the other ways that people try to define systemic risk are much less quantitative. One frequently hears explanations of systemic risk using analogies with classic runs on bank deposits by individuals or nonfinancial business firms. We know bank runs on deposits can be systemic because deposits are used for economic transactions, as explained earlier. The deposits are part of the payments system. The reason we have deposit insurance is to prevent such runs. But to assess the systemic nature of a run on nondeposit short-term debt, which is not used for transactions purposes, it is not enough to simply say, "If you want to see why a run on short-term debt is systemic, just go see the movie *It's a Wonderful Life*." Rather, one needs to explain and measure the impact of such a run on short-term debt, and show why or why not it is like a run on a depository institution. For example, could it create a serious credit crunch that would impact consumers and businesses, and how large would that crunch be?

Another approach to defining the systemic nature of financial propagation is to make physical analogies such as with the plumbing in a house: "The failure of this financial institution would clog the plumbing." Another analogy is mountain climbing. According to Kaufman and Scott (2003), Eddie George, the former governor of the Bank of England, would say that "direct financial exposures tie firms together like mountaineers: if one falls off the rock face, others are pulled off, too." Yet another analogy is falling dominoes. While certainly useful for some purposes, these metaphors do not provide a way to measure the systemic nature of the risk.

Several new ideas to define and measure systemic risk empirically have been proposed recently. However, most of them have purposes other than creating criteria to determine whether the creditors of a financial institution should be bailed out, or whether a particular firm is systemically important. They are therefore not operational in the sense I use the term here. Rather, the measures are useful for monitoring overall systemic risk in the financial system, a task for which the Fed is already responsible and for which the administration wants the Fed to take on more responsibility. This is the motivation for the measures proposed by Bhansali, Gingrich, and Longstaff (2008) and Huang, Zhou, and Zhu (2009). The Bhansali et al. proposal uses information available in financial as well as nonfinancial sectors, while Huang et al. look at primarily financial sector credit default swap (CDS) and equity prices.

Such systemic risk measures would also be needed for macroprudential regulation or for countercyclical movements in regulatory instruments. For example, some argue that there is a need for countercyclical regulation that raises capital requirements in booms and loosens them in slumps. Adrian and Brunnermeier (2009) develop a measure that can be used for such purposes. It generalizes the concept of value at risk for an individual firm. They call the measure CoVar, and they show how it can be used to measure risk in the financial system as a whole. However, without more cross-holdings data of the type Furfine (2003) has collected for interbank loans, it is not clear how this measure would help determine whether a bailout of a firm is warranted.

Qualified Financial Contracts in Bankruptcy

One of the arguments given in favor of a bailout rather than letting a firm go through bankruptcy proceedings is that the bankruptcy law gives exemptions from the automatic stays for derivatives and repos—so-called qualified financial contracts. Without the automatic stay, a bankruptcy would cause a run on the repos and fire sales of collateral underlying the derivatives.

Consider an example. Suppose there is a CDS that stipulates that Firm A will pay to Firm B if Firm C defaults on a bond. It is the counterparty relationship between Firm A and Firm B that we are interested in. Firm A will usually post collateral for part of the sum that must be paid in the event Firm C defaults on the bond. Now, suppose Firm A fails and goes into bankruptcy. If Firm B is in the money on the CDS, then Firm B can now demand the collateral on the CDS. Firm B can also be compensated for the replacement costs of the contract. While Firm B does not have to wait along with other creditors—because of the exemption of the automatic stay—the process still takes time. If there were no exemption to the stay, then Firm B would have to wait along with the unsecured creditors such as bond holders.

What is so bad about waiting longer? One concern is that prices of a replacement CDS or the collateral already pledged would change. If so, then the agreement could be to settle on the basis of prices at the time that the bankruptcy is declared. Some people, including Tom Jackson in chapter 11 of this book, have begun to ask why, if the exemption from the automatic stay is a problem, would the qualified financial transactions be exempt in the first place?

One answer might be that then the instrument would be less attractive. But that might be the cost of reducing systemic risk. In any case, this example shows that in the process of delving into the reasons for the systemic risk, one might find that good alternatives to the bailout are possible in a particular circumstance. It also illustrates that there is considerable debate about the nature and extent of systemic risk.

Learning from the Recent Crises

The recent crises show how far away we are from defining and agreeing on systemic risk. Regarding the triggering event, there is disagreement about whether it was the failure to bail out Lehman's creditors or actions by government itself. Regarding the macroeconomic impact, there is disagreement about whether the restriction of credit brought about the sharp decline in production or the reverse as the panic itself caused firms to pull back.

Understanding the events surrounding the Lehman bankruptcy is particularly important. Many now argue that the cause of the panic in the fall of 2008 was the government's failure to intervene and prevent the bankruptcy of Lehman. This view gives a rationale for continued bailouts and the expectation that any firm will be bailed out. Harvey Miller (2009), for example, testified to the House Judiciary Committee that "[i]n the context of the Lehman experience, it appears beyond reasonable controversy that it is in the best interests of the country and the global financial system for the Treasury and the Federal Reserve to have the authority to utilize federal funds to avoid potential systemic failure." And he provided his reasons:

It is important to keep in mind that until the weekend of September 12–14, 2008, the belief that Lehman would be the subject of a bankruptcy was beyond comprehension. Lehman was the fourth largest investment bank in the United States. It reported consolidated assets of over $600 billion and liabilities of almost that amount. It operated a massive, global business on a 24/7 basis. Through its highly developed network of subsidiaries and affiliates, and 25,000 employees, Lehman conducted hundreds of thousands of transactions each day at the speed of light and on a world-wide basis. It moved billions of dollars around the world for itself and its customers each and every day. If ever there was an institution that might have been deemed "too big to fail," Lehman was a prime candidate.

In contrast, Peter Wallison (2009) testified to the Congressional Oversight Committee that "[t]he Lehman example seems to demonstrate that even when a major institution fails at a time of profound market panic the actual systemic risks are minimal." In my view, the problem was not the failure to bail out Lehman Brothers but rather the failure of the government to articulate a clear, predictable strategy for lending and intervening into a financial sector. This strategy could have been put forth in the weeks after the Bear Stearns rescue, or even earlier, but it was not. Instead, market participants were led to guess what the government would do. After Bear Stearns, many guessed that Lehman and its creditors would be bailed out. The lack of a strategy continued during the confusing rollout of the Troubled Asset Relief Program (TARP) plan, which, according to event studies in interbank and equity markets, was a more likely reason for the panic than the failure to intervene with Lehman.

Additional evidence is accumulating that confusing and unpredictable government interventions made things worse. There was noticeable movement of interest rate spreads in the interbank market and the bank debt market around the time of the seizure by the FDIC of Washington Mutual and its sale to JPMorgan Chase. This was followed quickly by a sharp drop in the price of Wachovia's bank debt, its aborted FDIC-driven acquisition by Citigroup, and its eventual acquisition by Wells Fargo. The acquisition of Merrill Lynch by Bank of America has also come under scrutiny. The Special Inspector General for TARP (2009) now reports that Timothy Geithner, who was president of the Federal Reserve Bank of New York, did not view the contagion or chain reaction to AIG's credit default swap counterparties as reason to bail out AIG. But to many this was the assumed reason that AIG's failure would have had a systemic effect. So was there systemic risk here or not? If so, what was it? The case is evidently not so clear.

ASSESSMENT

This brief review leads me to conclude that there is no clear operational definition and measure of systemic risk at this time. I am not alone in this assessment. The three main international institutions with responsibility for systemic risk—the IMF, the Bank for International Settlements (BIS), and the Financial Stability Board—reached the same conclusion. Their report for G20 Finance Ministers and Governors (2009) finds that that current knowledge and understanding "limit the extent to which very precise guidance can be developed.

Assessments of systemic importance will necessarily involve a high degree of judgment." The problem, of course, is that judgments vary widely. A completely discretionary "I know it when I see it" approach is obviously not going to work to limit bailouts. Neither is relying on precedent, as in "Let's just assume the 19 financial institutions listed here are the systemic ones because they were in the government's stress test." To some people, virtually everything is systemic. To others, it remains very rare.

The 19 Financial Institutions in the Stress Test

1. JPMorgan Chase
2. Citigroup
3. Bank of America
4. Wells Fargo
5. Goldman Sachs
6. Morgan Stanley
7. MetLife
8. PNC Financial Services
9. U.S. Bancorp
10. Bank of New York Mellon
11. GMAC
12. SunTrust
13. State Street
14. Capital One Financial Corp.
15. BB&T
16. Regions Financial Corp.
17. American Express
18. Fifth Third Bancorp
19. KeyCorp

POLICY IMPLICATIONS

My assessment that systemic risk is still not well defined leads to three policy implications.

First, those reform proposals that rely on systemic risk to determine in advance whether a firm should be deemed systemically significant are not ready for prime time. They should be shelved until an operational definition is available. If we go ahead, we will make things worse by enshrining an inoperative concept. It is certainly inappropriate to preannounce which firms are systemically risky. This would make it obvious which firms would be bailed out and cause huge moral hazard problems. Moreover, the determination of whether a firm was systemically risky is time and state dependent. That is, it depends on the state of the cycle and the state of interconnections with other firms.

Second, a major effort should be undertaken to define and measure systemic risk. Since a proper examination of the causes of the recent financial crisis is part of this effort, perhaps the task could be subsumed under the Financial Crisis Inquiry Commission. But this is a big task requiring much data collection, analysis, and interpretation. In principle, we need to take what Furfine (2003) and Ashcraft and Duffie (2007) have done for the interbank market and apply it to the repo and derivative counterparties and any other link between financial firms. A large research effort should be devoted to the task of defining and measuring systemic risk.

Third, until the hard work of defining and measuring systemic risk is yielding results, policy makers have to find a framework for dealing with the bailout problem, recognizing these ambiguities. It may turn out that the reason why it is so difficult to define systemic risk is that it is much rarer than many now believe. But in the meantime, there is disagreement, and we need to recognize this. In my view, we need a highly transparent and accountable framework to ensure that the systemic risk concept is not abused in practice and fosters a shift away from the bailout mentality that still exists today.

A PROPOSED FRAMEWORK

There are three key elements of such a framework. First, using some set of *guidelines and criteria*, its goal should be to find an alternative to bailout once a case of systemic risk arises. This will help government officials avoid a bailout. Because of the lack of an operational definition at this time, the guidelines and criteria could be based on the general concepts described earlier, recognizing the imprecision and the various motivations people have to abuse the term. When and if the definitions and measures of systemic risk become operational, the guidelines and criteria would be tightened.

Second, for transparency and accountability, a report should be written about the case and made available to the public. The report would describe the rationale and justification for any bailout in detail, referring explicitly to how the criteria and guidelines apply and why the alternative to bailout was not used. A preliminary version of the report would be required within two weeks of the action, with a final report six weeks later.

Third, to make this process workable, *a credible alternative to the bailout should be made available to all market recipients*. As already noted, the report should say why these alternatives were not used. As an example, one alternative would be Tom Jackson's Chapter 11F.

This definition would improve incentives to monitor risk. If such a framework were laid out after the bailout of Bear Stearns creditors and if the management of Lehman reasoned that their firm might go into bankruptcy, then they would have been much more prepared and the Lehman bankruptcy would have been less severe, or it might never have occurred. The framework would create a virtuous circle where fewer firms would satisfy the definition, causing more to monitor their risk. It would end the vicious circle of bankruptcy and systemic risk we have now.

LEARNING FROM THE SUCCESS
OF ANOTHER FRAMEWORK

The framework I am proposing might be compared with the exceptional access framework the IMF instituted in 2003. Recall that the Mexican financial crisis of 1994–1995 brought about unprecedented bailouts by the IMF and the U.S. Treasury of the holders of Mexican dollar-linked government bonds (called *tesobonos*) through large-scale loans to Mexico to pay these creditors. So there are clear analogies between this intervention and the bailing out of the creditors of financial institutions now.

Almost immediately after the Mexican bailouts, many expressed concern about moral hazard. Expectations of similar bailouts could reduce due diligence on the part of investors and could also reduce incentives for emerging market countries to take steps to avoid circumstances that might lead to default. As a result of this moral hazard problem, as well as uncertainty about the nature of future policy actions, people worried that there could be more crises—more severe crises—in the future.

Reflecting these concerns, proposals were made to establish a new framework for limiting bailouts so that investors and borrowing countries would know the rules of the game. There were proposals by the British and the Canadians, for example, to put limits on access to large-scale loans from the IMF and to clarify the limits. These proposals were resisted during the 1990s by the United States and others. Doubts were expressed that any such limits could be adhered to. If limits were drawn, there was no credible way that they would be followed. In addition, some were concerned about the loss of discretion that such limits would entail. Agreement on such a framework could not be reached.

Without such a framework, interventions were erratic, and emerging market crises got worse and continued for another eight years. There was the Asian financial crisis and the Asian contagion with Korea, Thailand, Indonesia, and Malaysia. There was the Russian crisis with global contagion to Brazil and Argentina and even the United States as the Fed had to cut the interest rates in response. The erratic nature of the interventions was very visible in the case of Russia. After several years of support, loans were suddenly pulled in August 1998. I believe that the lack of predictability was as much a problem as the moral hazard.

But eventually a solution to the impasse was found. The solution was to introduce an alternative to either default or bailout. The alternative was to add new clauses to the sovereign bonds—collective action clauses—that would allow for an orderly workout of sovereign debt problems between a country and its creditors. The existence of such an alternative made it credible for the official sector to say no. Thus any guidelines set in advance would be more credible. The collective action clause alternative is, of course, analogous with the Chapter 11F alternative in the proposal made in this book by Tom Jackson.

And as soon as these clauses were put into the bonds, the IMF and its shareholders established a new exceptional access framework. The framework was much the same as the framework I am proposing here. After the framework was in place, emerging markets moved into a new era of stability. Emerging market crises, which were so common during the years since the Mexican intervention, ended in 2002; looking back, it is now clear that the terrible "eight-year crisis" ended. And in this recent crisis, which emanated from the developed countries, the emerging market countries have rebounded remarkably well. We never can prove cause and effect beyond a shadow of a doubt in economics, but the new framework had a role, in my view, both by clarifying the nature of future bailouts and by encouraging emerging market countries to follow policies that reduced the chance of crisis greatly.

REFERENCES

Adrian, Tobias, and Markus K. Brunnermeier. 2009. "CoVar." Unpublished paper, August.

Ashcraft, Adam B., and Darrell Duffie. 2007. "Systemic Illiquidity in the Federal Funds Market." *American Economic Review* 97, no. 2 (May): 221–225.

Bhansali, Vineer, Robert Gingrich, and Francis A. Longstaff. 2008. "Systemic Credit Risk: What Is the Market Telling Us?" Unpublished report, PIMCO.

Board of Governors of the Federal Reserve System. 2001. "Policy Statement on Payments System Risk." Washington, DC, May 30.

Chauffour, Jean-Pierre, and Thomas Farole. 2009. "Trade Finance in Crisis: Market Adjustment or Market Failure?" Unpublished paper, World Bank, June.

Diamond, Douglas W., and Raghuram G. Rajan. 2009. "Fear of Fire Sales and the Credit Freeze." Unpublished paper, University of Chicago.

Friedman, Milton, and Anna J. Schwartz. 1963. *A Monetary History of the United States, 1867–1960.* Princeton, NJ: Princeton University Press.

Furfine, Craig. 2003. "Interbank Exposures: Quantifying the Risk of Contagion." *Journal of Money, Credit, and Banking* 35, no. 1 (February), DOI: 10.1353/mcb.2003.0004.

———. 2006. "The Costs and Benefits of Moral Suasion: Evidence from the Rescue of Long-Term Capital Management." *Journal of Business* 79, no. 2.

G20 Finance Ministers and Governors. 2009. "Guidance to Assess the Systemic Importance of Financial Institutions, Markets and Instruments: Initial Considerations." Prepared by the staffs of the International Monetary Fund, Bank for International Settlement, Financial Stability Board, October.

Huang, Xin, Hao Zhou, and Haibin Zhu. 2009. "A Framework for Assessing the Systemic Risk of Major Financial Institutions." Board of Governors of the Federal Reserve System, Finance and Economics Discussion Series (FEDS), 2009-37, http://econpapers.repec.org/paper/fipfedgfe/2009-37.htm.

Kahn, Charles M., and William Roberds. 1998. "Payment System Settlement and Bank Incentives." *Review of Financial. Studies* 11: 845–870.

Kaufman, George G., and Kenneth E. Scott. 2003. "What Is Systemic Risk, and Do Bank Regulators Retard or Contribute to It?" *The Independent Review* 7, no. 3 (Winter): 371– 391.

Miller, Harvey R. 2009. "Too Big to Fail: The Role for Bankruptcy and Antitrust Law in Financial Regulation Reform." Testimony before the Subcommittee on Commercial and Administrative Law, House of Representatives, Committee on the Judiciary, October 22.

Rochet, Jean-Charles, and Jean Tirole. 1996. "Interbank Lending and Systemic Risk." *Journal of Money, Credit, and Banking* 28 (November): 733–762.

Romer, Christina D. 1992. "What Ended the Great Depression?" *Journal of Economic History* 52 (December): 757–784.

Special Inspector General for the Trouble Asset Relief Program. 2009. "Factors Affecting Efforts to Limit Payments to AIG Counterparties." SIGTARP-10-003, November 17, http://www.sigtarp.gov/reports/audit/2009/Factors_Affecting_Efforts_to_Limit_Payments_to_AIG_Counterparties.pdf.

Taylor, John B. 1995. "The Monetary Transmissions Mechanism: An Empirical Framework." *Journal of Economic Perspectives* 9 (Fall): 11–26.

Thomson, James B., and Joseph G. Haubrich. 2009. "Too Big to Fail and the Definition of Systemic Significance." FinReg21,www.finreg21.com, November 2.

U.S. Treasury Department. 2009. "Financial and Regulatory Reform." Washington, DC.

Wallison, Peter. 2009. "Testimony before the Congressional Oversight Panel." January 14.

5

Lessons Learned from the Lehman Bankruptcy

KIMBERLY ANNE SUMME

THE CARNAGE IS EVERYWHERE. Storied corporate histories have been dashed in the wreckage of the worst economic dislocation since the Great Depression. Many of the most globally recognized businesses have disappeared. Chrysler, a company previously resuscitated by the charismatic Lee Iacocca, has failed. General Motors, a 101-year-old company, now has the dubious distinction of being the largest industrial bankruptcy filing to date and is 60 percent owned by U.S. taxpayers. Waterford Wedgwood, a 250-year-old company known for its fine china and crystal, was placed

I wish to thank my husband, Philip, and our children for their patience, and Locke McMurray, Thomas Russo, Rebecca Simmons, and Scott Willoughby for their efforts to improve the quality of this chapter. Any errors are solely my own.

in administration in the United Kingdom. Countless other companies around the world, both large and small, suffered from the destructive forces of trillions of dollars in lost home values, stock market losses, and vanishing jobs.

The financial sector, which most blame for this crisis, suffered as well. The first notable casualty was Bear, Stearns & Co. Inc., a firm founded in 1923 that survived the stock market crash of 1929 without firing one employee. Bear Stearns, which once traded as high as $171 per share, was sold in March 2008 to JPMorgan Chase for $10 per share. Merrill Lynch, founded in 1914 as a partnership between Charles Merrill and Edmund Lynch, where Merrill's motto was "I have no fear of failure, provided I use my heart and head, hands and feet—and work like hell," disappeared into Bank of America in September 2008 to escape catastrophe. Lehman Brothers, an investment bank founded in Alabama in 1850 by two brothers from Bavaria, survived the Civil War and two world wars, but faltered in September 2008, taking with it the fragile U.S. and global economy.[1] While many companies hobbled by this recession had been steadily declining for some time, the financial institutions' failures were remarkable for the speed of their demise, adding to the complexity of their insolvencies and their disastrous effect on the global financial landscape.

Even the survivors have been badly wounded. AIG, the global insurance company founded in Shanghai in 1919 and once one of the world's largest companies, suffered devastating losses in its financial products subsidiary and has subsequently received U.S. taxpayer assistance of over $150 billion. The company continues to sell parts of its business in an effort to repay government loans. Bank of America, just three short years ago the world's largest bank, is mired in litigation and government investigations over its acquisition of Merrill Lynch, forcing the bank's CEO to step down in December 2009. Citigroup, once one of the world's largest banks and a top ten company by market capitalization, is now one-third owned by U.S. taxpayers and has a market cap less than that of Bank of Nova Scotia. Goldman Sachs and Morgan Stanley, venerable investment banks, became bank holding companies in an effort to ensure access to government funding in a difficult economic climate.

The stories of these corporations is just part of a gloomy worldwide recession. Millions of jobs have been lost, with the United States experiencing its highest level of unemployment since World War II. The price of a barrel of oil has leaped as high as $126.33 in June 2008, plunging to $32.94 by December 2008, and now it is on the climb again at $80 a barrel. And as with many past economic crises, Ponzi schemes have unraveled. Allen Stanford, the failed former bodybuilding gym owner, was arrested after a lengthy investigation into an $8 billion financial fraud. Bernard Madoff, a former chairman of NASDAQ, is now serving a 150-year sentence for defrauding investors of billions of dollars.

Policy makers have struggled with difficult choices in the wake of this devastation, urged on by a public outraged at the outsized compensation earned by many of Wall Street's leaders and blaming the financiers for "getting us into this mess." Along the way, derivatives, a once esoteric corner of finance, have been targeted by many for causing, or at the least contributing to, the collapse of the U.S. economy and triggering a global crisis. For years, while policy makers endeavored to keep pace with the innovation and creativity of Wall Street, regulation often lagged behind seminal developments in the financial industry.

While some may feel that the worst of the crisis is behind us, this sentiment should not dissuade policy makers from the laborious task of reconsidering our regulatory structure, particularly as it relates to systemically important financial institutions.[2] The precipitous disappearance of several of the largest financial institutions has concentrated risk in a far smaller number of entities, accentuated by the fact that the three largest derivatives portfolios are now held by the United States' three largest bank holding companies. Moreover, policy makers' pressure to utilize centralized counterparties, a concept that certainly offers potential solutions to some of the problems that plagued our financial system, risks assembling the ultimate concentration of risk if derivatives products are migrated in meaningful volumes to exchanges.

Without doubt, an abundance of policy areas deserve review. All agree that we must ensure that future failures of systemically important financial institutions are tolerable not only for our economy, but for the global economy as well. This chapter will focus on one of those areas: the resolution of systemically important financial institutions and, in particular, the treatment in bankruptcy of certain financial instruments known as qualified financial contracts. Qualified financial contracts encompass a variety of instruments, as discussed later.[3] This chapter will focus on two of those instrument categories: over-the-counter or privately negotiated derivatives and repurchase or "repo" transactions.

DIFFERENT BANKRUPTCY REGIMES
FOR DIFFERENT ENTITIES

History of U.S. Bankruptcy Laws

The history of bankruptcy in the United States makes for fascinating reading.[4] With the federal government choosing rather late in our country's history to create a central bank in 1914, the American banking system until then relied on state banks to serve in roles, such as the creation of paper money, that today are occupied by the Federal Reserve System. In the 1800s, state bank failures were commonplace, and local regulators developed a variety of approaches to handle bank insolvencies. In 1829, New York state, under the leadership of then governor, and soon-to-be president of the United States, Martin Van Buren, established the first insurance fund designed to protected bank depositors.

By the 1870s, a banking crisis in Europe led to the collapse of U.S. railroads, then the backbone of commerce. The tipping point was the failure in September 1873 of Jay Cooke and Company, a banking enterprise that had invested in the development of a transcontinental railroad to be built by the Northern Pacific Company. The U.S. stock market dropped sharply as a result of Cooke and Company's failure, and the ensuing recession lasted for five years. Three million people lost their jobs in the Panic of 1873, and family farms grappled with declining commodity prices and decades of resulting impoverishment.

The Panic of 1873 resulted in increased efforts by the judiciary to take the ideological lead in the development of reorganization plans for failed companies, and to this day, the United States continues to be a debtor-friendly jurisdiction. In general, U.S. bankruptcy law is designed to rehabilitate or to liquidate an insolvent entity. If rehabilitation is elected, the objective is to restructure the insolvent entity's business operations and/or capital structure to form a sustainable, productive enterprise. If liquidation is elected, the objective is to distribute losses equitably among creditors. Regardless of which approach is taken, preexisting creditor claims cease to accrue upon a company's bankruptcy filing, and the relative value of existing contracts is preserved.

For failed banks, however, the courts play a secondary role to the federal bank regulator who handles the insolvency, the Federal Deposit Insurance Corporation (FDIC). Unlike corporations, banks are a sort of franchise authorized by a state or the federal government, and their central role in the provision of credit, payment and settlement means that federal policies are the driving factor in any bank insolvency. As a consequence, the U.S. Bankruptcy Code does not address the insolvency of banks, savings and loans, and credit unions.

Contemporary financial institutions, particularly the most systemically important ones, often consist of dozens of separate legal entities operating globally, a mix of banks, broker-dealers, commodity brokers, futures commission merchants, Delaware corporations, and insurance companies. Upon insolvency, each of these component entities is potentially subject to its own insolvency regime, depending on its organizational form and sphere of activities. For example, the bankruptcy of Lehman Brothers, involving nearly one hundred entities operating globally, resulted in many of the larger businesses being handled either under Chapter 11 of the U.S. Bankruptcy Code (in the case of Lehman Brothers Holdings Inc., the parent holding company, Lehman Brothers Special Financing, Inc., the Delaware corporation that held much of the derivatives portfolio, and several other entities) or under Chapter 7 (in the case of Lehman Brothers Inc., the broker-dealer). Lehman Brothers also maintained insurance subsidiaries that were subject to unique insolvency laws.[5] There were also bankruptcy proceedings initiated in a variety of jurisdictions outside of the United States, including Australia, Japan, and the United Kingdom. Some Lehman Brothers entities did not file for bankruptcy, however. For example, Lehman Brothers operated a bank, today known as Aurora Bank FSB, which employs 1,700 people servicing over $100 billion in mortgages.[6]

The Current U.S. Insolvency Regime for Entities Engaged in Derivatives and Repurchase Transactions

Banks The Federal Deposit Insurance Act (FDIA) provides that the FDIC may operate as a conservator to preserve the value of a failing bank and return it to financial health or as a receiver in order to liquidate a failed bank. Unlike a proceeding under the U.S. Bankruptcy Code, an FDIC receivership or conservatorship is not subject to direct supervision by the courts. In large part, this policy choice was designed to ensure that bank failures were not subjected to the assumed-to-be lengthy proceedings under Chapter 11 of the U.S. Bankruptcy Code, and it placed more discretion with the FDIC to act expeditiously.

Three key principles relate to the treatment of failed banks, relative to qualified financial contracts. First, in view of the unique role of banks as depository institutions, upon the failure of a bank, depositors will receive priority over the bank's unsecured general creditors.[7] Second, the FDIC has limited repudiation and avoidance powers with respect to qualified financial contracts. For example, regardless of whether the FDIC is acting as a conservator or a receiver, it must either disaffirm or repudiate all or none of the qualified financial contracts between the failed bank and the same counterparty, together with associated credit support.[8] Third, the FDIC has the right to transfer qualified financial contracts, but unlike other contracts, the FDIC must transfer to the same transferee all the qualified financial contracts and related claims between the failed bank and the counterparty and its affiliates.[9] Furthermore, the FDIC may not transfer qualified financial contracts to a non-U.S. institution unless the counterparty's contractual rights are enforceable to the same extent as under U.S. law.[10] The time frame in which the FDIC must elect to transfer and provide notice is dependent on the capacity under which it is acting. If the FDIC is acting as receiver, it must provide notice of the transfer by 5:00 P.M. EST on the business day after its appointment as receiver.[11] At that time, the counterparty to the failed bank may elect to terminate the qualified financial contract (i.e., the nondefaulting counterparty to the failed bank could follow the termination and close-out provisions in the ISDA Master Agreement for derivatives transactions). If the FDIC is acting as conservator, there is no special time limit on its right to transfer qualified financial contracts, and the counterparty may not terminate the qualified financial contracts unless the conservator defaults to a degree that would permit termination under applicable noninsolvency law.

From available reports, it appears that in every recent case where a large U.S. bank has become subject to a receivership proceeding, all qualified financial contracts and associated margin of the failed bank were transferred in their entirety to a single bridge bank or third-party acquirer.[12] When the assets of Washington Mutual Bank, the largest U.S. bank failure to date, were sold in September 2008 to JPMorgan Chase, the FDIC transferred to JPMorgan Chase all qualified financial contracts to which Washington Mutual Bank was a party. However, while the FDIC has achieved a solid record in effectively handling failed banks with qualified financial contracts portfolios, none of those bank failures to date have involved a derivatives portfolio that approaches the size of Lehman Brothers' estimated $35 trillion notional derivatives portfolio.

Broker-Dealers Since 1978, the U.S. Bankruptcy Code has excluded broker-dealers from Chapter 11. The rationale was that a separate scheme was needed to protect the millions of brokerage customers across the United States, and that any reorganization of a brokerage through Chapter 11 would be costly and complex. Instead, customers of failed brokerages are subject to liquidation proceedings under Chapter 7 of the U.S. Bankruptcy Code and would share pro rata in the distribution of the failed brokerage's assets. Alternatively, the Securities Investor Protection Corporation (SIPC), created by the Securities Investor Protection Act of 1970 (SIPA),[13] could petition the bankruptcy court to appoint SIPC and allow it to administer the return of customer property. SIPC has been incredibly successful in the execution of its mission. According to its website, 99 percent of customers covered by

SIPA have been made whole in the over four hundred failed brokerage cases handled during the past thirty-eight years.[14] When Lehman Brothers Inc., the broker-dealer, filed for insolvency, SIPC transferred approximately 630,000 customer accounts representing over $142 billion of assets, mainly to the brokerage arm of Barclays Bank, Barclays Capital Inc., as approved by the bankruptcy court.[15] The protections of SIPA are explicitly focused on offering protection to individual brokerage customers, and as such, statutory protections do not extend to derivatives, repurchase transactions,[16] futures, and securities lending counterparties.

Corporates   Under the U.S. Bankruptcy Code, corporations and other entities within its scope can be reorganized under Chapter 11 or liquidated under Chapter 7. Section 362(a) of the U.S. Bankruptcy Code provides that upon the filing of a bankruptcy petition under the U.S. Bankruptcy Code, an automatic stay is applied such that secured and unsecured creditors of the debtor are prevented from making claims or taking other unilateral actions against the bankrupt entity to collect debts. Counterparties to qualified financial contracts, however, are permitted to exercise immediate contractual rights to terminate transactions and to offset or net termination values, without application of the stay.

Many financial institutions have historically engaged in derivatives transactions through an unregulated corporation. Lehman Brothers Special Financing, Inc. (LBSF), for example, was a Delaware corporation that engaged in the investment bank's derivatives business. As a result, when LBSF filed for bankruptcy on October 3, 2008, it was estimated that it was a counterparty to 930,000 derivatives transactions documented under 6,120 ISDA Master Agreements.[17] The ISDA Master Agreement gives the nondefaulting party, upon a counterparty's default (which includes voluntary and involuntary bankruptcy), the right to designate a date on which the portfolio will be valued and terminated, to terminate the transactions, and to liquidate and apply any collateral.

THE RATIONALE FOR PROTECTING QUALIFIED FINANCIAL CONTRACTS FROM THE STAY UNDER THE U.S. BANKRUPTCY CODE

Since 1978, an increasing range of trading contracts have been protected from the application of the automatic stay and other powers under the U.S. Bankruptcy Code.[18] Similarly, the Federal Deposit Insurance Act was amended to protect the rights of parties to qualified financial contracts. As a result, counterparties to qualified financial contracts are generally permitted to enforce default and termination provisions in those contracts without the need for relief from the automatic stay. In addition to the exercise of termination rights under the contractual terms applying to those qualified financial contracts, the debtor's counterparties may also liquidate collateral that has been pledged by the debtor. Any shortfall resulting thereafter will constitute unsecured claims against the bankruptcy estate, entitling creditors to share in any distribution.

The rationale for protecting qualified financial contracts has been to mitigate the systemic risk arising from cascading bankruptcies of other entities. By providing a safe harbor from the application of certain provisions of the U.S. Bankruptcy

Code or the FDIA to these contracts, the delays assumed to be inherent in the bankruptcy process would be avoided, and counterparties could reduce the losses that would otherwise result from the degradation of collateral pledged by the debtor.[19] Because qualified financial contracts would be terminated and netted quickly, financial market participants would be stabilized through the release of liquidity necessary to settle their obligations. As the FDIC stated in 2005:

> This is particularly important in the financial markets because, unlike loans or other financial contracts, the value of derivatives are [sic] based on fluctuating market values. If a counterparty is placed into bankruptcy or receivership, the stay on the termination of the contract and the liquidation of collateral could create escalating losses due to changes in market prices. As a result, the ability for the non-defaulting party to terminate the contract and net exposures quickly can be crucial to limit the losses to the non-defaulting party because such contracts can change quickly in value due to market fluctuations.[20]

Two well-known scholars offer another rationale for the treatment of qualified financial contracts under the U.S. Bankruptcy Code. These scholars argue that systemic risk concerns are not a sufficient rationale for protecting these contracts. Rather, because derivatives are not asset specific, they should not be subject to an automatic stay, which by its nature is designed to be specific in its safeguarding of assets. Thus, economic efficiency and value preservation are increased for contracts that are not subject to the application of the automatic stay.[21]

Systemic risk concerns were, however, the articulated reason for regulatory action taken in 1998 following the sharp losses experienced by the prominent hedge fund, Long-Term Capital Management. Losses resulting from the Russian ruble crisis earlier that year occurred at a time when the fund had $1.4 trillion of notional value of off–balance sheet derivatives positions with seventy-five counterparties.[22] Then president of the Federal Reserve Bank of New York, William McDonough, stated that the "abrupt and disorderly close-out of LTCM's positions would pose unacceptable risks to the American economy."[23] Rather than terminate the derivatives contracts, as the fund's counterparties would have been permitted to do under the specified protections afforded to swap counterparties, several of the largest counterparties, at the urging of the Federal Reserve, infused the fund with $3.6 billion in capital so that counterparties then had time to unwind their derivatives positions in an orderly fashion. Leading financial institutions felt that if Long-Term Capital Management, a Delaware company, had been allowed to file under Chapter 11, counterparties of the failed fund would have rushed to close out their transactions and to liquidate any collateral on hand.[24] Slower counterparties would have seen the value of their collateral diminish and found the replacement of hedged transactions meaningfully more challenging.

Once Long-Term Capital Management was successfully resolved, the regulators remained more concerned about systemic risk arising from limitations on termination than those arising from a precipitous termination. The President's Working Group on Financial Markets[25] published a series of recommendations in 2000 in an effort to improve the close-out netting regime for qualified financial contracts under the U.S. Bankruptcy Code. The President's Working Group noted that its recommendations were designed to "enhance market stability, limit counterparty exposure and . . . preserve market stability in the event of a failure of a financial institution."[26]

The effort to improve the close-out netting regime continued for the next several years, culminating in the expansion of protected qualified financial contracts in the Bankruptcy Abuse Prevention and Consumer Protection Act of 2005.[27] The act harmonized most provisions relating to the insolvency of banks, broker-dealers, investment banks, and companies while expanding the transaction types covered by the safe harbor and extending such protections to a larger array of nonfinancial companies. Master netting contracts were also included in the safe harbor under the act on the basis that the more counterparties that were able to net down their exposures free of Chapter 11 constraints, the less exposed they and the markets would be to the failure of a major participant.

POLICY CHOICES IN MAKING FAILURE TOLERABLE FOR SYSTEMICALLY IMPORTANT FINANCIAL INSTITUTIONS

The failure to prevent Lehman Brothers from filing for bankruptcy, which many regard as a historic error committed by the secretary of the Treasury and the Federal Reserve chairman, led to the Obama administration's proposal to migrate the treatment in bankruptcy of a systemically important financial institution from the U.S. Bankruptcy Code to a regime largely based on the FDIA. As noted, the United States does not have a single bankruptcy or regulatory regime that would permit the unified resolution of diverse financial groups such as Lehman Brothers. Many point to this fragmented approach as being partly responsible for the chaos that ensued from the Lehman Brothers bankruptcy, where the FDIA, Chapters 7 and 11 of the U.S. Bankruptcy Code, SIPA, state insurance law, and foreign laws applied to various bankrupt Lehman entities.

The Obama administration has issued a series of proposals, largely similar, beginning in March 2009 in an effort to apply resolution authority to "systemically important financial companies." The administration's initial proposal was revised in July 2009 and applied to "large, interconnected financial companies." On November 6, 2009, the administration issued yet another revision of its proposal, this time working in concert with the House Financial Services Committee (the "House Proposal").[28] Under the House Proposal, the proposed resolution authority would authorize the secretary of the Treasury, upon the recommendation of the Federal Reserve and the FDIC, to consult with the president to authorize the FDIC to exercise resolution powers as the receiver of an identified financial holding company in situations of systemic risk. An identified financial holding company is oddly not defined in the subtitle of the House Proposal addressing the proposed resolution authority, but rather is defined in the general definitions provision. There, identified financial holding company is broad in its sweep, capturing a wide array of financial and commercial companies, ranging from automobile manufacturers with financing subsidiaries to asset managers and hedge funds. The FDIC would be authorized to sell immediately any or all assets of the identified financial holding company or alternatively, if a buyer or buyers could not be found for those assets, the assets and liabilities of the company would be transferred temporarily to a bridge financial company and an orderly liquidation would follow.

The Obama administration's proposal would be largely irrelevant to the management of insolvency risks arising from derivatives. Insured depository institutions, broker-dealers subject to SIPC, and insurance companies are omitted from coverage under the House Proposal.[29] While the administration likely had Lehman Brothers–type entities in mind when creating its proposed resolution authority, such entities have largely disappeared. Bear Stearns and Merrill Lynch were folded into commercial banks, and Goldman Sachs and Morgan Stanley converted their charters to become bank holding companies in the fall of 2008. In other words, there are no systemically important entities (such as those identified in note 3 of this chapter) that conduct the significant majority of their derivative business out of an identified financial holding company. Rather, Bank of America, Citibank, and JPMorgan Chase each conduct their derivative trading out of their respective banks. JPMorgan Chase, for example, has a $79.94 trillion notional value derivative portfolio; arguably, with its $900 billion in deposits and its leading custodial business in the $5 trillion daily repo market, it would seem to be the type of systemically important entity that should be captured through a unified insolvency regime. Goldman Sachs and Morgan Stanley are still migrating their derivative business on the basis of their conversion to bank holding companies. For example, Goldman Sachs currently conducts its derivative business through Goldman Sachs International, a U.K. broker-dealer.[30] Morgan Stanley Capital Services Inc., one of Morgan Stanley's primary derivatives subsidiaries, will merge in 2010 into Morgan Stanley Bank N.A., a Utah bank, and the credit derivatives and interest rate swap business will be executed out of this entity. Morgan Stanley & Co. International plc, the U.K. broker-dealer, will engage in equity derivatives, while Morgan Stanley & Co. Incorporated, a U.S. broker-dealer, will transact in foreign exchange.

The challenge is pinning Lehman Brothers' collapse on its qualified financial contracts or, more broadly, its insolvency, as being directly responsible for the exacerbation of global financial instability.

Some may argue that this failure to capture insured depository institutions within the House Proposal does not matter. After all, the FDIC's resolution authority would already apply to commercial banks. However, the Obama administration has missed a unique opportunity to address the economic and procedural inefficiencies produced by our fragmented bankruptcy regime. If Lehman Brothers existed today, the House Proposal would apply to Lehman Brothers Holding Inc. but not to Lehman Brothers Inc., the broker-dealer that arguably was the more systemically important entity. Moreover, systemic risk has been too broadly defined in the House Proposal in the sense that many financial and commercial companies could be covered, and some or most of those companies may not be of truly systemic importance. In addition, the failure to identify explicitly those companies of systemic importance in advance of the application of any resolution authority suffers from a lack of legal clarity and will result in market participants making assumptions about whether any particular entity is or is not covered by the proposed resolution authority. True progress will be made when our bankruptcy regime reflects the diverse nature of contemporary financial groups. In order to ensure that future failures of systemically important entities are tolerable for the financial system, a unified bankruptcy approach must be adopted. In addition, policy choices must acknowledge that systemically important entities may unravel within a matter of days, so that clarity of action and process in a compressed, and likely aggravated market environment, is ensured. In addition to making policy choices that are designed with legal certainty and speed in mind, it is also important that operational challenges are considered. Over-the-counter derivatives and repurchase transactions are two of the more critical qualified financial contracts that systemically important entities engage in, and the operational infrastructure for these aspects of the institution are some of the most overworked and vulnerable. The Obama administration's failure to address the aforementioned concerns will not avert any systemic effects resulting from the future bankruptcy of one of our most critical institutions.

Over-the-Counter Derivatives: Remove the Safe Harbor and Impose a Stay?

Some on Wall Street remark quietly that the only way in the future to avoid the sort of chaos that resulted when Lehman Brothers failed is to remove the safe harbor for qualified financial contracts and apply an automatic stay. Harvey Miller, the architect of Lehman Brothers' bankruptcy filing, testified that "massive destruction of value" could have been averted if an automatic stay had been in place for these contracts.[31] Accordingly, Miller proposes that the termination and close-out netting rights that derivative counterparties rely on should no longer exist—at least not until such time as the automatic stay is lifted. Recent legislative proposals have incorporated this view. The House Proposal provides that qualified financial contract counterparties should be subject to the automatic stay for one business day. The proposal introduced by Senator Christopher Dodd would extend the application of the stay to three business days. Proponents of this view note that the qualified financial contracts safe harbor accelerated Lehman Brothers' demise by increasing demands for collateral and requests to close positions at the firm's most vulnerable moment. In other words, in their view, the safe harbor, which was ostensibly designed to prevent systemic risk, ended up creating systemic risk and hastened the bankruptcy process. Hence, proponents contend that the safe harbor should be removed and an automatic stay imposed for derivative transactions and other qualified financial contracts.

The congressional rationale for protecting qualified financial contracts from the automatic stay was to avoid systemic risk. Congress and regulators were keen to prevent a cascade of bankruptcies of financially interconnected entities by protecting qualified financial contracts and respecting the underlying agreement between counterparties to terminate those transactions. Unfortunately, at present, empirical evidence supporting or opposing the exemption of qualified financial contracts from the automatic stay does not exist. While studies of the Lehman Brothers bankruptcy are likely, what we do know is that none of Lehman Brothers' derivative counterparties filed for bankruptcy in the aftermath of Lehman's failure. It is also known that the derivatives market did not grind to a halt after Lehman Brothers' bankruptcy filing. Rather, the global derivative markets continued to trade quite actively, leading some to criticize the sizable profits earned from this trading by leading banks in the first two quarters of 2009.[32] In addition, while it was widely estimated in the lead-up to the October 10, 2008, credit default swap auction for bonds referencing Lehman Brothers that close to $400 billion in payments could be required in payments to settle outstanding contracts, in fact only $6 billion in net settlement payments were ultimately needed.[33]

It is also known that a mere five weeks after the Chapter 11 filing of several Lehman Brothers entities that were party to "derivative contracts," defined by the debtor to include securities contracts, forward contracts, repurchase agreements, and swap contracts, approximately 740,000 out of 930,000 derivative contracts—80 percent of the debtor's derivative contracts—had been terminated pursuant to the provisions in the underlying contract.[34] At this time, November 13, 2008, Lehman Brothers succeeded in its motion to assign and settle outstanding derivative transactions before the U.S. Bankruptcy Court for the Southern District of New York.[35] Lehman Brothers argued that some of the counterparties who had not elected to terminate their derivative transactions were out-of-the-money to the debtor and, as a result, the estate might best realize the value of those transactions through assignment. The Bankruptcy Court agreed and concluded that derivative transactions that had not been terminated could be assigned to third parties without the consent of the original counterparties.

By January 16, 2009, the Lehman Brothers estate filed a second motion to clarify that unterminated derivative transactions could be assigned without court intervention if the original counterparty so consented. At that hearing, Lehman Brothers noted that out of the 190,000 derivative contracts that had not been terminated at the time of its first motion in November 2008, now only 30,000 derivative contracts remained unterminated.[36] In other words, only 3 percent of all derivative contracts outstanding at the time of the Chapter 11 filing were unresolved roughly 106 days later.

As it relates to derivative transactions specifically, the debtor reported on November 18, 2009, that out of 6,355 ISDA Master Agreements (or other contracts supporting derivative trading) in place at the time of the bankruptcy filing, approximately 50 percent had been reconciled and concluded with respect to the valuation of the derivative portfolio.[37] A smaller percentage, 17 percent, had been settled.[38] At the same time, Alvarez & Marsal, appointed by the U.S. Bankruptcy Court to manage the Lehman Brothers estate, noted in its "State of the Estate" report that a remarkable enhancement to the value of the debtor's derivative book had occurred following the bankruptcy filing. Nearly $2 billion in cumulative cash collections were received to the credit of the derivative book by January 29, 2009; by November 6, 2009, that figure had risen to $8.023 billion.[39]

If the analysis is broadened to consider whether any of the top thirty unsecured claimants to Lehman Brothers were significant derivative counterparties or were entities who subsequently experienced bankruptcy, the answer is no. According to Schedule 1 of Lehman Brothers Holdings Inc.'s petition for bankruptcy, approximately $2.5 billion of bank loans represented the vast majority of unsecured claims, with a number of Japanese banks serving as the primary lenders to Lehman Brothers. None of those entities, at least according to this court record, were significant derivative counterparties to Lehman Brothers, nor did any creditor listed subsequently file for bankruptcy.

Debates over the valuations of terminated derivative transactions continue to vex the bankruptcy estate, however. In addition, a relatively small number of counterparties to LBSF, the primary U.S. derivative trading entity, have not fulfilled their obligations under the ISDA Master Agreement and have not terminated the derivative transactions, perhaps hoping that as out-of-the-money counterparties to Lehman Brothers that exposures will swing back in their favor. Lehman Brothers has successfully pursued one such counterparty, Metavante Corporation, a financial technology company. Metavante had entered into interest rate swap transactions with LBSF, and upon LBSF's Chapter 11 filing, it elected not to terminate those transactions, yet it did not make any further payments. LBSF petitioned the U.S. Bankruptcy Court for the Southern District of New York to compel Metavante to perform under the ISDA Master Agreement and declare that Metavante's termination rights were subject to the automatic stay. LBSF argued that pursuant to Section 365(e)(1) of the U.S. Bankruptcy Code, an executory contract could not be terminated or modified solely because of a provision in the contract that is conditional on the insolvency or financial condition of the debtor or the commencement of a case under Chapter 11.[40] Metavante countered that Section 2(a)(iii) of the ISDA Master Agreement, which provides that payment obligations to one's counterparty are conditional on there being no event of default, justified its decision to cease making payments to the estate since the guarantor's insolvency had not been cured. After eight months, Metavante owed LBSF more than $6.3 million in addition to default interest.

Judge James Peck was not persuaded by Metavante's argument. He determined that Metavante was required to terminate its positions or continue to fulfill its contractual obligations. Metavante could not benefit under its derivative contracts once it had suspended performance. Metavante was held to have had the right to terminate the derivative contracts, but it had waived that right by failing to exercise it within a reasonable period of time. The congressional history behind the safe harbor provisions indicated to Judge Peck that it was the intent that swap market participants would immediately, or at least "fairly contemporaneously," terminate qualified financial contracts in order to take advantage of the protections afforded by the safe harbor provisions.[41] Metavante is planning to appeal the decision, but for now, the implication is that counterparties do not have an unlimited window of time in which to exercise their termination rights with respect to derivative transactions, but the court refrained from imposing a specific time frame for such exercise.

What Does Lehman Brothers' Failure Mean for Qualified Financial Contracts and the Exemption from the Automatic Stay?   Lehman Brothers did not fail because of losses experienced in its derivative portfolio. Rather, Lehman Brothers failed because of a sharp lack of liquidity and poor management choices relating to its commercial real estate, mortgage, and leveraged loans business—areas the U.S. Bankruptcy Code cannot affect.

The acute problem for policy makers is that once a bank is in distress, its cash liquidity is threatened, its stock price is plummeting,[42] and no other market participants will extend credit or transact with the failing bank. The application of an automatic stay, while appearing to preserve the value of the "assets" of the failing entity, may be illusory as it relates to derivatives since derivative transactions and the collateral associated with those transactions are not really assets in the traditional sense, and the preservation of value may rapidly change, particularly in a distressed market. Moreover, the legal certainty afforded to the termination of these contracts, from the perspective of both the well-understood provisions of the ISDA Master Agreement and the application of the safe harbor provisions of the U.S. Bankruptcy Code, should not be discounted. Highly liquid derivative transactions, such as interest rate and foreign exchange derivatives (which constitute 80 percent of the $600 trillion notional value over-the-counter derivative market[43]), were terminated by many of Lehman Brothers' counterparties after the investment bank's failure, allowing those counterparties to reduce potential losses by entering into replacement transactions. The loss of an ability to hedge one's trading book because of the application of a stay would result in significant losses for qualified financial contract counterparties, causing a catastrophic decline in the activities of the financial markets.

Some would counter that giving derivative counterparties the right to terminate, while other creditors are frozen, may destabilize the failing entity further. However, this argument overlooks the fact that termination offers immediate liquidity and a transfer of wealth to occur, as payments are made between counterparties. In a situation of systemic risk, the application of a stay to derivative counterparties of a systemically important entity is unlikely to preserve significant value given the volatility of markets at that time. In a severe market dislocation, the value of a derivative portfolio may not be terribly differentiated on day one of the bankruptcy filing versus three business days later. In addition, contrary to the assertion that collateral is being drained from the failed entity, at least for systemically important entities such as banks, those banks rarely, if ever, post collateral to their nonbank counterparties, so there is simply nothing to liquidate, making it even more imperative to terminate the contracts as quickly as possible. Lastly, the imposition of a one-business-day stay as included in the House Proposal, or a three-business-day stay as proposed by Senator Dodd, is ineffective in terms of stabilizing the financial system and would only provide the FDIC with time to identify an appropriate entity to which the qualified financial contracts could be transferred. That said, it is not clear whether the FDIC, despite its ability in handling over one hundred bank failures this year, would be able to familiarize itself with a complex derivatives and qualified financial contracts portfolio within one or three business days.

Liquidity Crises and the Operation of the Repo Market

Beginning in the summer of 2007, significant fault lines were exposed in the funding methodology increasingly relied upon by investment banks. Unlike commercial banks, which may access temporary extensions of cash at a discounted rate through the Federal Reserve, investment banks such as Bear Stearns or Lehman Brothers borrowed cash from money market funds, among others, for a short duration of time, with those obligations typically collateralized by Treasury securities.

Bear Stearns, the first major victim of what was then the "subprime crisis," was heavily dependent on overnight repos to fund its less liquid assets, such as derivatives. At the same time, a deteriorating pool of collateral was being offered by Bear Stearns to its secured lenders. For example, highly rated but hard-to-value tranches of securitized pools of subprime mortgages and corporate securities were offered as collateral. This reflected the drive by investment banks and investors to boost their leverage and garner higher returns. Increasing haircuts on the collateral being posted were also becoming commonplace.

The strain that Bear Stearns faced was enormous and relentless, particularly given that the duration of the borrowing cycle was one day. At the same time, the firm was grappling with short selling and other pressures, all culminating in the ultimate erosion of confidence in Bear Stearns as a counterparty. As fractures grew in the repo market, Federal Reserve chairman Ben Bernanke, alarmed at the rapid unraveling of Bear Stearns, established the Primary Dealer Credit Facility on March 17, 2008. For the first time, investment banks such as Lehman Brothers were able to borrow directly from the Federal Reserve. Daily lending activity through this facility reached its peak in October 2008 at an average of $150 billion. Interestingly, though, is that the Federal Reserve reported on September 12, 2008, that neither Lehman Brothers nor any other dealer had tapped the facility, likely out of concern that it would signal a fundamental weakness.

While the Primary Dealer Credit Facility alleviated some pressure, operational risks in the settlement of repo transactions remained elevated. The market had migrated by 2007 to a triparty model for settlement, whereby a custodian bank physically controlled and managed the collateral. At the epicenter of the triparty model was JPMorgan Chase and the Bank of New York Mellon. On a combined basis, these two banks clear the vast majority of the $5 trillion daily repo market. Federal Reserve Chairman Bernanke recognized this second danger in March 2008, cautioning that there were significant dangers associated with having only two clearing banks support the financial system and stating that a central clearing system was worth considering.

However, once Lehman Brothers failed in September 2008, liquidity demands surged as counterparty concerns trumped everything. Approximately $2.68 trillion of Treasury settlement failures were recorded in October 2008, a consequence of a flight to the safety of Treasury securities. The macroenvironment had shifted so dramatically that as nominal interest rates fell, fewer securities were lent, resulting in a year-over-year decrease in the repo market of 50 percent.[44] Eventually, once the U.S. government increased liquidity in the financial system and banks were recapitalized, the fractures began to close.

Certainly, capital reserves are critical for systemically important financial institutions. Banks such as JPMorgan Chase, for example, rightly highlight on earnings calls their Tier 1 common capital, currently stated in its third quarter 2009 earnings call to be $101 billion. However, when a financial institution is under strain, its capital becomes inextricably linked to its liquidity. More capital could be required at just the moment in time when funding and investment are scarce. For example, Standard & Poor's reported that Lehman Brothers' Tier 1 capital ratio was 10.7 percent at the end of the second quarter 2008, in line with other investment banks such as Goldman Sachs, which was 10.8 percent at that time, and Lehman Brothers also had a liquidity pool of $42 billion in August 2008.[45] But as market participants learned in the aftermath of Bear Stearns and Lehman Brothers, liquidity management is no longer about how much cash is on hand but, rather, singularly focused on how much access to cash you have. Once counterparties, creditors, and customers lose confidence in their financial counterparty, the entity is unable to continue functioning.

Making Failure Tolerable

What should policy makers do to make future failures of systemically important financial institutions tolerable? First, policy makers need to agree on, and periodically reevaluate, what institutions are considered to be systemically important. Developing new regulatory and insolvency regimes without understanding the types of entities to which the label will apply is not prudent. Clarity on what institutions are considered by regulators to be systemically important will ensure that appropriate regulatory resources can be brought to bear as well as focusing heightened regulatory scrutiny of those entities' businesses. Greater risk awaits if our policy makers act as if no entity is too big to fail but then, once failure is close at hand, take actions that indicate they are, in fact, too big to fail.

In the case of Lehman Brothers, the majority of market participants did not act as if they knew the investment bank's failure was imminent. In fact, many market participants continued to believe that either an acquirer would step forward or the government would assist the troubled firm as it had Bear Stearns. Prominent news publications focused on the Korean Development Bank's interest in acquiring a stake in Lehman Brothers; consequently, Lehman Brothers' stock traded sharply up at discrete points in late August 2008. As late as September 2, 2008, the Korean Development Bank was on record confirming that it was in discussions with Lehman Brothers. By September 10, however, just four days before Lehman Brothers' bankruptcy filing, the Korean Development Bank ceased discussions, Lehman reported its second consecutive quarterly loss, and clients finally began to comprehend that maybe the impossible would become the possible. New business ground to a halt.

No one from the federal government was on record during the weekend prior to Lehman Brothers' bankruptcy commenting that bankruptcy was a possibility—that would have been untenable for a regulator to observe in any event. Rather, the regulators were on record stating that they were working around the clock to avoid the collapse of our financial system. Federal Reserve Chairman Bernanke subsequently testified on September 24, 2008, before the Senate Committee on Banking, Housing, and Urban Affairs that Lehman Brothers' distress had been well-known for some time and that credit default spreads were evidence that bankruptcy was likely. In fact, Lehman Brothers' spreads were oddly not indicative of such a state. As a paper published by the International Monetary Fund noted, Lehman

Brothers' default showed an exceptional case in which cash bond prices collapsed to around 20 cents as credit default swap spreads remained relatively low, leading to the unusual scenario where the basis was positive during distress.[46] A research report published by Barclays Capital noted:

> In recent financial institutions bankruptcies, CDS levels were clearly not the leading indicator. Lehman Brothers provides the best example, as its CDS remained in spread running the week of its bankruptcy filing. This actually resulted in some of the best basis trades ever in the credit market as the bonds cratered well before CDS.[47]

In addition, the chairman of the Financial Services Authority, Lord Turner, noted in remarks on October 29, 2009, that CDS spreads of financial institutions were at their lowest in spring 2007, precisely the point in time we now recognize was the most fragile.[48]

Moreover, Chairman Bernanke stated in Senate testimony on September 24, 2008, that "we judged that investors and counterparties had had time to take precautionary measures." This observation seems obvious in retrospect, but it was not so obvious in that delicate, ultimately unrecoverable moment, when a potentially failing institution was on the brink of collapse. Financial institutions, unlike other corporate entities, are unique in that they are more likely to suffer from an immediate "bank run" mentality. While the short-selling of Lehman Brothers was widely reported and even commented on by the firm itself in the summer of 2008, Lehman Brothers' derivative counterparties were not flooding it with hundreds of requests to assign their derivative transactions. The number of Lehman Brothers' counter-parties remained steady after Bear Stearns was folded into JPMorgan Chase in March 2008 and continued throughout much of the summer. Derivative trading volumes remained steady until there was a slight decrease in August, a normal occurrence for the industry. Moreover, less than 1 percent of Lehman Brothers' counterparties requested that the initial margin posted in connection with their derivative trades be segregated at a third-party custodian. If the market had been in agreement that Lehman Brothers was essentially failing, presumably CDS spreads would have reacted very differ-ently, many market participants would have terminated their derivative contracts or attempted to assign their positions to another counterparty willing to take that risk, and coun-terparties would have not waited until the week before the bankruptcy filing to do their documentation due diligence. Certainly, some counterparties did take these actions, but the vast majority of counterparties did not—6,355 counter-parties, to be precise.

Second, policy makers need to reconsider the existing bankruptcy reform proposals. Some have argued that the U.S. Bankruptcy Code, with its focus on creditors, is not capable of working effectively for systemically important entities, and that the FDIC is best placed to utilize its resolu-tion authority for systemically important entities. I disagree. The Bankruptcy Code offers well-conceived principles, established jurisprudence, a well-regarded bench, and, at least for recent large bankruptcies, a relatively efficient pro-cess. The expansion of the FDIC's resolution authority as contemplated by the House Proposal would result in lower recoveries for counterparties, as well as secured and unsecured creditors, thereby imposing a higher cost of credit on a wide array of businesses. In any event, the U.S. Bankruptcy Code is not likely to operate since the largest derivative participants are banks, already subject to the FDIA. Policy makers should consider whether the existing FDIC resolution regime is adequate to meet the challenges presented by the size, concentration, and complexity of these banks' derivative portfolios, particularly given the interconnected trading relationships among these institutions, as well as the banks' partial ownership of at least one exchange that potentially could benefit from migrating some over-the-counter derivatives to a central counterparty model.

Whatever enhancements are made to the regulatory and bankruptcy regimes, policy makers must ensure that legal certainty is paramount in their deliberations. A critical component of legal certainty is insisting on the continuation of a reliable and robust netting regime. Netting is an effective mechanism in the management of credit risk in that it reduces the credit and liquidity exposures through its elimination of individual transfers. Cross-product netting is critical in that it allows entities to net all their qualified financial contracts, assuming mutuality, under a single master agreement. With greater legal certainty for netting, market participants can more effectively evaluate their risks. To place netting under doubt would be massively counterproductive, generating substantial legal and operational uncertainty. Policy makers miss the point when they propose protections for limited classes of participants and/or products.

Third, in lieu of applying the automatic stay, policy makers should consider other tools that perhaps more effectively make failure more tolerable. For example, despite the impression given by the media, regulators have access to a wide array of trading data for systemically important financial institutions. Developments by the Depository Trust & Clearing Corporation in the provision of weekly derivatives data expands on what was available a year ago. The challenge is how to prioritize and evaluate that data on a real-time basis. Given the speed with which financial institutions can deteriorate, regulators need to develop a more effective mechanism for evaluating the health of systemically important financial institutions.

Fourth, a more stable liquidity environment must be created. A shift to term repo arrangements, particularly in a distressed market, should be considered as it could possibly relieve pressure on broker dealers and clearing banks that make the exchanges of securities and cash between dealers or fund managers. The challenge is that the documentation supporting repo arrangements should be amended as it is fairly easy to exit the arrangement. This is because "mini-close-out" provisions are not included in the industry standard Master Repurchase Agreement, although an optional form is available. A mini-close-out provision permits a nondefaulting party in a failed securities delivery in a repo transaction to elect to close out only the failing transaction. In addition, policy makers should continue to advance exploration of the proposal that a central clearing utility could replace the two clearing banks, and evaluate whether such a utility would serve as a better watchdog on limit risks and stem rapid withdrawals of credit or conversely, whether risk is concentrated in an intolerable way. The institutionalization of penalties for settlement failures should also be examined.

Fifth, regulators need to reexamine their organizational structures and optimize their staffs in such a way as to execute effectively and on a timely basis on their missions. Federal Reserve chairman Bernanke acknowledged this in a recent conference, observing, "Unfortunately, regulators and supervisors did not identify and remedy . . . weaknesses in a timely way."[49] Existing law already provides regulators with the power to restrict banking activity, but that power has not always been used. Congress passed the Financial Reform Recovery and Enforcement Act in 1989, allowing regulators to intervene earlier to prevent the buildup of bad loans in the system, but regulators failed to utilize this power in 2007 and 2008. Congress passed the Sarbanes-Oxley Act in 2002 after the collapse of Enron, but corporate governance and disclosure mandates contained therein have not resulted in the boards of failing institutions to query more effectively the risk management of those institutions.

Other Areas Requiring Policy Makers' Consideration

Too Big to Fail   Billions of dollars were lost as a result of Lehman Brothers' bankruptcy filing, impacting the firm's unsecured creditors such as holders of its bonds and commercial paper, as well as shareholders, thirty percent of whom were Lehman employees.[50] Market psychology experienced a seismic shift on September 15, 2008. While Secretary of the Treasury Timothy Geithner commented that the collapse of Lehman Brothers was not a cause of the economic collapse, but rather a symptom,[51] the panic was nevertheless palpable on Wall Street and elsewhere. The prospect that large financial institutions could now be allowed to default had a dramatic impact on the cost of borrowing for surviving financial institutions such as Goldman Sachs and Morgan Stanley, and each changed its charter to a bank holding company in an effort to stabilize its liquidity management within a week of Lehman Brothers' bankruptcy. Runs on the $3.6 trillion money market industry, which provided critical loans (commercial paper) for thousands of businesses for everyday expenses such as payroll, eventually required the Federal Reserve to step in with a $1.6 trillion backstop. All the while, jittery stock markets lost $2.85 trillion in value in three days.[52]

Whether Lehman Brothers' bankruptcy filing was a symptom or a cause of the economic crisis is likely irrelevant, but the undeniable disorder that was unleashed created an opening for policy makers to consider whether any institution was too big to fail. The reality is that there are several multijurisdictional financial institutions that, in my view, are too big to fail. Their significance to the U.S., and perhaps the global, economy is such that these institutions have extraordinary levels of concentration of trading activity, while at the same time constituting some of the largest institutions as measured by deposits. Some, such as George Shultz, former secretary of the Treasury and secretary of state, and Mervyn King, the Bank of England governor, argue that if an institution is too big to fail, it should be broken apart.

Large custodians such as the Bank of New York Mellon, State Street Bank, and PNC Bank are also too big to fail. The custodian's role in protecting the assets of customers, reaching into the trillions, means that disruptions to the safety of those assets would severely undermine confidence in the financial system and disrupt the ability of firms to regain control of their assets.

In addition, if over-the-counter derivatives trading activity is forced onto one or more exchanges, the concentration of risk for any one exchange will significantly dwarf the $35+ trillion notional value derivative book of Lehman Brothers. Policy makers are counting on the reduction in counterparty risk by having a central counterparty stand between the buyer and seller of each derivative trade, as well as the imposition of uniform margin requirements. But as preliminary research by the International Monetary Fund shows, even a very modest 1 percent weighted average initial margin requirement by a central counterparty would entail several billion dollars of collateral. The failure of this type of entity would be catastrophic, and policy makers must carefully evaluate whether sufficient fail-safes are in place before trading is required to migrate there.

Valuation Issues

Complex derivatives such as credit default swaps on asset-backed securities or collateralized debt obligations presented a major challenge for valuation when markets began to fall apart. Policy makers should consider whether complex derivatives remain suitable for a mark-to-market model.

Rating Agencies

It is appalling that nothing has effectively been done to reconfigure the way in which ratings are given. After all, it has been widely reported that the rating agencies' laxness in its models for certain types of real estate–connected transactions led to the presence of less collateral and more risk when those models failed. On October 28, 2009, the House Financial Services Committee passed the Accountability and Transparency in Rating Agencies Act. This bill would require the rating agencies to disclose any conflicts of interest in the provision of its services, to enhance transparency and disclosure and to have at least one-third of a rating agency's board of directors be independent. Policy makers should act to address more effectively the deficiencies of the rating agencies.

Organizational and Operational Issues

Harvey Miller, Lehman Brothers' lead bankruptcy counsel, noted that his firm was forced to organize, "on a moment's notice," the largest and most complex bankruptcy in history.[53] The U.K. administrators at PricewaterhouseCoopers, tasked with handling nineteen Lehman Brothers entities' bankruptcies, echoed that remark, noting that many were stunned by the complexity of the bankruptcy. Miller was right: Lehman Brothers had no insolvency plans prepared.[54] The guidance this author and other senior lawyers received on the eve of Lehman Brothers' bankruptcy filing was to "do your best." The legal department was not the only unit in a state of chaos. Basic corporate repositories of information were not widely available or were not reflective of the many tentacles that the organization had. For example, a comprehensive inventory of assets was not readily available, and once the acquisition by Barclays Bank of Lehman's brokerage business occurred, there was a loss of accounting systems, operational support, and manpower.

Systemically important financial institutions should be required to have detailed crisis management plans that take into account multijurisdictional operations. The House Proposal is helpful in this respect as it includes a proposal to require identified financial holding companies to prepare and to report periodically on plans for resolution. In the United Kingdom, the Financial Services Authority issued a discussion paper on October 22, 2009, that, among other things, proposes that systemically important banks prepare a "living will" that sets forth the bank's operational resolution in the event of its failure.

Moreover, the most sophisticated financial institutions lack the ability to assess risk across counterparties, products, and jurisdictions. Risk management and data systems have grown organically with business lines and while information may be captured for one product area, there is no real-time capability to track that exposure across products. Moreover, the thousands and thousands of financial contracts, including derivatives and repo agreements, are not easily catalogued by financial institutions. Home-grown repositories exist, but there is usually limited functionality associated with those systems.

In addition, given the role that the lack of liquidity played in the failure of Lehman Brothers, it may be worthwhile to consider requiring systemically important financial institutions to have a liquidity management plan. An effective liquidity management plan would at the least offer the failing institution a small window of time in which to make critical decisions. The Basel Committee on Banking Supervision has developed liquidity guidelines that are being incorporated into U.S. interagency regulatory guidance to determine adequate liquidity buffers.[55]

Multijurisdictional Bankruptcy

This chapter does not address the implications of a systemically important financial institution's failure outside the United States. However, with the demise of Lehman Brothers, the challenges associated with the lack of a multijurisdictional bankruptcy regime applicable to a major financial institution became apparent. Several significant jurisdictions, such as the United Kingdom, have materially different approaches to creditor rights in an insolvency than in the United States. In the United Kingdom, for example, no distinction is drawn between domestic and foreign creditors, and this system has not historically had a special insolvency regime applicable to banks. The Banking Act of 2009, however, was recently passed in the United Kingdom such that for the first time, banks now have a specialized statutory regime. UNCITRAL has developed a Model Law on Cross-Border Insolvency, but whether this is taken up by a sufficient number of significant financial jurisdictions remains to be seen. The critical point is that in today's world, a focus on domestic bankruptcy law to the exclusion of international law will continue the disrupted process under which financial institutions are treated.

CONCLUSION

Financial innovation has been an incredible, although largely invisible, engine of economic growth. Any insolvency and regulatory framework should ensure that effective capital allocation and economic growth are balanced in such a way as to avoid catastrophic economic collapse.

George Bernard Shaw once remarked, "We learn from history that we learn nothing from history." The failure of policy makers to develop a more robust and unified insolvency and regulatory regime that reflects the financial landscape would be intolerable. Let us hope that our policy makers choose not to legislate based on the caprice of public sentiment, and instead recall another observation of Shaw's that "we are made wise not by the recollection of our past, but by the responsibility for our future."

NOTES

1. Lehman Brothers entered bankruptcy with consolidated assets of $639 billion of assets and consolidated liabilities of $613 billion, making it the largest bankruptcy filing in U.S. history. (See Affidavit of Ian T. Lowitt Pursuant to Rule 1007-2 of the Local Bankruptcy Rules for the Southern District of New York in Support of First-Day Motions and Applications, September 14, 2008.) Lehman Brothers' consolidated assets exceeded the annual gross domestic product of all but the seventeen wealthiest nations (Ben Hallman, "A Moment's Notice," *American Lawyer*, December 1, 2008).

2. This chapter will not attempt to define a "systemically important financial institution," concluding that it is a task better left to the capable minds of others, but one that is imperative for policy makers to agree on in advance of any new resolution or other regime. Rather, the reader is asked to assume for purposes of this chapter that the term *systemically important financial institution* refers to a small number of the largest financial institutions, such as banks, custodians, asset managers, and insurance companies. If measured by a firm's centrality to the extension of credit, participation in the payment and settlement systems, clearing of transactions, and/or its significance in particularly interconnected financial markets such as the $600+ trillion notional over-the-counter derivatives market or the

$5 trillion daily repo market, such a list might include the following U.S. institutions: Bank of America (primarily a bank); Citigroup (a bank and an insurance company); Goldman, Sachs & Co. (a bank holding company, migrating a portion of its derivatives portfolio to the bank, a broker-dealer [repo], and other corporations); J.P. Morgan Chase Bank (primarily a bank); Morgan Stanley (a bank holding company migrating a portion of its derivatives portfolio to the bank, a broker-dealer [repo], and other corporations); and Wells Fargo (a bank). It should be noted that many of the aforementioned institutions also include some of the world's largest asset managers. Major custodians that operate as banks, including The Bank of New York Mellon, Northern Trust, PNC Financial Services Group, and State Street Corporation, should also be candidates for systemically important financial institutions. Lastly, a collection of critical exchanges, including the Chicago Mercantile Exchange and the Intercontinental Exchange, are also candidates for systemically important financial institutions, particularly given the possible migration and concentration of over-the-counter derivatives.

3. The term *qualified financial contract* captures a variety of transactions, including securities contracts, commodity futures, forward contracts, repurchase agreements, swap agreements, and master netting agreements. See 11 U.S.C. §§ 555, 556, 559, 560 and 561; and 12 U.S.C. § 1821(e)(8)(D).

4. Readers are encouraged to consult David A. Skeel Jr.'s seminal treatise on the subject, *Debt's Dominion: A History of Bankruptcy Law in America* (Princeton, NJ: Princeton University Press, 2001).

5. By historical anomaly, insurance companies are regulated by the states, and there is no federal insolvency regime applicable to insurance companies. Many, including me, believe insurance companies should be subject to federal regulatory and insolvency regimes.

6. Lehman Brothers' acquisition of the bank in 1999 allowed it to make home loans, which in turn were included in mortgage securitizations handled by the investment bank.

7. When the $32 billion IndyMac failed in July 2008, $18 billion of the bank's $19 billion of deposits were insured.

8. 12 U.S.C. § 1821(e)(11).

9. 12 U.S.C. § 1821(e)(9).

10. This restriction is understandable, but it could present systemic challenges if a systemically important U.S. bank fails and the remaining U.S. systemically important banks, likely to be limited in number, are operating in a distressed market, making the assumption of a large derivatives portfolio perhaps challenging. Of course, in such a scenario, there can be no guarantee that foreign institutions would be in any better position.

11. 12 U.S.C. § 1821(e)(10).

12. "Report to the Supervisors of the Major OTC Derivatives Dealers on the Proposals of Centralized CDS Clearing Solutions for the Segregation and Portability of Customer CDS Positions and Related Margin," June 30, 2009, 3, footnote 9.

13. 15 U.S.C. § 78 aaa *et seq.*

14. See www.sipc.org under "Our 38-Year Track Record for Investors."

15. "Testimony of Stephen P. Harbeck, President and Chief Executive Officer of SIPC, before the Committee on Financial Services, the United States House of Representatives," January 5, 2009. Interestingly, a bankruptcy court is authorized pursuant to Section 363(b)(1) of the U.S. Bankruptcy Code to approve sales only of the bankrupt estate's property. At the time of the sale of Lehman's brokerage to Barclays Bank, the Lehman brokerage had not yet filed for bankruptcy. Instead, SIPC engineered its liquidation process at the same time as the sale of assets to Barclays Bank was occurring, thereby preserving value for the business and ensuring that most customers' accounts were transferred seamlessly.

16. SIPC takes the view that repo counterparties are not securities "customers," but some courts have found them to qualify for SIPC protection (and priority in a U.S. Bankruptcy Code liquidation) if the facts suggest a broker-customer fiduciary relationship between the broker and the counterparty.

17. Lehman Brothers Holdings Inc., First Creditors Section 341 Meeting, January 29, 2009, 19–20 (www.lehmanbrothersestate.com).

18. See Bankruptcy Reform Act of 1978, Pub. L. No. 95-598 (adding, 11 U.S.C. §§ 362(b)(6) and 548(d)(2)(B)). In 1989, the qualified financial contract provisions were adopted as part of the Financial Institutions Reform Recovery and Enforcement Act (FIRREA). FIRREA amended the Federal Deposit Insurance Act (FDIA) provisions for U.S. bank insolvency. The U.S. Bankruptcy Code has been amended periodically to conform to the definitional provisions included in the other statutes. Generally, after the 2005 amendments to the U.S. Bankruptcy Code and FDIA, the scope of transactions covered are the same among the statutes, except that the FDIA includes some mortgage-related transaction types that are not included under the U.S. Bankruptcy Code.

19. The President's Working Group on Financial Markets, "Hedge Funds, Leverage, and the Lessons of Long-Term Capital Management," April 1999, 20.

20. Michael H. Krimminger, "Adjusting the Rules: What Bankruptcy Reform Will Mean for Financial Market Contracts," October 11, 2005, www.fdic.gov.

21. Franklin Edwards and Edward R. Morrison, "Derivatives and the Bankruptcy Code: Why the Special Treatment?" *Yale Journal on Regulation* (January 1, 2005).

22. Ibid., footnote 35.

23. "Testimony of William McDonough, before the Committee on Banking and Financial Services, the United States House of Representatives," October 1, 1998, 5.

24. While Long-Term Capital Management was organized as a Delaware corporation, trades were managed in Long-Term Capital Portfolio, L.P., a partnership organized in the Cayman Islands.

25. The President's Working Group on Financial Markets, formed in 1988, consists of the Board of Governors of the Federal Reserve System, the Securities and Exchange Commission, the Commodity Futures Trading Commission, and the secretary of the Treasury.

26. The President's Working Group on Financial Markets, "Recommendations by the President's Working Group on Financial Markets," April 11, 2000, 29.

27. Congress has expanded the transaction types entitled to special treatment over time. Commodity and forward contracts were initially considered qualified financial contracts in 1978, and as financial instruments developed, Congress expanded the safe harbors in 1982, 1984, 1990, and 2005. The Financial Netting Improvements Act of 2006 further strengthened netting (Pub. L. No. 109-390, 120 Stat.2693).

28. In November 2009, Senator Christopher Dodd, chairman of the Senate Banking Committee, released his competing 1,136-page proposal entitled "Restoring American Financial Stability Act of 2009" in which he labels a systemically important entity as a "specified financial company."

29. The House Proposal allows for financial companies, which are not covered by the definition of "identified financial holding company," to be designated as such if the new Financial Services Oversight Council acts under its emergency powers in systemic risk situations.

30. The Office of the Comptroller of the Currency's Quarterly Report on Bank Trading and Derivatives Activity Second Quarter 2009, table 1, notes that Goldman Sachs Bank USA is the second largest derivative participant with a $40.47 trillion notional value derivative portfolio. That figure is at odds with a wealth of contracts that exist in the market that continue to identify Goldman Sachs International, the U.K. broker-dealer, as the counterparty for derivative transactions. Morgan Stanley Bank is listed as the eighteenth largest commercial bank derivative participant, but table 2 indicates that Morgan Stanley as the bank holding company is the fourth largest derivative participant with a $40.59 trillion notional value derivative portfolio.

31. Testimony of Harvey Miller, before the Committee on the Judiciary, Subcommittee on Commercial and Administrative Law, U.S. House of Representatives, October 22, 2009, 3.

32. Christine Harper, Shannon Harrington, and Matthew Leising, "Wall Street Stealth Lobby Defends $35 Billion Derivatives Haul," Bloomberg, August 31, 2009. The authors note that the

estimated combined revenue from fixed income trading for Bank of America, Citibank, Goldman Sachs, JPMorgan Chase, and Morgan Stanley for the first two quarters of 2009 was $35 billion. The OCC reports that trading revenue as a percentage of gross revenue for Goldman Sachs in the second quarter of 2009 was 63 percent. See OCC's "Quarterly Report on Bank Trading and Derivatives Activities Second Quarter 2009."

33. Details on the Lehman Brothers auction, as well as other credit default swap auctions, can be found at www.creditfixings.com.

34. Debtors' Motion for an Order pursuant to Sections 105 and 365 of the Bankruptcy Code to Establish Procedures for the Settlement or Assumption and Assignment of Prepetition Derivatives Contracts, Lehman Brothers Holdings Inc., et al., No. 08-13555 (U.S. Bankr. Ct., S.D.N.Y. November 13, 2008).

35. Ibid.

36. Debtors' Motion for an Order Approving Consensual Assumption and Assignment of Prepetition Derivatives Contracts, Lehman Brothers Holdings Inc., et al., No. 08-13555 (U.S. Bankr. Ct., S.D.N.Y. January 16, 2009).

37. Alvarez & Marsal, "Lehman Brothers Holdings Inc.: The State of the Estate," November 18, 2009, 28.

38. Ibid.

39. Ibid., 27.

40. Several prominent U.S. hedge funds (Elliott Capital Management, King Street Capital, and Paulson & Co.) filed a statement in July 2009 in the Metavante proceeding noting that the U.S. Bankruptcy Code does not extend the safe harbor provisions to contractual provisions that are "in anticipation" of future termination and/or set-off rights under the ISDA Master Agreement. These funds argued that the wait-and-see approach of Metavante represented the forfeiture of its right to terminate the transaction under the protections afforded by the safe harbor provisions in the future.

41. *Re Lehman Brothers Holdings Inc.*, Case 08-13555 (U.S. Bankr. Ct., S.D.N.Y. September 15, 2009).

42. Lehman Brothers' stock price fell by 90 percent on September 12, 2008.

43. Bank for International Settlement, "Semiannual Over-the-Counter (OTC) Derivatives Markets Statistics," www.bis.org/statistics, June 2009.

44. Michael Mackenzie, "Bank Runs Left Repo Sector Exposed," *Financial Times*, September 10, 2009.

45. Tanya Azarchs and Scott Sprinzer, "Why Was Lehman Brothers Rated 'A'?" *Standard & Poor's Ratings Direct*, September 24, 2008, 5.

46. Manmohan Singh and Carolyne Spackman, "The Use (and Abuse) of CDS Spreads during Distress," International Monetary Fund Working Paper, WP/09/62, March 2009.

47. Barclays Capital Global Relative Value Research Note, "The State of the CDS Market," October 20, 2008.

48. Lord Adair Turner, "Examining the Causes of the Financial Crisis," speech given to the Economic Club of America and National Journal Group, October 29, 2009, www.fsa.gov.uk.

49. Ben S. Bernanke, "Financial Regulation and Supervision after the Crisis: The Role of the Federal Reserve," speech given at the Federal Reserve Bank of Boston 54th Economic Conference, October 23, 2009. Chairman Bernanke's footnote 1 points to a wealth of considered studies of regulatory failure.

50. These employee-owned shares included restricted stock awards.

51. Andy Serwer, Nina Easton, and Allan Sloan, "Geithner: 'We Were Looking at the Abyss,'" *Fortune*, September 10, 2009, http://money.cnn.com/2009/09/08/news/economy/geithner_lehman_bankruptcy.fortune/index.htm.

52. Reserve Primary Fund, one of the largest money market funds, had lent Lehman Brothers $785 million, about 1.3 percent of its assets, some of it in short-term loans that Lehman was unable to repay. In a two-day run on the fund, more than 60 percent of its money was withdrawn. The fund's net asset value fell below $1 a

share and "broke the buck" on September 16, 2008, subjecting investors to losses and triggering withdrawals at other funds.

53. Ben Hallman, "A Moment's Notice," *American Lawyer*,
December 1, 2008.

54. Practically speaking, a financial institution cannot be seen to
prepare for a possible insolvency filing as it will immediately lose its
access to financing and other stabilizing actions.

55. Basel Committee on Banking Supervision, *Principles for Sound
Liquidity Risk Management and Supervision*, (Basel, Switzerland: Bank
for International Settlements). The OCC, FDIC, and the Federal
Reserve System, among others, issued proposed *Interagency Guidance
on Funding and Liquidity Risk Management* in June 2009.

PART III

WHAT FINANCIAL FIRMS CAN DO

6

A Contractual Approach to Restructuring Financial Institutions

DARRELL DUFFIE

IN THIS CHAPTER, I BRIEFLY OUTLINE some approaches to the "automatic" out-of-court recapitalization of financial institutions whose distress may pose risks to the economy. The main objectives are (1) to reduce the incentive of a large financial institution to take socially inefficient risks while relying on the backstop of a government bailout and (2) to

I am grateful for extensive conversations with Mark Flannery, fellow members of the Squam Lake Group, Chris Culp, Andrew Gladin, Jason Granet, Barbara Havilcek, Dick Herring, Bev Hirtle, Tom Jackson, Bill Kroener, Phil Prince, Ernst Schaumberg, Alex Wolf, and many Stanford colleagues, particularly Peter DeMarzo, Joe Grundfest, Ken Scott, Kimberly Summe, and John Taylor. I especially benefited from a discussion of this chapter provided by David Skeel.

reduce the likelihood that, once distressed, the financial institution indeed suffers a severe failure with adverse spillover effects to the economy. I emphasize two mechanisms. The first is distress-contingent convertible bonds, which are claims to interest and principal that automatically convert to shares of equity if and when the financial institution fails to meet a stipulated capital requirement. The second mechanism is a regulation mandating an offer to existing shareholders to purchase new equity at a low price when the financial institution fails to meet a stipulated liquidity or capital requirement.

Other approaches that have been used in practice include the purchase by insurance and reinsurance firms of put options on their own shares that can be exercised when loss claims in designated lines of insurance exceed stipulated triggers, or bonds whose principal is contractually reduced in proportion to designated loss claims (Punter, 1999; Culp, 2009).

ROADBLOCKS TO REGULATION-FREE RECAPITALIZATION OF DISTRESSED FIRMS

When a financial institution has a low level of capital relative to its assets, there are several impediments to its recapitalization, absent regulation.

The existing equity owners of the financial institution are typically reluctant to issue new equity. The price at which new equity can be successfully issued is likely to be so dilutive as to be against the interests of those shareholders. Despite the potential for new capital to significantly reduce the firm's distress costs, a large amount of the total-firm value added by new equity capital would go toward improving the position of creditors, who would otherwise absorb losses at default. Current shareholders are not interested in "donating" wealth to debt holders. This roadblock to equity issuance is called "debt overhang" (Myers, 1984).

Furthermore, new shares offered to the market by a weak financial institution may be viewed by potential buyers as "lemons." A potential investor might ask, "Why would I pay $10 a share if the bank is willing to sell shares at that price? The bank knows more than me about the value of the new shares. Thus, if the bank is willing to sell at $10, then the shares could be worth at most $10, and possibly much less." This impediment to a sale is called adverse selection. It often follows, as suggested by Akerlof (1970) as well as Leland and Pyle (1977), that the new shares would need to be sold at such a low price that the existing shareholders would prefer that they are not offered at all.

Raising cash from the sale of assets is also unattractive to equity owners. By lowering the leverage of the financial institution, they would lose the advantage of profiting from any upside return on the assets and the advantage of the option to default if the return on assets is poor, in which case creditors (or taxpayers) would absorb the default losses. Furthermore, asset sales may themselves suffer from a severe "lemons" discount.

Faced with the prospect of severe bankruptcy costs, the creditors of the weakened financial institution might prefer to voluntarily reduce their contractual claims. For example, by offering to exchange each dollar of debt principal for a package of new debt and equity claims worth a market value of 75 cents, they would come out ahead if this avoids a bankruptcy in which they would recover only 50 cents in market value. Rarely, however, are the creditors of a firm headed for bankruptcy able to coordinate such an out-of-court restructuring. If all but one of them were to agree to this, for example, then the last has an incentive to hold out, given the likelihood that the restructuring would save the firm from default, leaving the hold-out creditor with a full payment of his original claim. Perhaps the remaining creditors would be willing to go ahead anyway, bailing out one or a few small hold-out creditors, but rarely would the remaining creditors avoid a defection in their own ranks. This situation is sometimes called a "prisoner's dilemma." Even though the creditors would be better off, as a group, to commit to a restructuring of their claims, it is unusual in practice to obtain the individual consents of sufficiently many of them.

Bankruptcy is normally an effective mechanism for breaking through the recapitalization "gridlock" just described. A distressed firm can emerge from bankruptcy with a new and less risky capital structure. More broadly, as has been shown in theoretical work by Innes (1990), Hart and Moore (1998), and DeMarzo and Duffie (1999), a conventional capital structure consisting of pure equity and pure debt, with a bankruptcy-style "boundary condition," is an efficient contractual approach for raising capital and for allocating a firm's cash flows and control rights. This theoretical foundation, however, does not consider costly systemic-risk externalities.

An alternative to the bankruptcy resolution of failures is government-coordinated receiverships or conservatorships, which can also consider the costs and benefits to the taxpayer and the general economy.

There are currently proposals to adapt one or both of these approaches, bankruptcy or government-led receiverships, for the restructuring of systemically important financial institutions (SIFIs). The objective of all proposals is to improve the balance between firm-level efficiency and economy-wide costs. My goal here is a further consideration of complementary prefailure restructuring mechanisms for resolving distressed SIFIs.

DISTRESS-CONTINGENT CONVERTIBLE DEBT

As originally envisioned by Flannery (2005), distress-contingent convertible bondholders receive equity shares in lieu of future claims to interest and principal if and when the issuer fails to meet certain capital requirements. There are a number of alternative designs for the distress trigger and for the conversion ratio, the number of shares of equity to be received in exchange for each dollar of bond principal. I will discuss these later. There are also various proposals for the degree to which such debt issues would contribute to meeting a financial institution's regulatory capital requirement. It is also an open question whether the issuance of these bonds would be a regulatory requirement or an optional method of meeting capital requirements, and if so, the quantitative formula by which distress-contingent convertible debt, equity, preferred shares, and other instruments would be weighted in measuring regulatory capital. If the issuance of such bonds is not required by regulation, an incentive to issue these "hybrid" securities could be based on an adjustment to tax codes that allows their preconversion interest payments to be deductible from income for tax purposes, just as for ordinary corporate debt. Historical precursors to the notion of distress-contingent securities, such as income bonds and stock cancellation schemes, are reviewed by Skeel (1993).[1]

In November 2009, Lloyds Bank announced that it would issue £7.5 billion of such bonds, called "CoCos," with conversion to common equity if the bank's Tier 1 capital ratio falls to 5 percent. The Royal Bank of Scotland is said to be planning a similar issuance. These announcements are part of a general recapitalization of these two banks that includes new equity rights issues and involves a participating investment by the United Kingdom. The president of the New York Federal Reserve, William Dudley, as well as the chairman of the Federal Reserve System, Ben Bernanke, have recently spoken in favor of the general concept of distress-contingent convertible debt for SIFIs (Dudley, 2009; Bernanke, 2009). The governor of the Bank of England, Mervyn King, although more skeptical, has said that these instruments are "worth a try."

If the trigger for automatic conversion is an accounting capital ratio, such as the Tier 1 capital trigger used in the design of the Lloyds Bank issuance, there should be some concern over the failure of accounting measures to capture the true financial condition of the bank. For example, Citibank, a SIFI that did receive a significant government bailout during the recent financial crisis, had a Tier 1 capital ratio that never fell below 7 percent during the course of the financial crisis and was measured[2] at 11.8 percent at roughly its weakest moment in December 2008, when the stock market capitalization of Citibank's holding company fell to around $20 billion, or about 1 percent of its total accounting assets. Because of the limited-liability treatment of equity and because of significant prevailing uncertainty over the true valuation of

Citibank's assets, this stock market valuation suggests that Citibank's assets probably had a market value well below its debt principal in late 2008. Nevertheless, any reasonable Tier 1 capital-based tripwire for distress-contingent convertible debt would probably not have been tripped.

If restricted to accounting measures of capitalization, perhaps a more effective trigger could be based on the ratio of tangible common equity (TCE) to tangible assets, a measure that excludes preferred shares and intangible assets such as goodwill and tax shields from net operating loss carry-forwards, all of which are relatively useless assets during a solvency crisis. At the end of 2008, Citibank had tangible common equity of only $31 billion,[3] for a TCE ratio of about 1.5 percent, effectively signaling that Citibank was substantially less well capitalized than most of its peer SIFIs. (Among large banks, only Bank of New York–Mellon had a similarly low tangible common equity capital ratio.) The "S-Cap" stress tests, by which the U.S. government measured shortfalls in the capitalization of large banks in the spring of 2009, were based instead on accounting common equity (which includes goodwill). Even tangible common equity reacts slowly to market conditions, given the typical lag in marking down bad loans for accounting purposes.

Nevertheless, a trigger based on tangible common equity seems worthy of serious consideration. There have also been proposals that triggers should be based in part on the existence of a general financial crisis (Squam Lake Working Group on Financial Regulation, 2009).

If, instead, the envisioned debt is converted to equity when the market value of equity falls to a sufficiently low level, then short sellers may, depending on the conversion price and the number of new equity shares created, be tempted to "attack" the issuer's stock in order to trigger the conversion and profit from the resulting dilution or the reduction in the market value of equity shares associated with a reduced value of the option to default. Short sellers might further increase their profits by acquiring the convertible debt in advance of attacking the stock, so as to obtain new shares cheaply through conversion. Even in the absence of such an attack, merely a rational assumption by some shareholders that sales of shares by other shareholders might trigger a conversion could indeed lead many shareholders to fulfill this prophecy, through the resulting short-term impact of sudden sales on share prices. Markets need not be so efficient that bargain-hunting buyers of shares would react quickly enough to offset the downward price impact caused by sellers.

Such a self-generating decline in share prices, sometimes called a "death spiral," could be mitigated by a trigger that is based instead on a trailing average share price—for example, the average closing price of the shares over the preceding 20 business days. In that case, any adverse price impact on a given day would receive a weight of 1/20 toward the trailing average price used in the conversion trigger.

Flannery (2009) explains that the incentive for a speculative attack is lessened or eliminated by a sufficiently high contractual conversion price P, according to which each dollar of principal of debt is converted to $1/P$ shares. Flannery notes that if the conversion price is higher than the trigger price of equity (that market price for shares at which conversion is contractually triggered), then conversion is effectively antidilutive, raising the price of shares. This leaves open the question of how to set the trigger price and the conversion price so that, despite any antidilutive effect of conversion, the original equity holders have a strong incentive to keep the financial institution well capitalized.

The presence of distress-contingent convertible debt in the capital structure of a dealer bank is unlikely to stop a liquidity crisis once it begins (Duffie, in press). Short-term creditors, over-the-counter derivatives counterparties, and prime-brokerage clients who anticipate the potential failure of the bank are unlikely to be dissuaded from a "run" merely by the fact that the future principal and interest claims of the bonds have been converted to equity. This conversion does nothing for the immediate cash position of the bank. Once a rush for the exits begins, it is rational that it would continue in a self-fulfilling manner. The trigger that converts the debt to equity should be set so as to eliminate the debt claims before a liquidity crisis is likely to begin, and hopefully with a sufficiently strong impact on the balance sheet to forestall a self-fulfilling presumption of a liquidity crisis.

One could also contract so that the cash proceeds of a contingent-convertible debt issue are escrowed, say, in a trust, and become available to the issuer in cash only when the debt is converted to equity.[4] This improves the cash position of the bank at a time of distress, albeit at the cost to the bank of idling the cash raised until that time.

MANDATORY RIGHTS OFFERINGS OF EQUITY

Distressed financial institutions, among other firms, sometimes offer rights to existing shareholders to purchase new shares at a price that is typically well below the current market price. Given the effects of dilution, debt overhang, and adverse selection, an offering price near the current market price is unlikely to be exercised by many shareholders. When offered at a sufficiently low price, however, many existing shareholders would subscribe, given that a failure to do so would result in a costly dilution of their share claims and an effective transfer of wealth to those who do subscribe. Any shareholders without the cash necessary to take up the offer would do best by selling their shares before the expiration of the offer to those who do have the cash. Thus, a mandatory rights offering at a sufficiently low price is likely to be well subscribed, so long as the issuer indeed has some value left in its business for long-run equity investors.

Table 6.1 provides a list of major bank equity rights offerings during the recent financial crisis. (The data are gathered from press reports and are preliminary.) The discounts

TABLE 6.1   Crisis Period Bank Equity Rights Offerings

Bank	Date	Size ($ billions)	Discount	Take-up
Société Générale	March 08	8	39%	100%
UBS	May 08	16	31%	100%
RBS	April 08	24	46%	100%
HSBC	March 09	18	48%	100%
HBOS	June 09	8	45%	8%
Barclays	July 09	9	10%	19%
BNP	September 09	6	29%	TBD
Lloyds	November 09	22	60%	100%
ING	November 09	11	52%	TBD

shown are in each case the ratio of the offering price to the closing market price on the day prior to the announcement of the offering. The "take-up" is the fraction of the offer that was subscribed by shareholders. In both of the cases shown in which the take-up was less than 100 percent, the rights offering had been underwritten or otherwise guaranteed, so that the bank received the full proceeds of the planned offering. Equity rights offerings are more common for firms in financial distress, particularly firms with a relatively concentrated share ownership. The lack of rights offerings by major U.S. banks during the recent financial crisis is not easily explained, but it could be related to the relatively dispersed ownership of these banks, which raises a risk of undersubscription of the offering.

A rights offering at a low price largely finesses the adverse-selection problem that I described earlier. In effect, the buyers and the sellers of the new shares are the same investors. Nevertheless, because of debt overhang, the existing shareholders may in many cases prefer not to conduct such a mandatory rights offering. Thus, due to the social costs of systemic risk, it may be appropriate to introduce a regulation that forces an automatic rights offering as soon as a financial institution hits specified tripwires in its measured financial condition.[5] If the short-term creditors, clients, and other counterparties of a financial institution know that a rights offering of sufficient size will occur at stipulated liquidity triggers, they may view a liquidity crisis to be sufficiently unlikely that they are unlikely to start one with a run.

Even under existing U.S. regulations, banks are required to issue new shares, or otherwise raise new regulatory capital, when they do not meet stipulated capital-adequacy standards. In practice, however, most banks that have failed have not been forced to raise new capital under these regulations. Presumably, the triggers are not sufficiently well designed, or regulators have used excessive forbearance.

As opposed to the conversion of debt to equity, a mandatory rights offering provides new cash that may reduce the risk of a liquidity crisis. Indeed, the presence of a regulation mandating a rights offering when the capital position of a financial institution deteriorates may forestall the self-fulfilling prophecy of a run by creditors and others who have the discretion to drain cash from the weakened institution. Because of the time lag between the offering and the cash settlement of the new share purchases, however, even a mandatory rights offering is unlikely to stop a run in progress. The triggers must be set so that the new shares are sold before the cash is likely to be needed. Thus, as opposed to the case of distress-contingent convertible debt, there should be a bias toward triggers that are based on the cash liquidity of the financial institution, as opposed to overall balance sheet solvency.

Distress-contingent equity rights offerings also offer the potential for more powerful incentives for shareholders to exert pressure on their firms to avoid risky behavior. (Whether shareholders can coordinate, through boards of directors, for example, so as to effectively apply this pressure is a concern.) Moreover, in the course of a financial crisis, the banking sector may need significant amounts of new capital in order to continue to provide credit to the broader economy. Equity rights offerings could recruit new capital that would otherwise remain "on the sidelines" because of the market imperfections that I have described—debt over-hang and adverse selection.

At the start of this chapter, I mentioned another approach to the automatic restructuring of distressed financial institutions: the purchase by financial institutions of put options on their own shares. The puts could have a contractually stipulated exercise event, as has been the case for certain insurance companies such as Aon and Swiss Re, that is based on designated business losses. An alternative would be American options that could be exercised at the discretion of the financial institution. Obviously, the exercise price should be designed so as to recapitalize the financial institution before a liquidity crisis.

Unfortunately, however, a financial institution relying on such put options is also relying on the credit quality of the seller of the puts. If the source of distress is a general financial crisis, the put seller may itself be distressed and unable to honor the obligation to purchase shares. Some insurance firms have opted to buy their put options from a special-purpose entity that is required to invest in relatively safe assets that could be used to cover the exercise costs, as explained by Culp (2009). Mandatory rights offerings of shares are also effective, in this respect, because once granted to existing shareholders, they can be sold to any investor with the cash necessary to exercise the rights. Thus, a distressed financial institution making a rights offering at a sufficiently low share price has access to the entire pool of investible cash held in global capital markets. This reduces the adverse impact of flights to quality during financial crises by funneling capital back to providers of credit.

CONCLUDING REMARKS

In new work, I plan to examine the design of triggers for debt conversion and equity rights offerings from the viewpoint of the incentive of financial institutions to take inefficient risks.

NOTES

1. For a summary of the literature on stock cancellation schemes of Bradley and Rosenzweig (1992) and Adler (1993), see Skeel (2001: 226).

2. Citibank's Tier 1 capital ratio was 7.1 percent in the fourth quarter of 2007. See, for example, http://seekingalpha.com/article/115374-citigroup-inc-q4-2008-earnings-call-transcript?page=1.

3. See www.citibank.com/citi/fin/data/090807a.pdf.

4. This possibility was suggested to me by Joe Grundfest.

5. I am grateful to Peter DeMarzo for suggesting this approach.

REFERENCES

Adler, Barry. 1993. "Financial and Political Theories of American Corporate Bankruptcy." *Stanford Law Review* 45: 311–346.

Akerlof, George. 1970. "The Market for 'Lemons': Quality Uncertainty and the Market Mechanism." *Quarterly Journal of Economics* 84: 488–500.

Bernanke, Ben S. 2009. "Financial Regulation and Supervision after the Crisis: The Role of the Federal Reserve." Remarks Given at the Federal Reserve Bank of Boston Fifty-fourth Economic Conference, October 23, Chatham, MA.

Bradley, Michael, and Michael Rosenzweig. 1992. "The Untenable Case for Chapter 11." *Yale Law Review* 101: 1043–1095.

Culp, Christopher L. 2009. "Contingent Capital versus Contingent Reverse Convertibles for Banks and Insurance Companies." Working paper, Compass Lexecon and The University of

Chicago Booth School of Business. *Journal of Applied Corporate Finance* 20, no. 4 (Fall).

Dudley, William. 2009. "Some Lessons from the Crisis." Remarks at the Institute of International Banks Membership Luncheon, October 13, New York City.

Duffie, Darrell. In press. "The Failure Mechanics of Dealer Banks." *Journal of Economic Perspectives*.

Duffie, Darrell, and Peter DeMarzo. 1999. "A Liquidity-Based Model of Security Design." *Econometrica* 67: 65–99.

Flannery, Mark J. 2005. "No Pain, No Gain? Effecting Market Discipline via 'Reverse Convertible Debentures.'" In *Capital Adequacy Beyond Basel: Banking, Securities, and Insurance*, ed. Hal S. Scott. Oxford: Oxford University Press.

———. 2009. "Market Valued Triggers Will Work for Contingent Capital Instruments." Solicited Submission to U.S. Treasury Working Group on Bank Capital, University of Florida.

Hart, Oliver, and John Moore. 1998. "Default and Renegotiation: A Dynamic Model of Debt." *Quarterly Journal of Economics* 113: 1–41.

Innes, Robert. 1990. "Limited Liability and Incentive Contracting with Ex-Ante Choices." *Journal of Economic Theory* 52: 45–67.

Leland, Hayne, and David Pyle. 1977. "Informational Asymmetries, Financial Structure, and Financial Intermediation." *Journal of Finance* 32: 371–387.

Lloyds Bank. 2009. "Lloyds Banking Group PLC Announces Exchange Offer to Eligible Investors of Certain Existing Securities for Enhanced Capital Notes." Press release, November 3.

Myers, Stewart C. 1984. "The Capital Structure Puzzle." *Journal of Finance* 39: 575–592.

Punter, Alan. 1999. "The Spectrum of Alternative Risk Financing Opportunities." In *The Changing Risk Landscape: Implications for Insurance Risk Management*, ed. Neil Britton. Proceedings of a conference sponsored by Aon Group Australia Limited.

Skeel, David. 1993. "Markets, Courts and the Brave New World of Bankruptcy Theory." *Wisconsin Law Review* 2: 465–521.

————. 2001. *Debt's Dominion: A History of Bankruptcy Law in America.* Princeton, NJ: Princeton University Press.

Squam Lake Working Group on Financial Regulation. 2009. "An Expedited Resolution Mechanism for Distressed Financial Firms: Regulatory Hybrid Securities." Policy paper, Squam Lake Working Group, April.

7

Wind-down Plans as an Alternative to Bailouts:
The Cross-Border Challenges

Richard J. Herring

Bailouts of systemically important financial institutions (SIFIs) have required interventions in the United Kingdom, United States, and euro area totaling over $14 trillion, equivalent to about a quarter of the global GDP (Haldane, 2009).[1] SIFIs are deemed too big or too complex or too interrelated to be permitted to cause loss to creditors or counterparties, although generally these institutions are referred to as simply "too big to fail," which ignores some of the most important dimensions of the problem. One of the most unfortunate legacies of the current crisis is the lesson that policy makers drew from the market chaos in

The author is grateful to participants in the Stanford seminar and particularly to Ken Scott for comments on an earlier draft.

the aftermath of the bankruptcy of Lehman Brothers, the one SIFI that was permitted to cause loss to creditors and counterparties. The ministers of the G-20 appear to have decided that they would provide whatever subsidy necessary to avoid the disruptions that might occur in subjecting any other SIFI to the bankruptcy process, with the headline in the *Financial Times* stating, "Ministers pledge 'no more Lehmans'" (Guha, 2008).[2]

Leaving aside the troublesome but important problem of identifying SIFIs,[3] reliance on bailouts of all creditors and counterparties not only has been very costly to taxpayers but has purchased financial stability in the short run at the cost of a heightened risk of larger, more frequent, costlier crises in the future. When all creditors and counterparties are protected from loss, they have reduced incentives to monitor SIFIs. Moral hazard increases because managers can take greater risks without having to pay higher risk premiums. Indeed, as the stake of equity holders declines to zero, managers may be tempted to play "go for broke" on the basis of the implicit guarantee from taxpayers. As Mervyn King (2009:4), governor of the Bank of England, has noted, "The massive support extended to the banking sector around the world . . . has created possibly the biggest moral hazard in history."

The costs of financial crises should not be measured simply in terms of their impact on public finances, the destruction of wealth, and the loss of jobs and output, but also in the loss of trust in the fairness and efficiency of the financial system. This has been particularly true over the last two years in which the principal, direct beneficiaries of bailouts have been sophisticated counterparties (often other SIFIs), which benefited greatly from the preceding boom and should have been in the best position to monitor and exercise market discipline over their peers. Distrust in the fairness of the financial system is only exacerbated when SIFIs that have repaid their subsidies from the Troubled Asset Relief Plan then pay bonuses that dwarf the lifetime earnings of many taxpayers.

Not only do bailouts impose heavy costs on taxpayers and increase incentives for risk taking, but they also waste resources by sustaining huge, zombie-like institutions that warehouse large amounts of dodgy debt, rather than serving as useful intermediaries. This delays economic recovery and the creative destruction that is the essence of dynamic capitalism.

Moreover, after the crisis is over, the expectation that an institution would be likely to receive a bailout in the future provides an unwarranted competitive advantage to SIFIs that bears no relationship to their ability to allocate capital efficiently or serve their customers more effectively. Confidence in implicit government backing permits SIFIs to fund themselves more cheaply and collect revenues from issuing guarantees they are not prepared to honor. This distortion of competition favors the large and complex financial institutions relative to smaller, simpler institutions that may serve their customers and society more efficiently.

Thus, bailouts provide incentives for institutions to become increasingly large, interconnected and complex in order to benefit from this implicit government subsidy. Perversely, governments often explicitly subsidize the creation of larger SIFIs as, for example, in the merger of Bear Stearns with JPMorgan Chase, or Merrill Lynch with Bank of America. And, had it not been for a change in the interpretation of the tax law that permitted Wells Fargo to claim $16 billion in tax losses from merging with Wachovia, the government would have subsidized the merger between two floundering giants—Wachovia and Citibank. In 1998, the five largest banks controlled 8 percent of global banking assets; now they control more than 16 percent (Haldane, 2009).

Why do officials feel compelled to provide bailouts? It is often because they lack tools to unwind the affairs of a SIFI without creating feared intolerable spillovers to the rest of the financial system. The principal, perceived channels of contagion include (1) interconnections with other SIFIs that are often extremely opaque and can change almost instantly, so that the collapse of one SIFI may possibly lead to the collapse of others;[4] (2) the inability to continue systemically important services such as third-party repo market making, custody, clearing and settlement during a wind-down of nonessential activities; (3) the inability to deal with international corporate complexity. The latter point is little discussed but deserves special attention. The sixteen large, complex international financial institutions identified by the IMF and the Bank of England have 2.5 times more majority-owned subsidiaries than the sixteen largest multinational manufacturing firms. This difference is undoubtedly due to the fact that banks have greater flexibility in avoiding taxes by booking business in tax havens than most manufacturing firms and because banks can often avoid burdensome regulations by conducting activities abroad. This suggests that the first-best solution to this problem might be for the tax and regulatory authorities to eliminate the incentives they have created, often inadvertently, for banks to adopt complex corporate structures.

The most complex SIFI has 2,435 majority-owned subsidiaries, 50 percent of them chartered abroad (see Herring and Carmassi (2009)). As emphasized later in this chapter, this international corporate complexity presents a formidable challenge to an orderly unwind, because countries differ with regard to virtually every aspect of how they resolve a failing financial institution. But even within one country, a SIFI may be subject to multiple regulators, each of which has different objectives and different procedures for dealing with a failing institution. In the absence of an *ex ante* agreement on the sharing of losses, it is likely that most regulatory authorities will ring-fence the assets that they can control in order to make sure that they fulfill their responsibilities to the groups they are charged with protecting, which inevitably leads to lengthy litigations.

For example, in the United States, a financial conglomerate may be subject to separate resolution actions by multiple entities—each with a different process, different objectives, and different timetables. A failed depository institution will be subject to Federal Deposit Insurance Corporation (FDIC) procedures constrained by least cost resolution requirements and domestic depositor preference laws. A failed broker/dealer will be subject to Securities Investor Protection Corporation (SIPC) procedures. An Edge Act subsidiary could be liquidated by the Federal Reserve Board (Fed), or the Fed may choose to turn it over to the bankruptcy courts. A failed insurance subsidiary would be subject to separate, state-specific procedures in each of the states in which it operates. The parent holding company and most other subsidiaries would be subject to normal bankruptcy processes. These separate proceedings serve different policies with different priorities and objectives. The United States is not alone in this respect. The Report and Recommendations of the Cross-Border

Resolution Group (2009:18) notes even, "At the national level few jurisdictions have a framework for the resolution of domestic financial groups or financial conglomerates."

What can be done to end bailouts? Two alternatives are currently under consideration: (1) accept the fact that we will have an increasing number of SIFIs, but subject them to much tougher capital regulation and more intensive supervision in an attempt to prevent all failures, or (2) require that each SIFI devise a wind-down plan that will assure its board, primary supervisor, and college of supervisors (if any), that it can be wound down without creating intolerable spillovers. Each will be examined in turn.

HIGHER CAPITAL REQUIREMENTS AND MORE INTENSE SUPERVISION

The G-20 has agreed that all banks will be subject to higher capital requirements and will be required to meet these requirements with higher-quality capital that can serve as a buffer against loss. Based on past performance, it is difficult to be optimistic about this approach. The five largest U.S. financial institutions that either failed or were forced into government-assisted mergers in 2008—Bear Stearns, Washington Mutual, Lehman Brothers, Wachovia, and Merrill Lynch—were each subject to Basel Capital standards, and each disclosed Tier 1 capital ratios ranging from 8.3 percent to 11.0 percent in the last quarterly report before they were effectively shut down (Bloomberg, 2009). These capital levels were from two to almost three times the regulatory minimums.

More capital is a very slender reed to sustain the stability of the financial system. As these examples show, capital can decline at an alarming rate in a crisis. This is partly because of accounting conventions that permit banks to conceal losses in a variety of ways until the end is near and partly because regulators often prefer to forbear rather than force losses to be recognized. The main problem, however, is that any reasonable level of capital may be simply overwhelmed by the losses that can occur in a crisis. Moreover, higher capital requirements can motivate greater risk taking unless precisely calibrated.

In addition, reliance on capital requirements ignores the remarkable ability of financial institutions to devise new ways to engage in regulatory capital arbitrage. A recent case is the attempt by the Basel Committee to impose punitive capital charges against resecuritizations to discourage banks from holding CDOs and other complicated, resecuritized assets. For the example, a BB-rated tranche of a mortgage-backed security incurs a risk weight of 350 percent under the Basel II standardized approach. Under the new rules, the BB-rated tranche of a resecuritized asset incurs a capital charge of 650 percent. Similarly, an AAA-rated tranche of an original securitization receives a 20 percent risk weight, while a resecuritzed tranche receives a 40 percent risk weight.

The market quickly responded to this increase in capital requirements by devising a new resecuritization technique called a Re-Remic.[5] Re-Remics have been used to resecuritize senior, private-label MBS tranches that have been downgraded from their original AAA ratings to BB. In a typical Re-Remic, a downgraded tranche is subdivided into a new, resecuritized AAA-rated senior tranche and a lower, mezzanine resecuritized tranche rated BB. Additional credit enhancement is provided by an option for the new senior tranche to be resubdivided into two exchange classes of securities in the event the resecuritized Senior AAA tranche loses its AAA rating. A typical Re-Remic structure is depicted in figure 7.1 in the appendix to this chapter. Even if the bank retains the complete resecuritization on its books, its required capital will fall relative to the initial situation in which it would be charged 350 percent against the full amount of the downgraded security. This remains true even if the bank exercises the exchange option. Moreover, banks can and do simply exchange downgraded securities in a Re-Remic transaction, and each ends up with less capital required to support the same amount of risk.

More troubling still is evidence that bank examiners, who are the front line of the supervisory system and are supposed to be making candid evaluations of the institutions they monitor, may be giving more lenient treatment to SIFIs. The primary tool of bank supervision is the CAMELS rating assigned to each bank, which is based on the examiner's assessment of the bank's capital adequacy, asset quality, management, liquidity, and sensitivity to market risks. These ratings are shrouded in secrecy and, until last June, have been more successfully protected than nuclear secrets. But the CAMELS rating for a very large SIFI was revealed last June in material subpoenaed by Congress from the Federal Reserve Board (see Keoun and Mildenberg, 2009). This SIFI had received a $34 billion bailout and had an order to raise $34 billion more in capital. It had made two disastrous acquisitions, and its CEO was in trouble with the SEC and being sued by shareholders. Moreover, the board had made no succession plan for departure of the CEO, surely one of the most fundamental responsibilities of good corporate governance. Nonetheless, this firm received a CAMELS rating of 2, which is used to designate banks that present "few, if any supervisory concerns" (Lopez, 1999). It is hard to imagine that a non-SIFI with similar problems would have received nearly as favorable a CAMELS rating.

Unfortunately, neither the Obama administration's proposal nor the G-20 proposals address the underlying causes of poor supervisory performance. Supervisors are burdened with a wide variety of ill-defined objectives, making it very difficult to hold them accountable for any particular objective. Moreover, their compensation system is generally not designed to motivate strong performance in protecting the interests of taxpayers (see Herring, 2009).

Wind-down Plans[6]

Fortunately, the G-20 has proposed another approach that may turn out to be more promising. The G-20 has agreed to force SIFIs to "develop internationally consistent, firm-specific . . . resolutions plans" (G-20, 2009a). Although the G-20 has so far supplied few specifics about what such plans should contain, based on interviews with bankruptcy practitioners and bankruptcy lawyers, I will speculate about what an ideal plan should contain.

The wind-down plan should be designed to accomplish a number of different objectives. First, it should protect taxpayers from the necessity of bailing out SIFIs by providing an alternative resolution method that will not require a taxpayer subsidy or impose intolerable spillovers on the rest of the financial system. Second, it will make clear to SIFIs, the market in general, and creditors and counterparties in particular that no SIFI need be bailed out. This should increase market discipline and help level the playing field by removing the implicit government guarantee. Third, making a credible wind-down plan will force SIFIs to anticipate and internalize some of the spillover costs that might occur if they should become insolvent. Ideally, maintaining a credible wind-down plan should be viewed as much a part of good governance as maintaining a business continuation plan. Fourth, it will make the primary supervisor aware of what they must be prepared to do if a SIFI approaches insolvency. Fifth, it will make the college of supervisors (if any) aware of the measures they must take to minimize spillovers that might otherwise occur if a SIFI should become insolvent. This will have the dual advantages of forcing each member of the college to reveal to each other what they are likely to do in the event a SIFI becomes insolvent, and, over time, it may provide an impetus for harmonizing at least some resolution procedures.

The wind-down plan begins with the assumption that the SIFI is insolvent.[7] The SIFI should write a plan that would specify precisely what it would do in the event of insolvency. (Note that in contrast with the British living will concept, which takes into account plans for averting insolvency, this wind-down plan begins with the assumption of insolvency.) The wind-down plan, in my view, should contain several mandatory elements. First, the SIFI must map its lines of business into the corporate entities that must be taken through some sort of resolution process in the event of insolvency, and each of these separate entities must be justified to the board and, ultimately, the primary supervisor.[8] The resolution procedures must be described for each entity, including an estimate of how long they will take. The dialogue between the SIFI and the primary supervisor is likely to be contentious at first because it will represent a dramatic change from past practice. As Lord Turner, chairman of the Financial Services Authority in Britain, has noted, "In the past, authorities around the world have tended to be tolerant of the proliferation of complex legal structures designed to maximize regulatory and tax arbitrage. Now we may have to demand clarity of legal structure" (Giles, Jenkins, and Parker, 2009).

Second, the SIFI must identify key interconnections across affiliates such as cross-guarantees, stand-by lines of credit, or loans that link the fate of one affiliate to that of another. The plan should also identify operational interdependencies such as IT systems, liquidity, and risk management procedures that would impede the separation of one unit from another.

Third, the SIFI will be required to develop and maintain a virtual data room that contains information that an administrator or resolution authority would require to make an expeditious resolution of the entity. This is likely to require investment in new management information systems that can provide information such as organizational structures, loan exposures, and counterparty exposures disaggregated by borrower or counterparty and by legal entity.[9]

Fourth, the SIFI must identify key information systems, where they are located, and the essential personnel to operate them. Plans must be made to make these systems available to all entities during the resolution process, whether they are operated by the SIFI or are outsourced to a third party. As a practical matter, this may require that IT operations be segregated in a separate subsidiary that could continue to function while the rest of the firm is being resolved.

Fifth, the SIFI must identify any activities or units it regards as systemically relevant and demonstrate how they can continue to operate during a wind-down. This will usually require that they be separately incorporated and capitalized and easily detached from the group, so that some other entity can keep the systemically important function going.

Sixth, the SIFI must consider how its actions may affect exchanges, clearinghouses, custodians, and other systemically important elements of the infrastructure. Ideally it should identify ways it can disconnect from these highly automated systems without creating serious knock-on effects. This will require cooperation with these systemically important parts of the infrastructure. A particularly good example of this in the past was the effort to make the Clearing House Payments System able to sustain the failure of its four largest members.

Seventh, the SIFI must identify precisely the procedures it would follow in a wind-down. This report should be quite detailed, including at a minimum a list of bankruptcy attorneys and administrators who might be consulted, individuals who would be responsible for press releases and the various notifications, and a good faith estimate of the time it would take to unwind each separately chartered entity.

Eighth, the unwind plan must be updated annually, or more often if a substantial merger or acquisition or restructuring introduces additional complexity. Of course, this deals with issues of legal structure, not risky positions, which may change very rapidly.

Management of the SIFI must demonstrate to its board that the unwind plan is complete and feasible. Boards should recognize that oversight of wind-down plans is as much their responsibility as oversight of business continuation plans. Indeed, when the SIFI approaches insolvency, the board's fiduciary duty becomes one of maximizing the bankruptcy estate that can be passed on to creditors.[10] If the board finds the plan is excessively complex or time-consuming, it has a duty to require management to simplify the corporate structure of the firm, invest in more powerful and comprehensive IT systems, or reduce the geographic range or scope of its activities so that it can be wound down in a reasonable amount of time.[11] This process may also have a useful side benefit. Considerable research in cognitive psychology shows that decision makers are likely to be more risk averse when they are forced to confront worst case scenarios even if they consider them unlikely to happen (see Guttentag and Herring, 1984, and references therein).

Next, the primary supervisor must evaluate the wind-down plan in detail (if appropriate with a national college of supervisors). It must certify that the plan is feasible, and the estimated time for the wind-down is plausible and acceptable. In addition, it must ensure that all systemically important activities have been identified and properly insulated, so that they could be spun off to another firm in the event of insolvency. If the primary supervisor finds the plan is not feasible or would take an unacceptable amount of time to execute, it should have the power to compel the SIFI to simplify its corporate structure or improve its IT infrastructure or spin off activities that cannot be unwound without creating intolerable spillovers.

This is a highly controversial point, but unless some authority has the power to compel action,[12] no meaningful action is likely to be taken, and the entire exercise will become a senseless and costly ticking of boxes. It may even prove counterproductive to the extent it encourages market participants to believe that a problem has been solved, when in fact it has not. It would be undesirable for regulators to force a cookie-cutter structure on a SIFI purely for supervisory convenience, but supervisors should be empowered to meet the goals of a good wind-down process, perhaps by raising the costs of supervising complex institutions, substantially and in proportion to their complexity. Institutions could then have some degree of choice over the way in which they become less complex.[13]

Many experts would prefer a much softer approach in which the supervisor would send the plan back to the board and management with comments noting perceived deficiencies and asking for remedial action or an explanation, which might be publicly disclosed. Unfortunately, this more gentle approach, akin to moral suasion, is unlikely to be very effective, particularly when we start from a position in which so many financial firms have become much too complex to take through any kind of resolution procedure in a reasonable amount of time. Moreover, it seems naive to expect that firms would willingly give up the complexity that virtually assures them access to the safety net and a competitive edge over other smaller, less complex institutions.

Imposing constraints on the size or structure of firms has traditionally been justified on grounds of competition policy, not as a way of enhancing financial stability. But what was once unthinkable is now being widely discussed. As former secretary of state and of the Treasury George Shultz has said, "Any bank that is too big to fail is simply too big."

In addition, Alan Greenspan, former Fed chairman, has recently spoken in favor of breaking up banks that are too big to fail because they interfere with the creative destruction that is essential to a dynamic economy.[14] Phillip Hildebrand (2009), vice governor of the Swiss National Bank, has stated the case a bit more cautiously:

> Size restriction would, of course, be a major intervention in an institution's corporate strategy. . . . For this reason, the advantages and disadvantages of such a measure would have to be examined and weighed very carefully. Nevertheless, in the case of the large international banks, the empirical evidence would seem to suggest that these institutions have long exceeded the size needed to make full use of these advantages.[15]

Perhaps, most surprisingly, Jamie Dimon, CEO of JPMorgan Chase, has endorsed a resolution mechanism that would wipe out shareholders and impose losses on creditors but protect the financial system when a SIFI fails. "We think everything should be allowed to fail . . . but we need a resolution mechanism so that the system isn't destroyed. To dismantle a bank in a way that doesn't damage the system should be doable. It's better than being too big to fail" (quoted in Sender, 2009).

Moreover, such restrictions can be justified on grounds of competition policy. Indeed, the EU has a mechanism for doing so. In recent months European Commissioner for Competition, Neelie Kroees, has required that ING, the Royal Bank of Scotland, and Lloyds downsize to compensate for the anticompetitive effects of the subsidies they have received. The Competition Commissioner can force banks to do many things, including "divest subsidiaries or branches, portfolios of customers or business units, or to undertake other such measure . . . on the domestic retail market. . . . In order for such measures to increase competition and contribute to the internal market, they should favor the entry of competitions and cross-border activity. . . . A limit on the bank's expansion in certain business or geographical areas may also be required" (European Union, 2009: C15). The United States lacks any mechanism for considering such issues. And although this is action taken after the extension of a bailout, it seems preferable to the frequent pattern in the United States of subsidizing the merger of a very large bank with another even larger bank without any regard for competitive effects.

During this process, the primary supervisor will gain an understanding of the regulations and tax provisions that provide SIFIs with incentives to adopt such complex corporate structures. It may be excessively optimistic to hope that these insights will help inform future regulatory, accounting, and tax reforms, but it would be useful, nonetheless, to confront regulators with some of the unintended consequences of their actions.

The potential benefits from developing wind-down plans are substantial. First, the process should reduce moral hazard by making it clear to creditors and counterparties that a SIFI can be resolved in such a way (see chaps. 9 and 11 in this volume) that it may impose losses on them without catastrophic consequences for the rest of the financial system. In its reaction to the "living will" proposal in the United Kingdom, Moody's provided indirect evidence that this might be quite effective. It warned the British authorities that such an approach "would remove the necessity to support banks as banks would no longer be too interconnected or complex to fail. This could potentially result in rating downgrades where ratings currently incorporate a high degree of government support" (quoted in Croft and Jenkins, 2009).

Second, gaining approval of the wind-down plan will cause SIFIs to simplify their corporate structures and make preparations so that less of the bankruptcy estate is consumed by a frantic, last-minute attempt to formulate and execute a wind-down plan. These amounts can be quite substantial. The administrators of the Lehman bankruptcy have estimated that at least $75 billion (Cairns, 2009: 115) was wasted because of the lack of any preparation for bankruptcy.

Third, developing the plan may cause SIFIs to reduce their risk exposures because of greater awareness of the board, more thorough analysis by supervisors, and greater discipline by creditors and counterparties.

Fourth, it will help level the playing field between SIFIs and smaller, less complex institutions so that profits and market share flow to institutions that provide the best services most efficiently rather than to institutions that benefit from an implicit guarantee.

Of course, wind-down plans may have both private and social costs as well as these benefits. With regard to private costs, it will certainly increase the compliance costs for SIFIs. But some of the upgrades in IT systems may enable them to manage their businesses more effectively, as well as facilitate a wind-down.[16] It may also reduce the efficiency with which the SIFI can deploy its capital and liquidity, but often these

efficiencies have proven illusory in a crisis,[17] to the extent
that capital and liquidity may be ring-fenced by regulators
(both domestic and foreign) who believe their main duty
is to protect the customers of the SIFI in their domain. It
may increase capital requirements and tax payments to the
extent that corporate simplification requires the elimination of entities used to engage in regulatory arbitrage and
tax avoidance. But this is a private cost, not a social cost.

With regard to social costs, there is a danger that wind-
down plans could limit potential economies of scope and
scale. But there is little evidence of either in the academic
literature for institutions of even $20 billion,[18] much less the
multitrillion-dollar institutions that we have encouraged.
Moreover, at any given scale, the difference in efficiency
between the least-cost and the highest-cost producers dwarfs
any gains from economies of scope or scale. In any event,
technology-intensive activities, which because of their
heavy fixed costs, do appear to create genuine economies of
scale in some lines of business, could be spun off and operated as utilities so that firms of all sizes could benefit.

By reducing leverage, wind-down plans may increase
the costs of intermediation. But since excessive leverage is
heavily implicated as a cause of the recent crisis, this may
actually be a benefit rather than a cost.

The most substantial obstacle to devising a credible
wind-down plan, however, may be the profound differences
across countries in the way in which financial institutions are
resolved.[19] Most SIFIs have significant international operations that complicate any wind-down plan. Of the sixteen
Large Complex Financial Institutions (LCFIs) identified by
the Bank of England and the IMF, one had 96 percent of

its majority-owned subsidiaries chartered abroad. We should have learned about these problems from earlier crises, but there is very little evidence of officials having taken measures to deal with these issues more effectively when they arise again, as they inevitably will.

CROSS-BORDER OBSTACLES TO WIND-DOWN PLANS

A series of close calls has given us a glimpse of the damage that can occur in the collapse of an internationally active financial institution, but until very recently these cross-border issues have not had a prominent place on the international regulatory agenda. All of this has changed with the bankruptcy of Lehman Brothers. But many of the difficulties could have been anticipated from earlier collapses.

The closure of Bankhaus Herstatt in 1974 provided one of the first examples in the post-World War II era of the complications in a cross-border collapse. Herstatt was notorious for overtrading. When the German supervisors found that it was insolvent, it was closed at the end of the German business day, which was during the middle of the clearing and settlement process at the Clearing House Interbank Payments System in New York, where the dollar leg of most large-value foreign exchange transactions is settled. The consequence was that several institutions that had sold European and Asian currencies to Herstatt earlier in the clearing day, in the expectation of receiving dollars, found that they had unexpectedly become claimants in a German bankruptcy proceeding that extended for decades. Even though Herstatt was not a large institution, the disruption it caused in the foreign exchange market caused the largest foreign exchange market at the time (the dollar/Deutsche-mark market) to nearly collapse for several months.

This event also highlighted the importance of differences in time zones. A regulator in one country can affect the distribution of losses by the time it chooses to close a financial institution. To avoid similar disruptions in the foreign exchange markets, the authorities have usually tried to be careful to close banks over weekends to minimize the disruption of the clearing and settlement process. Finally, some thirty years later, the foreign exchange problem was largely solved with the launch of the Continuously Linked Settlement Bank and the extension of clearing and settlement hours by key central banks.

The Lehman collapse serves as reminder, however, that the foreign exchange market is not the only critical market in which the clearing and settlement process is vulnerable. Lehman's bankruptcy has led to civil proceedings on three continents where transactions were aborted in the middle of the clearing and settlement process. In the four Lehman subsidiaries that are being administered by PwC in London, about forty-three thousand trades are still "live" and will need to be negotiated separately with each counterparty (see Hughes, 2008).

The Lehman collapse also reminds us that a regulatory authority can still affect the international distribution of losses by when it chooses to initiate closure. Lehman managed its cash position on a global basis, sweeping all of the cash balances into the holding company in New York and then sending cash out to each subsidiary at the beginning of the next business day. Because the U.S. authorities chose to send the holding company to bankruptcy court before the open of business in Asia,[20] many of the solvent foreign subsidiaries were immediately forced into bankruptcy because they lacked liquidity to meet margin calls or complete transactions. Most are now suing the holding company.

The collapse of Banco Ambrosiano in 1979 taught investors and counterparties that a claim on the headquarters is not equivalent to a claim on a foreign subsidiary. But this lesson was lost on many of the counterparties to, clients of, and lenders to Lehman Brothers, who were unable to prove where their claims resided. The Lehman Brothers group consisted of 2,985 legal entities that operated in 50 countries. Most of these entities were subject to regulation by the host country as well as oversight by the SEC. The integration of the organization was such that a trade performed in one company could be booked in another, without the client necessarily being aware that the location of the asset had shifted. When subsidiaries entered insolvency proceedings, the shared systems for intercompany information were shut down, causing a total breakdown in financial reporting for the worldwide group. Because the IT system was decentralized and considered the property of some entities but not others, several subsidiaries have experienced serious difficulties in determining what their assets and liabilities actually are. Indeed, the hasty sale of the American broker/dealer to Barclays impeded the resolution of the other entities because Barclays gained property rights to many of the IT systems, and other subsidiaries have had to bargain with Barclays in much of Europe and Asia, Nomura to gain access to crucial data for unwinding in their piece of the remainder of the group.

The near collapse of LTCM in 1998 exposed the darker side of close-out netting rules that permit nondebtor counterparties to avoid stays in bankruptcy proceedings. Pressure from these counterparties caused the Federal Reserve Bank of New York to convene LTCM's major creditors to arrange what was, in effect, a prepackaged bankruptcy to avoid triggering the close-out netting rules promoted by the International Swap Dealers Association and supported by the Treasury and the Federal Reserve to permit nondebtor counterparties an exemption from the stay in bankruptcy proceedings. In the case of Lehman, permitting nondebtor counterparties to avoid stays in bankruptcy proceedings caused a massive destruction of value at Lehman. As of the bankruptcy date, derivative counterparties numbered 930,000, of which 733,000 sought to terminate contracts.[21]

But perhaps most revealing of all was the collapse of BCCI in 1991, which demonstrated the incredible complexity of international bankruptcy proceedings. It showed differences across countries with respect to the entity that initiates insolvency proceedings, the philosophy of bankruptcy (the separate entity doctrine versus the single entity doctrine), differences in goals, differences in procedures such as the right of set-off, and the possibility for bankruptcy proceedings to be trumped by criminal charges. In the case of BCCI, the United States initiated RICO proceedings that recovered a substantial amount of assets that might never have been discovered.

Since that time, many countries have modernized their bankruptcy and restructuring procedures, but the bankruptcy of Lehman showed that substantial differences remain.[22] Under Chapter 11 liquidation of LBHI in the United States, the debtor remains in possession and is authorized to continue operations and can seek debtor-in-possession (DIP) financing to continue operations. Chapter 11 provides a stay on past debts and gives the debtor the ability to restructure all debt and bind hold-out creditors subject to judicial approval.

In contrast, administration of Lehman Brothers UK Holdings Ltd. meant that a licensed insolvency practitioner took over and was more focused on trying to establish and realize value for creditors rather than continuing operation of the subsidiaries. The administrator was not authorized to seek superpriority rescue financing. U.K. law does not provide for a stay, but it does permit a moratorium on legal action. The administrator may choose not to pay past debts but may make "hostage" payments when additional services are needed.

In Germany, the court initially appoints a preliminary administrator independent from the debtor. The powers of the administrator are restricted until formal opening of proceedings within three months of application. With the formal opening of proceedings, the administrator has the power to administer and dispose of the debtor's assets and can benefit from an automatic stay of legal actions and enforcement against the debtor. The administrator can implement an insolvency plan if approved by a majority of the creditors. Although DIP financing is not permitted, the state provides a wage subsidy for the first ninety days. While this provides major help for some firms, wages were a very small proportion of Lehman's cash needs, and so it was obliged to liquidate.

In Japan, stakeholders can choose bankruptcy, reorganization, or civil rehabilitation. Rehabilitation, like Chapter 11, provides for DIP financing. But the courts have adopted a standard time line—six months—with an option to extend up to two months. This time frame is often insufficient for a complex restructuring like the Lehman subsidiary and, thus, usually results in the disposition of assets as quickly as possible, in contrast to the United States and the United Kingdom. In addition, all participants in the process are lawyers, who tend to rely on legal criteria rather than commercial criteria in selling assets from the bankruptcy estate.

Finally, in Korea, rehabilitation proceedings can be initiated by the insolvent debtor, creditors, or shareholders. Lehman initiated rehabilitation proceedings for one subsidiary. The court may appoint anyone as a rehabilitation receiver, but since most of the staff had already transferred to Nomura, it proved difficult to find a suitable receiver. Moreover, court approval has been necessary for virtually every decision, which has created very long lags.

In short, although there have been numerous indications since the bankruptcy of Herstatt in 1974 that regulators are unprepared for the resolution of a large complex financial institution with numerous international affiliates, virtually nothing has been accomplished to prevent such an event from leading to an international financial crisis.[23] Instead, we have permitted—indeed, encouraged—financial institutions to become increasingly large, complex, and interrelated in ways that are often obscure even to the institutions themselves.

WHAT IS BEING DONE?

The Financial Stability Board (FSB; then named the Financial Stability Forum) has produced a set of principles for

Cross-Border Cooperation on Crisis Management, endorsed by the G-20. The FSB reported that more than thirty supervisory colleges had been formed for international financial institutions.[24] The primary supervisor is responsible for convening a meeting of the college of supervisors at least once a year. The college is to play a role in monitoring and sharing information about the institution. We learned in the case of BCCI that this is unlikely to be effective. Some supervisors are constrained by bank secrecy laws and privacy laws. And most are constrained by the knowledge that once they share bad news with their peers, they lose their scope for discretion in dealing with the problem institution and may even precipitate an outcome they hoped to avoid.

But the document also mandates that supervisors should work to identify obstacles to effective management of a crisis involving the institution. The agreement also would "[s]trongly encourage firms to maintain contingency plans and procedures for use in a wind-down situation . . . and regularly review them to ensure that they remain accurate and adequate." If this requirement were strengthened and the college of supervisors were required to simulate a wind-down, this might be a huge advance.

Ideally, the college of supervisors should also review and sign off on the wind-down plan produced by management, endorsed by the board, and vetted by the primary supervisor. With such diversity in approaches to resolution, the college of supervisors is in an ideal position to verify whether the assumptions that the SIFI has made about how the activities that take place within its domain can be unwound are accurate and feasible. In addition, each member must make clear whether it would ring-fence the SIFI's operations in its country. If a member of the supervisory college does not believe that it has sufficient control over the activities of a branch of the SIFI, it should be empowered to require that it operate as a subsidiary with its own capital and liquidity requirements.

Ideally, the college of supervisors can identify resolution concepts and approaches that would lead to a cooperative solution.[25] But if, as seems likely, each country and regulator would ring-fence the assets of the SIFI in its domain, the whole panoply of consolidated supervision and regulation should be fundamentally reconsidered. If capital and liquidity cannot be moved across borders in the event of a crisis, it is foolhardy to base regulation and supervision on the assumption that they can.

Appendix

TABLE 7.1 Support Packages

($ Trillions)	U.K.	U.S.	Euro
Central Bank			
• "Money creation"	0.32	3.76	0.98
• Collateral swaps	0.30	0.20	0.00
Government			
• Guarantees	0.64	2.08	>1.68
• Insurance	0.33	3.74	0.00
• Capital	0.12	0.70	0.31
Total (% GDP)	74%	73%	18%

Note: Exchange rate used: FSR euro/U.S. dollar exchange rate of 0.710; sterling/U.S. dollar exchange rate of 0.613. Money creation includes both monetary and financial stability relations.

Source: Bank of England, *Financial Stability Report*, June 2009. Figures for United Kingdom updated to November 4, 2009.

8

TABLE 7.2 The List of SIFIs Reported by the *Financial Times*

1. In the United States: Goldman Sachs, JPMorgan Chase, Morgan Stanley, Bank of America, Merrill Lynch, and Citigroup
2. In the United Kingdom: HSBC, Barclays, Royal Bank of Scotland, and Standard Chartered
3. In Canada: Royal Bank of Canada
4. In Switzerland: UBS and Credit Suisse
5. In France: Société Générale and BNP Paribas
6. In Spain: Santander and BBVA
7. In Japan: Mizuho, Sumitomo Mitsui, Nomura, and Mitsubishi UFJ
8. In Italy: UniCredit and Banca Intesa
9. In Germany: Deutsche Bank
10. In the Netherlands: ING
11. Insurance groups: Axa, Aegon, Allianz, Aviva, Zurich, and Swiss Re

Source: Patrick Jenkins and Paul Davies, "Thirty Groups on Systemic Risk List," *Financial Times*, November 29, 2009.

TABLE 7.3 Differences across Five Largest Countries in EU with Regard to Insolvency Resolution

Country	Closure Decision Controlled by	Claim Notification and Verification	Authority Controlling Resolution	Legal Payment Requirements for Insured Deposits
France	Commision Bancaire's notice prior to court's declaration	Customers notified by fund and have 15 days to respond	Resolution overseen by banking supervisor	3 months with the possibility for the Supervisory Commission to extend by 3 months again
Germany	Petition filed by Financial Supervisory Authority to court	Creditors are notified by German compensation scheme within 21 days of notification of insolvency, and claims must be filed in writing by creditors with the German compensation scheme within 1 year.	Financial Supervisory Authority	Payments must be made within 3 months.

TABLE 7.3 Differences across Five Largest Countries in EU with Regard to Insolvency Resolution (Continued)

Country	Closure Decision Controlled by	Claim Notification and Verification	Authority Controlling Resolution	Legal Payment Requirements for Insured Deposits
Italy	The courts have the legal power to declare the insolvency status. However, the Bank of Italy, independently from the courts' declaration, can propose to the minister of the economy and finance the compulsory administrative liquidation of a bank in each of the following cases: exceptionally serious violations of prudential requirements, exceptionally serious irregularities in the bank's administration, exceptionally serious financial losses.	FITD subrogate to the right of depositors and carries out pay-offs directly.	The 1993 Banking Law Bank of Italy appoints liquidator.	The reimbursement of depositors shall be made, up to the equivalent of 20,000 euros, within 3 months of the compulsory liquidation order. The Bank of Italy may extend this term in exceptional circumstances or special cases, for a total period not to exceed 9 months.

TABLE 7.3 Differences across Five Largest Countries in EU with Regard to Insolvency Resolution (Continued)

Country	Closure Decision Controlled by	Claim Notification and Verification	Authority Controlling Resolution	Legal Payment Requirements for Insured Deposits
Spain	Bank of Spain petitions court	Depositors are not required to file a claim. The insurer makes a record of the depositors who are entitled to compensation and informs depositors of the events through ordinary mail of their right to compensation.	General insolvency laws and Discipline and Intervention of Credit Institutions Law. Authority to impose sanctions for very serious infractions shall rest with the minister of economy and finance at the proposal of the Bank of Spain, except for revocation of authorization, which shall be imposed by the Council of Ministers.	Will start as soon as possible and shall take place within a maximum of 3 months of the date on which deposits become unavailable; the funds may apply to the Banco de España for a maximum of three further extensions of the time limit, neither of which shall exceed 3 months.

TABLE 7.3 Differences across Five Largest Countries in EU with Regard to Insolvency Resolution (Continued)

Country	Closure Decision Controlled by	Claim Notification and Verification	Authority Controlling Resolution	Legal Payment Requirements for Insured Deposits
United Kingdom	The FSA	The Financial Services Compensation Scheme will contact or transfer insured deposits to a healthy private sector bank.	U.K. Banking Act 2009, including a special resolution regime and enhanced bank insolvency procedure	Aim for a fast and orderly payout of depositors' claims under the Financial Services Compensation Scheme

Source: Extracted from Eisenbeis and Kaufman (2008) and Brierley (2009).

FIGURE 7.1 Regulatory Capital Arbitrage

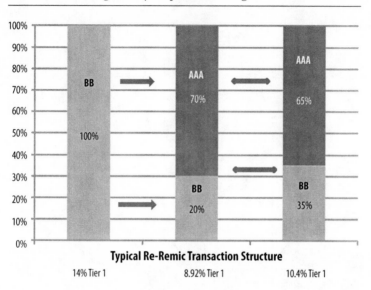

Typical Re-Remic Transaction Structure

14% Tier 1   8.92% Tier 1   10.4% Tier 1

NOTES

1. See table 7.1 in the end-of-chapter appendix for a disaggregation of the total amount of support.

2. It is telling in this regard that there was no criticism of the decision by the U.S. authorities, taken two days after the Lehman bankruptcy, to provide enormous subsidies to AIG, which now amount to $183 billion. Although during the most recent meeting of the G-20 in St. Andrews, Scotland, the leaders of the G-20 discussed ways of imposing the costs of future bailouts on the financial sector, they produced no practical plan to do so (see G-20, 2009b).

3. Some believe that SIFIs should be identified *ex ante* to impose additional regulatory burdens on them. Some believe they should not be identified *ex ante* because it would exacerbate moral hazard. Some believe that they cannot be identified *ex ante* because whichever institution turns out to be systemically important will always

depend on the context. This chapter assumes that at least some SIFIs can and should be identified *ex ante* for the purpose of preparing wind-down plans. The *Financial Times* claimed to have identified the Financial Stability Board's (FSB's) list of SIFIs (which are listed in table 7.2). The FSB has not confirmed the accuracy of this list, much less that such a list even exists.

4. Policymakers are understandably risk-averse when they think withholding a bailout may set off a systemic crisis, and so they are vulnerable to being bullied by SIFIs that may have superior information (and have an obvious interest in collecting subsidies).

5. For additional information on Re-Remics, see IMF (2009: chap. 2). This is also the source for figure 7.1.

6. The British prefer to call these "Recovery and Resolution Plans" although they are popularly known as living wills. The Obama administration has referred to the concept as rapid resolution plans, and sometimes they are known simply as funeral plans. I prefer to use the term *wind-down plan* to distinguish it from these other concepts. The plan I describe would be equally useful to a bankruptcy administrator or a resolution authority.

7. The British approach mixes this with a recovery plan that complicates the process with a number of very subjective assumptions. Institutions have strong incentives to devise recovery plans, but almost none to devise wind-down plans.

8. This notion has generated a considerable amount of controversy in Britain, with bankers generally taking the view that the supervisory authorities have no business monitoring their tax avoidance strategies and with Alistair Darling, chancellor of the Exchequer, tartly responding, "I do worry when an organization is structured for tax purposes rather than for the efficiency of its business and the strength of its business" (quoted in Giles et al., 2009).

9. This will undoubtedly be a contentious point as demonstrated by the years it has taken the FDIC to gain authority to require insured banks to identify insured deposits to facilitate rapid payouts. Banks successfully resisted for a number of years, claiming that it would be an overwhelming technological challenge.

10. The absence of a plan would be presumptive evidence of a failure to carry out this fiduciary duty.

11. Precisely what is "a reasonable amount of time" will likely change as the approach is implemented. The ultimate goal ought to be a plan that can be implemented over a weekend, but earlier iterations will clearly be much longer.

12. Of course, this power should not be without constraint. One way to curb arbitrary or inefficient use of such powers would be to give the institution the right to appeal a supervisory decision by presenting an alternative way of reducing the time to wind down the institution that would be equally effective but less costly.

13. Lord Turner has said that he hopes living wills will be a "forcing device for the clarification and simplification of legal structures" (Giles et al., 2009).

14. Transcript of a speech to the Council on Foreign Relations, October 15, 2009.

15. Paul Betts and Joe Leahy (2009) have put the case more forcefully: "The lesson of gargantuan institutions—the likes of Citigroup—is that these banks have become too big to succeed, impossible to run as well as too big to fail. And the bigger the group the bigger the systemic risk in the event of a financial meltdown."

16. Robert Eisenbeis pointed out to me that like the preparations for Y2K, which enabled a number of banks to deal more effectively with the shock of 9/11, this improvement in IT systems may have unexpected benefits.

17. The collapse of AIG provides a good example of this fallacy of consolidation. Presumably the ratings agencies granted the derivatives unit an AAA rating on the basis of the capital of the AAA-rated parent. But when losses at the derivatives unit spiraled, regulators would not permit capital to be upstreamed from the solvent insurance subsidiaries over to the derivatives affiliate. Instead, the burden fell on taxpayers. Moreover, the current allocations may seem optimal, given the regulations in place, but prove suboptimal if various authorities ring-fence in a crisis.

18. See, for example, Berger and Mester (1997). Although numerous empirical studies attempt to quantify economies of scale, all are subject to criticism because of the paucity of relevant data. This is, of course, particularly true for enormous banks. But it does seem clear that scale economies cannot be the main driving force behind the creation of trillion-dollar banks. A more robust and perhaps more relevant empirical regularity is that the compensation of senior executives tends to increase proportionately with scale. See, for example, Frydman and Saks (2007).

19. Even within an area as homogeneous as the European Union, there are significant differences across countries. Table 7.3 summarizes differences across the five largest countries in the EU with regard to several aspects of resolution policy.

20. According to Cohan (2009: 442):

> Paulson not only told McDade and Lowitt that Lehman had no choice but to file for bankruptcy, he also apparently told them the firm had to file for Chapter 7 liquidation by 7 p.m. Sunday. . . . "The words," remembered one participant in the meeting, "Bart used when he came into the board meeting were 'We were mandated to file. We were mandated to file.' He was very, very, very clear on that. . . . What if the board decided to defy Paulson and not file for bankruptcy protection? Because the Fed controlled Lehman's access to the money it needed to open for business the next day, the point was moot. . . . Christopher Cox, the SEC chairman phoned into the meeting from Washington. . . . [H]e had been told by Paulson to call to reinforce the idea that Lehman should file for bankruptcy." In fact the holding company Lehman Brothers Holding, Inc. filed for Chapter 11 bankruptcy at 1:45 a.m. Monday morning to keep the operating companies out of bankruptcy long enough for Barclays to buy them.

21. "Statement of Harvey Miller before the Subcommittee on Commercial and Administrative Law of the House of Representatives,

Committee on the Judiciary, 111th Congress, 1st Session for Hearings on 'Too Big to Fail: The Role for Bankruptcy and Antitrust Law in Financial Regulation Reform,'" October 22, 2009. Miller emphasized that as a result of the safe harbor provision of the Bankruptcy Code, nondebtor counterparties to derivatives contracts are permitted to exercise certain contractual rights triggered by a debtor's bankruptcy filing or financial condition, including the right to terminate the contract and take advantage of positions in their favor, and leave in place contracts in which they owe money to the debtor. The debtor usually has no right to terminate and remains exposed to such contracts.

22. The following five paragraphs are drawn from observations made by Ann Cairns (2009), managing director of Alvarez and Marcel, the firm that has taken the lead in managing the unwind of Lehman.

23. With, perhaps, the important exception of the European Union's Credit Institutions Reorganization and Winding-Up Directive in 2001 that adopted a single entity regime for any bank incorporated in the European Economic Area (EEA) applying to the parent bank and all of its branches in the EEA.

24. As noted in the progress report from the St. Andrews summit of the G-20 (2009b).

25. Although it is, perhaps, pleasant to contemplate international harmonization of resolution procedures, I regard it as the equivalent of expecting Esperanto to be adopted as the international language. Still, it may be possible for a handful of key countries or an integrated economic region like the EU to move toward harmonization at least with regard to the treatment of SIFIs.

REFERENCES

Bank of England. 2009. "Financial Stability Report." June.

Berger, Alan, and Loretta Mester. 1997. "Efficiency and Productivity Change in the U.S. Commercial Banking Industry: A Comparison of the 1980s and 1990s." Federal Reserve Bank of Philadelphia Working Paper No. 97-5/R.

Betts, Paul, and Joe Leahy. 2009. "Bankers Must Resist Temptation to Think Bigger." *Financial Times*, October 28.

Brierley, Peter. 2009. "The U.K. Special Resolution Regime for Failing Banks in an International Context." Bank of England, Financial Stability Paper No. 5.

Cairns, Ann. 2009. "Breaking the Insolvency Mould." *International Corporate Rescue* 6, no. 2: 115. Chase Cambria Publishing.

Cohan, William D. 2009. *House of Cards: A Tale of Hubris and Wretched Excess on Wall Street*. New York: Doubleday.

Croft, Jane, and Patrick Jenkins. 2009. "Moody's Warns over 'Living wills.'" *Financial Times*, September 23.

Cross-Border Bank Resolution Group of the Basel Committee. 2009. "The Report and Recommendations of the Cross-Border Resolution Group."

Eisenbeis, Robert A., and George G. Kaufman. 2008. "Cross-Border Banking and Financial Stability in the EU." *Journal of Financial Stability* 4, no. 3 (September).

European Union. 2009. "Commission Communication of the Return to Viability and the Assessment of Restructuring Measures in the Financial Sector in the Current Crisis under the State Aid Rules." *Official Journal of the European Union*, August 19.

Frydman, C., and R. Saks. 2007. "Executive Compensation: A New View from a Long-Term Perspective, 1936–2005." Federal Reserve Board Technical Report No. 2007-35.

G-20. 2009a. "Pittsburgh Summit: Progress Report on the Actions to Promote Financial Regulatory Reform." September 25.

———. 2009b. "St. Andrews Summit: Progress Report." November 7.

Giles, Chris, Patrick Jenkins, and George Parker. 2009. "Living Wills to Be Forced on Banks." *Financial Times*, September 15.

Guha, Krishna. 2008. "Ministers Pledge 'No More Lehmans.'" *Financial Times*.

Greenspan, Alan. 2009. "Speech to the Council on Foreign Relations." October 15.

Guttentag, Jack, and Richard Herring. 1984. "Credit Rationing and Financial Disorder." *Journal of Finance* 39, no. 5: 1359–1382.

Haldane, Andrew. 2009. "Banking on the State." Paper presented at the Twelfth Annual Federal Reserve Bank of Chicago International Banking Conference.

Herring, Richard. 2009. "The Known, the Unknown, and the Unknowable in Financial Policy: An Application to the Subprime Crisis." *Yale Journal of Regulation* 26, no. 2 (July).

Herring, Richard, and Jacopo Carmassi. 2009. "The Corporate Structure of International Financial Conglomerates: Complexity and Its Implications for Safety and Soundness." Chapter 8 in *Oxford Handbook of Banking*. Oxford: Oxford University Press.

Hildebrand, Phillip. 2009. "Current State of the Financial System of Switzerland." Introductory remarks at the half-yearly media news conference, Berne, June 20.

Hughes, Jennifer. 2008. "Lehman Creditors to Face Years of Waiting." *Financial Times*, November 14.

International Monetary Fund. 2009. "Global Financial Stability Report." October.

King, Mervyn. 2009. Speech to Scottish business organizations, Edinburgh, October 20.

Keoun, Bradley, and David Mildenberg. 2009. "Bank of America Has Second-Highest 'CAMELS' Rating." Bloomberg.com, June 25.

Lopez, Joseph. 1999. "Using CAMELS Ratings to Monitor Bank Conditions." *Federal Reserve Bank of San Francisco Economic Letter*, 99-109, June 11.

Sender, Henny. 2009. "Dimon Backs Means to Close Down Banks." *Financial Times*, October 28.

8

Wind-down Plans, Incomplete Contracting, and Renegotiation Risk:
Lessons from Tiger Woods

Joseph A. Grundfest

The recent financial crisis has focused regulators on the difficulties encountered when attempting to shut down large, complex, systemically important financial institutions. A frequently cited statistic observes that Lehman Brothers had 2,985 distinct legal entities strewn across the globe, and that its collapse has spawned a bankruptcy proceeding of Brobdingnagian proportions. To address these concerns, regulators in Europe and the United States are promoting the concept of "wind-down" plans for all systemically important financial institutions (SIFIs).

The basic concept behind a wind-down plan is simple. SIFIs would be required to define, in advance, how they can be efficiently shut down, restructured, or sold off in pieces without causing or increasing systemic risk. These wind-down plans would be subject to governmental review and approval. A common observation is that plans of this sort should cause firms to map their lines of business more rationally to their complex corporate structures, identify and manage operational interdependencies that might impede a breakup or dissolution of the firm (e.g., shared information technology systems, cross-guarantees, or intracorporate loans), and maintain an operational plan that would allow regulators quickly to take control of the SIFI in order to shut it down or break it up with minimum muss and fuss. The goal is to transform SIFIs from complex webs of intricately linked international operations that are as hard to untangle as a giant bowl of spaghetti into simpler, modular structures that can be snapped apart like a large set of Lego blocks.

Governance experts also suggest that the adoption of wind-down plans would have salubrious effects even if they are never implemented. Boards forced to consider and review these plans might cause banks to focus more closely on core lines of business, shed operations that are overly complex and difficult to wind down, rationalize internal financial flows, and simplify corporate structures. To some, if a bank is too complex to manage through a wind-down procedure, it is also probably too complex to operate on a day-to-day basis.

Opponents of wind-down plans offer many criticisms of the concept. *The Economist* suggests that "the whole idea of an "orderly failure" is a bit fantastical" for if a "death panel seeks to unwind a bank it will induce, not prevent, panic among its counterparties and creditors."[1] Other critics see wind-down plans as a means of forcing SIFIs to establish ring-fenced subsidiaries in each country in which the SIFI operates. That would make life easier for regulators but potentially less profitable for bankers. Some observe that wind-down plans are intended more to make it difficult for banks to engage in tax or regulatory arbitrage than actually to facilitate a smooth wind-down of troubled SIFI operations.

For present purposes, I remain entirely agnostic as to whether wind-down plans are a good or bad idea. In practice, I suspect that the merit of the concept will depend critically on the details of its implementation. Because wind-down plans can be done poorly or well, and because my observations relate to limitations on wind-down plan operations even under the best of circumstance, I accept the utopian assumption that regulators will adopt and enforce optimally structured wind-down plans that take into account the costs and inefficiencies that these plans might impose on SIFIs before they fail, or on SIFIs that do not fail. My concern, instead, is on a different question. Will even the best designed wind-down plan ever operate as intended?

INCOMPLETE CONTRACTS AND RENEGOTIATION RISK

German Field Marshall von Molte famously observed that no battle plan withstands contact with the enemy. Similarly, no wind-down plan is likely to withstand contact with a systemic financial crisis. Two predictable forces will likely prevent wind-down plans from operating as crafted, even if the plans are drawn with the greatest care and precision by the most competent legal and financial engineers.

First, wind-down plans cannot possibly anticipate every set of circumstances that arise in the midst of a systemic failure. Wind-down plans are therefore incomplete contracts. But every contract is, in some sense, incomplete, either because it is inefficient to contract for every foreseeable contingency or because unforeseen contingencies arise. Simply observing that a contract is incomplete is therefore an insufficient critique: there must be some *ex ante* reason to expect that the contract is incomplete in a manner likely to cause a material operational failure when time comes to execute on the agreement. Put another way, in order for incompleteness to constitute a meaningful criticism, there has to be good cause for the contracting parties to know at the time of execution that they are signing on to a plan that is unlikely to be implemented in accordance with its terms in the event it is ever executed.

Here, that condition is satisfied because systemic crises are largely unanticipated. If the regulatory, financial, and legislative systems accurately anticipated the circumstances of a looming systemic crisis, then they could take steps to prevent that crisis. Systemic financial crises are therefore, by their very nature, surprises. Wind-down plans will be unable to anticipate (and therefore to contract for) the nature of the surprise that requires that the plan be implemented, or the circumstances that arise in the midst of the crisis that could implicate the operation of the wind-down plan. Wind-down plans are thus profoundly incomplete in the sense that they are likely to be needed most under circumstances that are expected least and that maximize the probability of a problem generated by the incomplete nature of the agreement.

The legal system also tends to operate on the basis of precedent. The outcome of litigation that raises novel questions of law can be very difficult to predict. Because systemic financial crises occur infrequently (we hope), it is impossible, as a practical matter, to build a body of legally cognizable precedent that would provide guidance as to how the legal system in the United States, or any other nation, would address the challenges posed by a wind-down plan. This simple fact compounds the incomplete contracting problem by adding an additional layer of uncertainty.

This critique should not, however, be overinterpreted. Wind-down plans might well operate exactly as planned in the event of an isolated failure that is unrelated to a systemic crisis. Also, even if a systemic crisis renders a wind-down plan profoundly incomplete, the plan might usefully resolve many issues that would be left up in the air in the absence of a plan, and a partial resolution is likely better than none at all. Nonetheless, regulators and market participants should be suitably modest regarding their expectations as to how these plans will operate in the event of a systemic crisis.

Renegotiation risk is the second factor likely to prevent wind-down plans from being implemented as intended. A wind-down plan is, in large part, a contract between a financial institution and a government. Governments, however, are able unilaterally to renegotiate contracts, or to impose post hoc terms and conditions, with a facility that eludes the vast majority of private sector counterparties. Governments can unilaterally renegotiate a wind-down plan's terms by enacting legislation, adopting new regulations, amending existing regulations, or exercising moral suasion, among many other techniques. Incentives for governments to renegotiate are particularly strong in the midst of systemic financial crises when global financial and political risks are elevated. This simple fact further increases the risk that a wind-down plan will not be implemented as anticipated.

Again, the presence of renegotiation risk is not an argument against all forms of wind-down plans. Indeed, to the extent that a wind-down plan is in place and has been previously approved by regulatory authorities, the plan's presence could help constrain governmental action by persuading regulators to allow the plan to operate as initially intended. The presence of a preapproved wind-down plan can also operate as a focal point, or anchor, in later negotiations, and reduce the uncertainty that could otherwise exist if financial institutions and regulators were forced to start working with a blank piece of paper in the event of a systemic crisis. The presence of significant governmental renegotiation risk is, instead, counsel for caution, and suggests that drafters understand that their work can be most easily undone precisely at the time that it might be needed the most.

WIND-DOWN PLANS, PRENUPTIAL AGREEMENTS, AND TIGER WOODS

Wind-down plans are also known as recovery and resolution plans, living wills, rapid resolution plans, and funeral plans. A better analogy might, however, be to prenuptial agreements. And, the best example of incomplete contracting and renegotiation risk in a prenup that anticipates the problems likely to arise in wind-down plans might well involve Tiger

Woods, a figure who, until not long ago, was also viewed as too big and too connected to fail.

Prenups, like wind-down plans, are implemented only in the event of institutional failure. They are then used to divide and reallocate assets in a predetermined manner designed to minimize resolution costs and externalities on third parties. Couples with simpler, segregated physical and financial assets find it easier to implement prenup agreements. Couples with hard-to-value unvested stock options and other contingent claims, or balance sheets that are overweight in nondivisible assets, such as real estate, encounter more difficulties when implementing prenups. The parallel to financial sector wind-down plans is frighteningly close.

When prenups were in their infancy, they were fraught with legal and operational risk. How much disclosure do parties have to make regarding their assets and earnings potential in order that a prenup be binding? Do the parties to a prenup have to be represented by competent counsel in order to execute a binding agreement? How much time does a person need in order to review a proposed prenup so that the agreement won't later be thrown out for being obtained under conditions of duress? Springing a prenup on the bride while standing at the altar might be out of the question, but does that mean the prenup has to be signed, sealed, and delivered a week prior to the blessed day? How about a month in advance? Longer? And, when do the terms of a prenup become so one-sided that courts will refuse to enforce the agreement as against public policy? Experienced practitioners are today able to answer these and many other questions about the optimal structuring of enforceable prenups because the courts have sufficient experience with failed marriages that they have been able to generate a body of precedent that provides useful guidance to the newly, but skeptically, betrothed. There is no equivalent body of experience or precedent relevant to wind-down plans.

Assume for the moment that Tiger Woods and his wife had a state-of-the-art prenup that would be deemed enforceable by any court in the land. If Mr. Woods so desired, he would be able to institute divorce proceedings and cause the plan to be implemented precisely according to its terms in short order and at low cost.

Mr. Woods's problem, however, is that his infidelities have exposed the incomplete nature of his state-of-the-art prenup. They have also generated a form of renegotiation risk that was almost certainly unanticipated prior to the wedding. When the prenup was drafted, it is safe to assume that neither Mr. Woods nor his counsel anticipated that he would one day be the wealthiest sports figure ever to have two young children with a sympathetic bride while the tabloids race to number his dalliance into the double digits. Simply divorcing Mrs. Woods and implementing the prenup seems to be an unattractive alternative for Mr. Woods, as is made evident by his decision to take an indeterminate leave from the sport of golf while he seeks to rededicate himself to family values.

Instead, press reports suggest that Mr. Woods is attempting to renegotiate arrangements with his wife in order to induce her to remain in the marriage and not to trigger the existing prenup. According to these reports, Mrs. Woods is being offered increasing sums as an inducement for her not to instigate divorce proceedings. The unforeseen circumstances thus seem to have given birth to an entirely new concept: the anti-prenup agreement, or an agreement not

to trigger a valid preexisting prenup because of an unanticipated, uncontracted-for change in circumstance that gener-
ates an unanticipated systemic risk.

Given that the incomplete nature of the original contract
now forces Mr. Woods to deal with a counterparty who has
no obligation to agree to any terms, and who has good emo-
tional reason to want to cause pain to Mr. Woods, Mr. Woods
now finds himself confronted with profound renegotiation
risk. The analogy in the financial markets is that unforeseen
events related to a systemic crisis can cause governments to
want to force SIFIs not to implement their wind-down plans
as initially drafted, and to drive a fundamental renegotiation
of terms because of those changed circumstances.

To be sure, none of this it to argue that Mr. Woods should
not have had a prenup in place or that SIFIs should not
have wind-down plans. Mr. Woods may well be better off
because the existing prenup provides a rational focal point
for further negotiations, just as the existence of a carefully
crafted wind-down plan can provide a reasonable starting
point for the renegotiation of terms in light of unforeseen
circumstance. The point is, instead, more modest. Just as
Mr. Woods is likely surprised by the current operation of
his marital wind-down plan, we should all be ready to be
surprised by the operation of SIFI wind-down plans in the
midst of a systemic financial crisis.

INCOMPLETE CONTRACTS AND
RENEGOTIATION RISK IN THE RECENT CRISIS

While the Tiger Woods example is entertaining, it is, no
doubt, a stretch from the reality of the recent market crisis.

For better or worse, it is possible to point to several recent events that underscore the reality of incomplete contracting and renegotiation risk in the face of systemic financial crisis.

The dispute between Iceland and Britain over the application of British antiterrorism legislation to freeze the assets of Icelandic banks operating in Britain is, perhaps, the most public example of the circumstances under which incomplete contracting and renegotiation risk can arise during a systemic financial crisis. Icelandic banks had more than three hundred thousand customers in Britain with deposits in excess of five billion euros when they failed in October 2008. When it became apparent that the banks would fail, British authorities assured depositors that they would be made whole on their Icelandic accounts, even in amounts in excess of the preexisting deposit guarantees. To prevent the bank from transferring assets out of Britain, the British government froze the Icelandic bank assets, as well as the assets of Central Bank of Iceland and government of Iceland relating to the failed banks. The freeze was implemented pursuant to the provisions of Britain's Anti-Terrorism, Crime, and Security Act of 2001, and it was effected because the British Treasury "believed that action to the detriment of the UK's economy (or part of it) had been or was likely to be taken by persons who are the government of or resident of a country or territory outside the UK."[2]

Iceland was both surprised and offended by Britain's decision to respond to the financial crisis by declaring Iceland to be the equivalent of a terrorist threat, and Britain's actions have led to long a difficult negotiations between the two nations as they try to mend relations and address the consequences of the financial crisis. From Britain's perspective, however, it merely did what was necessary in order to safeguard its domestic financial interests in the midst of a serious global financial crisis. British statutory and regulatory authority was incomplete in the sense that the appropriate freeze authority existed nowhere other than in its antiterrorism legislation, and if in order to protect its interests the British government had to label Iceland a terrorist threat, then so be it. It was, to Britain, far the lesser of the evils. Furthermore, if Icelandic banks thought that they would be able to extract funds from the failed British institutions because there appeared to be nothing in British financial law that might have precluded the transfer, the actions of the British government demonstrated that sovereign renegotiation risk is a real threat because governments in crisis can generally find a rationale that supports their desired conclusion.

It is easy to conceive of situations in which financial institutions might attempt to implement wind-down plans that could be viewed as inimical to the interests of one nation in which the institution does business, and that the offended nation would take action to prevent implementation of the wind-down plan as written. The implications of such interference—whether pursuant to traditional banking authority or through imaginative application of alternative legal regimes—are essentially impossible to predict in the abstract.

The U.S. government's involvement with the Chrysler bankruptcy provides a further example of contractual arrangements not operating in accordance with all parties' expectations. There, secured creditors, including Indiana state pension funds, complained that the federal government's bailout plan violated their priority positions by favoring the United Auto Workers, which was scheduled to receive a 55 percent equity interest in the reorganized firm;

Fiat, which was scheduled to receive a 35 percent stake; and the governments of the United States and Canada, which would receive a 10 percent interest. The secured debt holders would receive 29 cents on the dollar for their holdings when, they asserted, there clearly was additional value available that could be used to pay off their secured, priority interests. Some observers suggested that the financial interests of the secured creditors were being subordinated in favor of the financial interests of the United Auto Workers, a union closely allied with the administration.

Supreme Court Justice Ruth Bader Ginsburg initially issued an order temporarily staying the transaction, but she quickly lifted the stay and allowed the deal to move forward, the transaction having already been approved by the lower courts. To be sure, the lower courts found no reason to invalidate the transaction notwithstanding the concerns of the secured creditors, but the very nature of the dispute underscores the extent to which friction and acrimony can arise in these sorts of transactions, and the extent to which wind-down plans will not necessarily operate in a manner that is universally agreed as in accordance with its terms.

The Chrysler transaction underscores a related and important point regarding the operation of the legal system in the course of a fast-moving systemic financial crisis: even if the operation of a plan is not changed by the intervention of the legal process, judicial proceedings add complexity and introduce risk that can be highly counterproductive. As a related example, consider the recent litigation over the operation of the automatic bankruptcy stay in connection with repurchase agreements that covered loans and associated loan servicing rights.[3] The court there concluded that the repurchase agreements satisfied the requirements for the Bankruptcy Code's safe harbor provisions and would therefore not be subject to the stay. The court, however, also concluded that the associated loan servicing rights were not sufficiently integrated into the repurchase agreement so as to qualify for the safe harbor and were therefore subject to the stay. Thus, the value of the assets in question had to be bifurcated in order to determine which would be subject to the stay in the bankrupt's estate and which would not.

The question regarding the scope of the assets subject to the repurchase agreement appears to have presented a question of first impression that was unanticipated by the drafters of the Bankruptcy Code, and it therefore presents an additional example of an incomplete contract. In the event of a systemic crisis, we should expect that many such questions of first impression will arise; and if we have to wait for each of these questions to be resolved through the legal process, then wind-down plans will, almost by definition, fail to operate as quick and efficient means of crisis resolution. Close attention will therefore also have to be paid to the extent to which persons adversely implicated by the operation of wind-down plans will have a right to litigate in a manner that could derail, delay, or distort the operation of these plans. The simple fact that material litigation is pending can be enough, in some circumstances, to cause a plan to fail to operate as intended, even if the litigation challenge ultimately fails.

CONCLUSION

Wind-down plans, properly implemented, may well be a good idea. The probability that these plans will be implemented according to their terms in the midst of a systemic financial crisis is, however, modest because of the dangers posed by incomplete contracting and renegotiation risk. The drafters of any wind-down plan would therefore be wise to consider the limitations inherent in their enterprise and not to overstate the likely benefits of any wind-down plan.

NOTES

1. *The Economist*, "Death Warmed Up: Are Living Wills Really the Answer to Banks That Are Too Big to Fail?" October 1, 2009, 87.

2. "UK Govt Launching Legal Action against Iceland," Citywire, October 8, 2008, www.citywire.co.uk/personal/-/news/markets-companies-and-funds/content.aspx?ID=316803&re=3902&ea=180442.

3. In re: *American Home Mortgage, Calyon New York Branch, v. American Home Mortgage Corp.*, 379 B.R. 503 (Br. Del. 2008).

PART IV

BANKRUPTCY VERSUS RESOLUTION AUTHORITY

9

Expanding FDIC-Style Resolution Authority

WILLIAM F. KROENER III

IN THIS CHAPTER, I CONSIDER THE expansion, with modifications, of FDIC resolution–type authority as an alternative to use of the general bankruptcy laws for the resolution of systemically important nondepositary financial intermediaries. This topic has become one of extensive discussion and is the subject of legislative consideration in the House and the Senate. Detailed proposals for a bank resolution–type approach have been made by others, including the Federal Reserve Bank of Kansas City (see chap. 10) and the Pew Financial Reform Task Force,[1] and it is the basis of the Obama administration's proposal. I will consider here some advantages, as compared to bankruptcy, of the bank resolutions model as currently implemented by the Federal Deposit Insurance Corporation (FDIC) under the Federal Deposit Insurance Act (FDIA); the manner in which that model generally operates in situations involving systemic risk and the identification of such situations; whether, as suggested in pending legislative proposals, including that by the Obama administration, the bank resolutions model can and should be adapted to the resolution more generally of nondeposit systemically important financial institutions (SIFIs); and some of the major issues arising with respect to such adaptation. I will also specifically consider whether the bank resolutions model, as adapted, has the potential to avoid some of the disadvantages of a bankruptcy approach without deteriorating into ad hoc bailouts and how the model can be implemented legislatively in a manner that avoids excessive and unnecessary use. I would suggest that the adaptation of the bank resolutions model, in some form, offers real promise for what George Schultz has suggested: "the clear and creditable measures . . . that convince everybody that failure will be allowed [and] bailouts, and the expectations of bailouts, will recede and even disappear" (see chap. 1).

Many of the precise details of the adaptation of the bank resolutions model of course can be varied. These include whether the FDIC or another government entity is the authority that conducts the systemic resolution, the details of decision making to invoke systemic resolution instead of the use of bankruptcy, whether resolution costs arising from nonbank systemic resolutions are paid from an *ex ante* fund or financed by the U.S. government with an *ex post* assessment on financial intermediaries (or a subset thereof), the financial intermediaries subject to any such assessment, and a number of other factors. I regard these as beyond the scope of this chapter. I believe for purposes here the key points are whether the bank resolutions–type model can be adapted in some form to systemic nonbank resolutions (1) so as to minimize external systemic economic effects without overprotection of creditors, and the consequent loss of market discipline, and (2) so as to be limited to truly systemic situations and not overused.

Whatever the precise details, the bank resolutions model has a number of advantages compared to the bankruptcy model. I would suggest that its expanded use provides an alternative to bankruptcy as a route to avoiding ad hoc bailouts such as those in the fall of 2008 with respect to nonbank financial intermediaries such as AIG. The principal advantages of the bank resolutions model, which are reciprocal with the disadvantages of the bankruptcy model, include (1) speed of resolution; (2) low relative administrative costs, since assets are returned to the private sector, or at least to private sector management, immediately without contested adversary proceedings or formal judicial consideration and decision; (3) a higher likelihood of ownership and management being placed in the hands of experienced and capable successors rather than some interim administration selected by preexisting creditors; (4) explicit consideration and focus on specific nonfirm general costs in considering whether the situation is systemic and requires special resolution; and (5) immediate decisions on the details of resolution.

Because of these advantages, there is widespread support in the current legislative debate for an orderly resolution regime for nonbank financial intermediaries patterned on the bank resolutions model. The most important advantage in bank resolutions is the speed, and resulting preservation of value, due to earlier intervention and the absence of an automatic stay. In bankruptcy, by comparison, there is an automatic stay of uncertain but possibly considerable duration while a plan is developed by creditors and submitted for judicial approval. However much this period can be shortened, there is time for values to vary and dissipate, and for external systemic losses to increase, in a bankruptcy proceeding. By comparison, the bank resolutions model operates to effect a solution, even if it is only the temporary solution of a bridge institution, immediately. (The longest "stay" in the bankruptcy sense is one business day with respect to qualified financial contracts in a receivership to permit consideration of their orderly transfer.[2]) In bank resolutions, there is an explicit focus on spillover systemic effects. This is a significant advantage where the principal purpose of the operation is to protect against systemic external effects not explicitly taken into account in bankruptcy proceedings. In addition, in most bank resolutions experienced management is immediately put in place. And there is a form of expert decision making involved, by experienced financial agency personnel, rather than an Article III judge, in determining the nature of the resolution. (As noted, the entity conducting the resolution need not be the FDIC, although by experience it is well adapted for this role.)

On the other hand, there are also some disadvantages to the bank resolutions model as compared to bankruptcy. These include (1) a less clear and predictable set of rules on creditor priorities, since these may be varied to accommodate the situation; (2) an essentially political decision whether the situation is one involving "systemic" risk;

(3) based on experience, a bias toward a finding of systemic risk in order to minimize disorder and disruption; and (4) timing uncertainties and very broad governmental discretion. Moreover, there is general agreement that the bank resolutions model works less well, and higher losses are realized, in sudden liquidity failures.[3] Even in these cases, however, the decision-making process is faster and there is more financial expertise brought to bear than may be the case in bankruptcy. Another major disadvantage of the bank resolutions model that has been widely identified is the fixed, nonnegotiable treatment of, and possibly inadequate consideration of, creditor claims. The problem seems to be that although there is a fixed and clear priority scheme, there is much less opportunity, if any, for *ex post* correction in the value of claims. Some also claim a degree of arbitrariness in the claims process as administered by the FDIC. I believe this is a by-product, perhaps a necessary one, of the speed and certainty of the bank resolutions model.

There is a significant set of questions as to how an "insolvency/failure" regime patterned on the bank resolutions model should work for SIFIs that are not banks. Systemic cases are currently identified by an assessment of anticipated adverse effects on the national or regional economy. The trigger mechanism involves a supermajority vote of the FDIC and Federal Reserve Boards, and approval of the secretary of the Treasury after consultation with the President. The test advanced by the administration in proposed legislation is very similar for SIFIs that are nondeposit institutions, but it is tighter by requiring adverse effects on the national or international economy. A serious potential disadvantage, as many have noted, and as suggested by the

Wachovia experience and by the FDIC's own administrative history, is that there can be a tendency—political or otherwise—to be overly quick in determining that a "systemic" situation exists and action is needed to prevent market disorder. This tendency would seem to me to be stronger if there is an *ex ante* fund available for such systemic resolutions, as proposed by the FDIC and others and included in the most recent version of the House proposal. And of course there is extraordinary discretion as to both timing and nature of the resolution.[4] Some proposals, including one considered in the House, seek to further strengthen the test in order to prevent overuse. The Obama administration has proposed essentially an extension of the bank resolutions model with a regime analogous to the FDIA for SIFI entities.[5] The most recent variation in the House sets a very high standard for the decision that a situation is systemic. The decision whether a particular situation may present systematic risks would be made in a manner similar to the current FDIA procedure involving supermajority sign-off by the relevant regulator (FDIC or SEC) and the Fed, and approval by the Secretary of the Treasury after consultation with the President. Treasury would then determine in systemic cases whether the resolution would be conducted by the FDIC or the SEC, presumably depending on the nature of the organization. A number of variations are possible, including a bifurcation into globally systemic and smaller but possibly systemic institutions, as suggested recently by the Kansas City Fed (see chap. 10). Recently, in amendments to the Frank bill, the circumstances where there is authority to make this determination have been proposed to be limited to *overall* systemic risks to the entire economy in order to control the possibility of overuse. I would suggest that this may be too stringent a test and that a single entity in at least some circumstances could pose systemic risks. I believe it may be shortsighted to try to limit situations that may be "systemic" too closely to those similar to the events of 2008. It would be preferable, in my view, to create additional flexibility since it may be needed. If systemic situations are too closely circumscribed by legislation, there is a risk of further defaults to ad hoc bailouts.

A variety of *ex ante* or *ex post* funding schemes are possible. As initially proposed by the Treasury, funding would be fronted by the U.S. government but come ultimately from all financial intermediary holding companies rather than only institutions that have been previously identified as potential SIFIs. As noted previously, in my view the creator of an *ex ante* fund would risk overuse of systemic resolution authority.

As compared to the other potential SIFI resolution regime—bankruptcy—the bank resolutions model appears to have the same advantages and disadvantages as the FDIA does for banks. The question is whether the advantages of control, low transaction costs, and others outweigh the potential disadvantages of higher potential political influence or a likely rush to find systemic situations in non-bank cases. Extending the bank resolutions regime to SIFIs in appropriate circumstances would also bring a variety of additional issues that would have to be considered and dealt with in the new construct. These include the focus on a broader group of stakeholders, not just depositors, and the possible need for an examination and enforcement functions in some form extending to SIFIs.

A major issue is whether and how to identify SIFIs in advance and whether particular types of SIFIs (other than depository institutions) should be subject to different rules. Identification in advance has the advantage of allowing special regulatory requirements to be imposed on SIFIs or potential SIFIs—higher capital requirements, closer supervisory scrutiny, and the like. A major disadvantage, however, may be a further tendency to expand the "too big to fail" category and thereby reduce market discipline. I would suggest that a further and very important possible method of preventing overuse, and instituting continuing market discipline, is a requirement that any systemic resolution, including those involving bridge authority, be accomplished through a receivership rather than a conservatorship. This would serve to assure that there are appropriate costs imposed on management and general creditors.

Special mention should be made of qualified financial contracts (QFCs). There are particular advantages to the FDIC bank resolutions regime, as compared to existing bankruptcy law, in dealing with QFCs since it is possible to preserve a book of business, or at least the "in the money portion," in an FDIC resolution process. The existing FDIA provisions effectively allow transfer of QFCs if completed by the close of business on the business day after failure. By comparison, QFCs are quickly closed out and unavailable as part of a continuing business or preservation of goodwill in bankruptcy.[6] I would suggest that in systemic nonbank resolutions the provisions related to QFCs should be modeled on those in bank resolutions.

The question at the end remains whether, for nondeposit SIFIs, an FDIA-type regime is preferable to bankruptcy and can successfully avoid ad hoc bailouts. I think it is fair to say that the discussions leading to this workshop have produced something of a convergence in trying to capture and combine advantages of the bank resolutions and bankruptcy resolutions in dealing with systemic financial intermediaries. Those that advocate the bankruptcy regime are looking for modifications that produce speed, expertise, and sensible limits on the automatic stay. These already exist in the bank resolutions model. Those that are attracted to the bank resolutions model need to deal with risks of overuse and discipline on the decision process so as to avoid reducing the process to ad hoc bailouts and overprotection of creditors. I believe from my experience that the bank resolutions model can be adapted to protect business values and limit spillover effects, appropriately penalize managers and shareholders, and instill creditor discipline in a way that is more effective than a bankruptcy-based model.

NOTES

1. Rodgin Cohen and Morris Goldstein, "The Case for an Orderly Resolution Regime for Systematically Important Financial Institutions," Pew Financial Reform Task Force, Briefing Paper #13.

2. Any "automatic stay" is limited only to certain qualified financial contracts, and only to a single business day, so values do not dissipate with continuing market adjustments.

3. Indymac is an example. There it was necessary for the FDIC, which lacked bridge back authority for OTS institutions at the time of the failure, to use a pass-through receivership to a conservatorship because of the absence of bidders. Such authority was added in federal housing legislation at the request of the FDIC in the week following the failure.

4. The prompt connective action provisions put in by FDICIA in the early 1990s after the thrift crisis have had only limited impact because bank accounting remains largely tied to historic cost conventions and therefore is generally backward looking and slow to recognize economic problems.

5. U.S. Treasury Department, "A New Foundation: Rebuilding Supervision and Regulation," *Financial Regulatory Reform*, Treasury White Paper, June 17, 2009, pp. 76–78.

6. Indeed, a technical problem in the Bear Stearns resolution was the need for a JPMorgan Chase guarantee of all transactions, initially drafted overbroadly and then revised a week later. It should be noted that there have been recent changes to the FDIC rule on QFCs that may undermine this advantage by allowing the FDIC to pick and chose the QFCs that are transferred based on the net overall position with a counterparty and its affiliates. 12 CFR 371, 73 Fed. Reg. 78162 (December 22, 2008).

10

The Kansas City Plan

Thomas M. Hoenig,
Charles S. Morris,
and Kenneth Spong

Under current law, financial regulators do not
have the authority to resolve financial holding companies
and nondepository financial companies that are in default
or serious danger of default, as they do with depository institutions. Although the normal bankruptcy process is a very
effective process for most nondepository financial companies that default on their obligations, it is not effective for
the largest financial companies whose failure poses systemic
risks to the financial system and overall economy. This chapter[1] outlines key components of a "rule of law" based process
for resolving financial institutions currently considered "too
big to fail" that ensures (1) a continuation of critical services
and a stable financial environment and (2) that a financial
company's senior management, shareholders, directors, and

creditors account for the costs of their decisions and are held accountable when those decisions lead a company to default on its obligations. Key differences between the proposed resolution process and the process proposed by the Department of Treasury in July 2009 (hereafter referred to as the "Treasury proposal") also are discussed.

A. DEFINITIONS

1. Alternative Resolution Process—The administrative resolution process described in this document as an alternative to bankruptcy under the United States Code for financial companies that meet specific criteria.

2. United States Financial Company—A financial holding company or bank holding company or any other company, including a nonregulated subsidiary of a holding company, which is incorporated or organized under the laws of the United States and engaged in financial activities in the United States.

3. Foreign Financial Company—A financial holding company or bank holding company or any other company, including a nonregulated subsidiary of a holding company, which is incorporated or organized in a country other than the United States and engaged in financial activities in the United States.

4. Appropriate Regulatory Agency—The consolidated federal regulatory agency for a bank holding company or financial holding company, the primary federal regulatory agency for a financial company, or state regulatory agency if there is no federal regulatory agency (e.g., insurance company) for a financial company.

Comment   The intent of this definition of the Appropriate Regulatory Agency is to allow the regulatory authority with the most detailed supervisory knowledge of a company to make the determination that the company is in default or danger of default. In contrast, the definition in the Treasury's proposal is that the appropriate regulatory agency is the Federal Deposit Insurance Corporation (FDIC) unless the holding company's largest subsidiary is a registered broker or dealer, in which case it is the Securities and Exchange Commission (SEC).

Covered Financial Company—A United States or Foreign Financial Company (other than an insured depository institution, registered broker or dealer that is a member of the Securities Investor Protection Corporation, or insurance company) that is subject to or may be subject to the alternative resolution process.

Comment   This definition differs from the Treasury's proposal. The Treasury's proposal uses an *ex post* definition in which the secretary of the Treasury determines that a financial company already in default or in danger of default poses systemic risk and is eligible for emergency assistance and/or an alternative resolution process based on a set of proposed criteria. In contrast, the definition used here is *ex ante* because it is for a predefined group of financial firms based on criteria discussed later. Also, the Treasury's proposal uses the terminology of a covered "bank holding company," which may or may not own a bank or be a holding company because it is defined as (1) a bank holding company as defined in the Bank Holding Company Act, (2) a Tier 1 financial company, or (3) certain nonbank subsidiaries of such companies.

Tier 1 Covered Financial Company—A Covered Financial Company that is predetermined to be subject to the alternative resolution process.

Tier 2 Covered Financial Company—A Covered Financial Company not designated as Tier 1, which would be subject to the alternative resolution process if, at the time it is in default or danger of default, it is determined to pose a systemic risk to the financial system or overall economy.

B. DESIGNATION OF COVERED FINANCIAL COMPANIES AND TIER LEVEL

1. Covered United States Financial Company—Any United States Financial Company that has (a) $50 billion or more in assets, (b) $100 billion or more in assets under management, or (c) $2 billion or more in gross annual revenue.

2. Covered Foreign Financial Company—Any Foreign Financial Company that has (a) $50 billion or more in assets in the United States, (b) $100 billion or more in assets under management in the United States, or (c) $2 billion or more in gross annual revenue in the United States.

Comment on Designation as a Covered Financial Company   The criteria for designation as a covered financial company is largely based on the Treasury's criteria for determining whether a financial company would be subject to *consideration* for designation as a Tier 1 financial company (Title II, Consolidated Supervision and Regulation of Large, Interconnected Financial Firms, Sec. 6, paragraphs a(2)A and a(2)B). The difference from the definition used here is the Treasury used $10 billion for criterion (a). The larger dollar amount is used here because it is unlikely that the failure of an institution with less than $50 billion in assets that does not meet criteria (b) or (c) would have systemic effects on the economy or financial system.

3. *Tier Designation*—The Board of Governors of the Federal Reserve System (Board), on a nondelegable basis, will designate any Covered Financial Company as a Tier 1 Covered Financial Company if it determines that material financial distress at the company could pose a threat to global or United States financial stability or the global or United States economy during times of economic stress.

a. Criteria for the determination includes, but is not limited to, factors such as a company's amount and nature of financial assets and liabilities, reliance on short-term funding, off-balance sheet exposures, transactions and relationships with other major financial companies, and importance as a source of credit to the United States economy and liquidity for the financial system.

b. For foreign companies, the criteria would depend on United States assets, liabilities, and activities.

c. All Covered Financial Companies that are not designated as Tier 1 will be designated as Tier 2.

Comment on Covered Financial Companies   The criteria for designation as a Tier 1 covered financial company is largely the same as the Treasury's criteria: Title II, Consolidated Supervision and Regulation of Large, Interconnected Financial Firms, Sec. 6, paragraphs a(1)A and a(1)B. The Treasury's proposal does not include a Tier 2 designation for a covered financial company.

4. *Consultation*—If a Covered Financial Company has one or more functionally regulated subsidiaries, the Board shall consult with the Appropriate Regulatory Agency for each subsidiary before making any determination.

5. *Reevaluation*—The Board shall at least annually reevaluate whether a Covered Financial Company is Tier 1 or Tier 2.

6. *Notice and Opportunity to Contest*—The Board shall provide a Covered Financial Company notice of its designation as Tier 1 or Tier 2. Within 30 days of its notice of designation, the Company can contest its designation and request a hearing.

C. RESOLUTION DETERMINATION

1. *Determination of Default or Danger of Default*—The Appropriate Regulatory Agency of a Covered Financial Company, in consultation with the consolidated regulator if the company is a subsidiary of a bank holding company or financial holding company, shall determine if the company is in default or danger of default.

2. *Default or in Danger of Default*—A Covered Financial Company shall be considered to be in default or danger of default if

   a. the company has filed, or likely will promptly file, for bankruptcy under title 11, United States Code,

   b. the company is critically undercapitalized as determined by the Appropriate Regulatory Agency,

   c. the company has incurred, or is likely to incur, losses that will deplete all or substantially all of its capital, and there is no reasonable prospect for the company to avoid such depletion without government assistance,

d. the company's assets are, or are likely to be, less than its obligations to creditors and others, or

e. the company is, or is likely to be, unable to pay its obligations (other than those subject to a bona fide dispute) in the normal course of business.

3. Determination of Resolution Process—The resolution method for a Covered Financial Company in default or danger of default will be

a. the Alternative Resolution Process if the company is a Tier 1 Covered Financial Company, or

b. the bankruptcy process under title 11, United States Code for a Tier 2 Covered Financial Company unless the Board and the Secretary of the Treasury (Secretary), in consultation with the President, jointly determine that the default of the company poses a threat to global or United States financial stability or the global or United States economy, in which case the Alternative Resolution Process would be used.

Comments on Resolution Determination

- Tier 1 covered companies are those covered companies for which the Board has determined that material financial distress at the company could pose a threat to global or U.S. financial stability or the global or U.S. economy during times of economic stress. In the Treasury's proposed resolution process, these companies would be treated like any other company in default or danger of default—that is, they would be subject to the alternative resolution process only *after* a recommendation is made to the Treasury secretary that their resolution through bankruptcy poses a systemic threat *and* the secretary determines *ex post* to use the alternative resolution process. In the proposal being advanced here, it is recommended that Tier 1 covered companies are predetermined to always be resolved by the alternative resolution process because it already has been determined that their problems could have systemic consequences. In addition, by predetermining the resolution process for Tier 1 companies, creditors would know in advance what their rights will be if the company fails, and the market would have confidence that they will be resolved in a timely and safe manner.

- The Tier 2 covered companies are those whose failure could have systemic consequences, but because they do not meet the criteria necessary for a Tier 1 designation, they would not automatically be resolved by the alternative process. In this proposal, Tier 2 covered companies normally would go through the bankruptcy process if they default, but they would be subject to the alternative resolution process if it is determined at the time they are in default or danger of default that it would have systemic consequences. The benefit of this option is that a Tier 2 company's cost of debt may be lower than if it is automatically subject to the alternative process because, if it defaults, creditors have more rights under the normal bankruptcy process than under the alternative resolution process. In addition, creditors know in advance that they might be subject to the alternative resolution process. A potential problem with this approach is that if a Tier 2 company becomes a Tier 1 company, existing creditors lose virtually all of their rights in the resolution process even though they had no influence on the company's decisions that led to its designation as a Tier 1 company.

- An alternative is for Tier 2 companies normally to go through the alternative resolution process unless at the time they are in default or danger of default it is determined that it would *not* have systemic consequences. The benefit of this option is that potential creditors know in advance they are subject to the worst-case scenario of an administrative process if the company defaults, but that they may actually have more rights if instead the company goes through the normal bankruptcy process. In addition, this option would be more equitable to existing creditors if a company changes from a Tier 2 to a Tier 1 company because the presumed resolution process would always be the alternative process, in which case creditors would never be moved to a resolution process where their rights are more restricted. A potential cost of this approach is that potential creditors will likely require a higher interest rate to lend to the company.

- As defined earlier, a financial company may also be a nonbank (nonregulated) subsidiary of a holding company. The resolution designation for these subsidiaries would be the same as for their parent holding companies because it would be possible for a subsidiary to be in default or danger of default and to have systemic implications by itself. Moreover, in the case of a limited liability subsidiary, the subsidiary could fail without necessarily putting the parent holding company in default, assuming the reputational and liquidity effects of the subsidiary's failure could be managed. This would be particularly true for subsidiaries that operate outside the cross guarantee and source of strength provisions that might be imposed on affiliated banks and their parent company. Consequently, it is important to have authority to directly resolve a subsidiary that could threaten financial stability whether or not it is possible to pursue a resolution at the parent company level as well.

D. RESOLUTION

1. Resolution Authority for the Alternative Resolution Process—The FDIC will be the resolution authority for the alternative resolution process.

2. Receivership—If the appropriate regulatory agency for a Covered Financial Company determines that the company is in default or danger of default, and it is determined that the alternative resolution process should be used, the appropriate regulatory agency will appoint the FDIC as receiver.

3. Minimize Overall Cost of Resolution—In taking any actions as receiver of a covered financial firm in default or danger of default, the FDIC must minimize the overall cost of the resolution, taking into consideration the action's effectiveness in mitigating potential adverse effects on the financial system or economic conditions, cost to the general fund of the Treasury, and potential to increase moral hazard on the part of creditors, counterparties, and shareholders of financial companies.

E. JUDICIAL REVIEW

If a receiver is appointed, the Covered Financial Company may, not later than 30 days thereafter, bring an action in the United States district court for an order requiring that the receiver be removed. The court shall, upon the merits, dismiss such action or direct the receiver to be removed.

F. POWERS AND DUTIES OF THE RECEIVER

1. Successor to the Covered Financial Company—The FDIC as receiver for a Covered Financial Company will succeed to all rights, titles, powers, and privileges of the Covered Financial Company and any of its stockholders, members, officers, or directors with respect to the company and its assets. At a minimum, the FDIC must replace the directors and members of senior management responsible for the company's condition.

2. Operate the Covered Financial Company—The FDIC as receiver for a Covered Financial Company may

a. take over the assets of and operate the company with all the powers of the members or shareholders, the directors, and the officers and conduct all business,

b. collect all obligations and money due the company,

c. perform all functions of the company in the name of the company,

d. preserve and conserve the assets and property of the company, and

e. provide by contract for assistance in fulfilling any function, activity, action, or duty of the FDIC as receiver.

3. Actions Taken by the Receiver—Upon its appointment as receiver of a Covered Financial Company, and subject to the minimum overall cost of resolution requirement in Section D, paragraph 4, the FDIC may

a. make loans to, or purchase any debt obligation of, the Covered Financial Company or any covered subsidiary,

b. purchase assets of the Covered Financial Company or any covered subsidiary directly or through an entity established by the FDIC for such purpose,

c. assume or guarantee the obligations of the Covered Financial Company or any covered subsidiary to one or more third parties,

d. acquire any type of equity interest or security of the Covered Financial Company or any covered subsidiary,

e. take a lien on any or all assets of the Covered Financial Company or any covered subsidiary, including a first priority lien on all unencumbered assets of the company or any covered subsidiary to secure repayment of any financial assistance provided under this subsection, or

f. sell or transfer all, or any part thereof, of such acquired assets, liabilities, obligations, equity interests or securities of the Covered Financial Company or any covered subsidiary.

4. Functions of Covered Financial Company's Officers, Directors, and Shareholders—The FDIC as receiver may provide for the exercise of any function by any member or stockholder, director, or officer.

5. Additional Powers as Receiver—The FDIC as receiver of the Covered Financial Company may place the company in liquidation and proceed to realize upon its assets in such manner as the FDIC deems appropriate, including through the sale of assets, the transfer of assets to a bridge financial company established under this Act, or the exercise of any other rights or privileges granted to the receiver.

6. *Organization of New Companies*—The FDIC as receiver may organize a bridge financial company. (The definitions and rules governing the organization of a bridge financial company would be defined as part of the legislation and likely modeled after the legislation that allows the FDIC to organize a bridge national bank.)

7. *Debt-for-Equity Exchange*—As part of its powers as receiver of a Covered Financial Company under paragraphs F(5) and F(6), the FDIC may offer creditors the opportunity to exchange their debt for equity as a means for raising new equity capital and a prelude for the timely reprivatization of the company.

Comment   The existing resolution process for insured depository institutions has a least cost requirement for the FDIC to use the resolution method that is least costly for the deposit insurance fund, but it includes a systemic risk exception to the least cost requirement. There is little need for a systemic risk exception to the requirement proposed in section D, paragraph 4 to minimize the overall cost of resolution because the FDIC can carry on critical financial functions through a bridge holding company and take other steps to mitigate systemic risk, although if deemed necessary, an exception could be added with restrictions that allow it to be used only in very limited circumstances.

8. *Merger and Transfer of Assets and Liabilities*—The FDIC as receiver of the Covered Financial Company may

(a) merge the company with another company, or (b) transfer any of its assets or liabilities.

9. *Payment of Valid Obligations*—The FDIC as receiver of the Covered Financial Company shall, to the extent funds are available, pay all valid obligations of the company that are due and payable at the time of the appointment of the FDIC as the resolution authority.

10. *Disposition of Assets*—In exercising any right, power, privilege, or authority as receiver, the FDIC should conduct its operations so as to

a. maximize the net present value return from the sale or disposition of assets,

b. minimize the amount of any loss realized in the resolution of cases,

c. minimize the cost to the general fund of the Treasury,

d. mitigate the potential for serious adverse effects to the financial system and the United States economy,

e. ensure timely and adequate competition and fair and consistent treatment of offerors, and

f. prohibit discrimination on the basis of race, sex, or ethnic groups in the solicitation and consideration of offers.

11. *Shareholders and Creditors of the Covered Financial Company*—Notwithstanding any other provision of law, the FDIC as receiver for a Covered Financial Company shall terminate all rights and claims that the stockholders and creditors of the company may have against the company's assets or the FDIC arising out of their status as stockholders or creditors, except for their right to payment, resolution, or other satisfaction of their claims as permitted under this section.

12. Coordination with Foreign Financial Authorities—The FDIC as receiver for a Covered Financial Company shall coordinate with the appropriate foreign financial authorities regarding the resolution of subsidiaries of the company that are established in a country other than the United States.

G. AUTHORITY OF THE FDIC TO DETERMINE CLAIMS

1. The FDIC as receiver may
   a. determine claims,
   b. determine rules and regulations for the determination of claims, including the use of the regulations used by the FDIC for insured depository institutions.

2. Priority of Expenses and Unsecured Claims—In general, unsecured claims against a Covered Financial Company or the FDIC as receiver for the company shall have priority in the following order:

   a. Administrative expenses of the FDIC.

   b. Any amounts owed to the United States.

   c. Any other general or senior liability of the Covered Financial Company that is not a liability described under clauses (d) or (e).

   d. Any obligation subordinated to general creditors that is not an obligation described under clause (e).

   e. Any obligation to shareholders, members, general partners, limited partners or other persons with interests in the equity of the Covered Financial Company arising as a result of their status as shareholders, members, general partners, limited partners or other persons with interests in the equity of the company.

3. *Creditors Similarly Situated*—All claimants of a Covered Financial Company that are similarly situated under paragraph G(2) shall be treated in a similar manner, except that the FDIC may take any action (including making payments) that does not comply with this section if

a. the FDIC determines that such action is necessary to maximize the value of the assets of the company, maximize the present value return from the sale or other disposition of the assets of the company, minimize the amount of any loss realized upon the sale or other disposition of the assets of the company, or to contain or address serious adverse effects on financial stability or the United States economy, and

b. all claimants that are similarly situated under paragraph G(2) receive at least the amount they would have received if

i. the alternative resolution process had not been used to resolve the Covered Financial Company, and

ii. the company had been liquidated under title 11, United States Code, any case related to title 11, United States Code, or any State insolvency law.

4. *Secured Claims Unaffected*—The claims priority in this section shall not affect secured claims, except to the extent that the security is insufficient to satisfy the claim and then only with regard to the difference between the claim and the amount realized from the security.

5. *Additional Priorities in a Financial Crisis*—The FDIC as receiver of a Covered Financial Company may place a higher claims priority on short-term (maturity 180 days or less) unsecured general or senior liabilities than on other

general or senior liabilities in the creditor class described in clause G(2)c

  a. if the FDIC, Board, and Secretary (in consultation with the President) jointly determine that such action is the best course of action to mitigate potential adverse effects on the financial system or economic conditions, taking into consideration the cost to the general fund of the Treasury and potential to increase moral hazard on the part of creditors, counterparties, and shareholders of financial companies, and

  b. subject to the other conditions of this section.

Note The additional priority for short-term liabilities does not apply to repurchase agreements because they are qualified financial contracts (as described in section H) and not a liability.

Comments on Allowing a Higher Claims Priority for Some Unsecured Short-Term Liabilities

- The rationale for the proposed exception to the normal claims priority for unsecured liabilities with maturities of 180 days or less is that many short-term liabilities of financial companies have become an important component of the daily financial flows required for the smooth functioning of the financial system and the economy. For example, many short-term instruments, such as commercial paper and repurchase agreements, are used by financial and nonfinancial firms as cash management instruments, or serve as backing for cash management instruments such as money market mutual fund shares. As a result, if a covered financial company were to go into receivership, the inability of customers and counterparties to access their short-term funds, or the potential loss of a portion of those funds, could intensify market disruptions and contribute to systemic risk.

- The systemic risks and market disruptions that arise from excessive reliance on short-term funding, and therefore the likelihood of needing to use this claims priority exception, can be significantly reduced by strengthening liquidity and/or capital requirements as part of the prudential supervisory process. Specifically, legislation providing for a systemic risk regulator and/or increased authority for consolidated supervisors of financial holding companies should mandate regulations that covered financial firms meet specific minimum liquidity requirements, supplemented by a required capital surcharge if liquidity is insufficient, explicitly tied to short-term funding.

- The rationale for requiring a capital surcharge only after assessing a firm's liquidity condition is that the underlying systemic problem with short-term funding is an asset-liability maturity mismatch that prevents firms from meeting short-term obligations in a crisis; that is, the firm either cannot access short-term funding or has to sell illiquid assets to meet the withdrawal of funds. For example, firms whose asset and liability maturities are perfectly matched would not need to hold additional capital because they would be able to meet all short-term obligations. A perfect match is not realistic since all financial intermediaries fund assets with longer maturities than the liabilities to some extent, so the liquidity requirement established by regulators would allow for a "reasonable" mismatch in asset-liability maturities, including liquidity risk management measures. For firms that do not meet the liquidity requirement (i.e., they have an excessive asset-liability maturity mismatch), a capital surcharge requirement would increase the cushion available to meet short-term obligations through the sale of longer-term or illiquid assets at the discounted values that may occur in a crisis.

- Listed next are suggestions for liquidity and capital surcharge regulatory requirements that legislation could require supervisory authorities to impose on covered financial firms.

  - *Minimum liquidity*—Covered firms must hold high-quality assets of comparable maturities that are at least equal to a specified percentage (e.g., 25 percent) of its liabilities with a maturity of 180 days or less. High-quality assets for purposes of this liquidity requirement are U.S. Treasury and government agency securities, claims on or unconditionally guaranteed by Organisation for Economic Co-operation and Development (OECD) central governments, deposits in U.S. depository institutions or banks in OECD countries, and claims collateralized by cash on deposit or securities issued or guaranteed by OECD central governments or United States government agencies.

  - *Capital surcharge*—Covered firms that fail to meet or only marginally exceed the minimum liquidity requirement must maintain *additional* Tier 1 capital based on (1) the shortfall that they have in matching short-term liabilities and assets, and (2) a specified percentage (e.g., 100 percent) of the minimum Tier 1 tangible capital ratio requirement. For example, if the minimum Tier 1 tangible capital requirement is 5 percent of tangible assets and the capital surcharge is 100 percent of the minimum Tier 1 tangible capital requirement, a firm would have to hold an extra amount of Tier 1 tangible capital equal to 5 percent of the shortfall of short-term liabilities. Tier 1 tangible capital (as currently defined) is common stock, noncumulative perpetual preferred stock, and minority interests in the equity accounts of consolidated subsidiaries less goodwill and other intangible assets.

- An additional benefit of tying specific liquidity and capital surcharge requirements to short-term funding (maturity of 180 days or less for the remainder of this comment) is that it could mitigate pricing distortions from changing the normal claims priority.
  - The potential that creditors holding a covered financial firm's short-term unsecured liabilities could receive a higher claims priority in receivership reduces their risk relative to longer-term creditors, which could lower the firm's cost of short-term funding relative to longer-term funding. This distortion could lead to a greater asset-liability maturity mismatch for covered firms and, therefore, an increase in the systemic risks associated with excessive short-term funding.
  - In addition, short-term unsecured creditors of covered firms would have additional protection not available to creditors of other (i.e., smaller) firms. This distortion perpetuates the view that investments

in the short-term debt of financial firms are safer at the largest financial firms than at smaller firms, which gives the largest firms a competitive advantage in the short-term funds markets, particularly in times of financial stress.

• However, these cost distortions would be mitigated by the additional costs incurred by covered firms in meeting the proposed minimum liquidity and/or capital surcharge requirements.

H. PROVISIONS RELATING TO CONTRACTS ENTERED INTO BEFORE APPOINTMENT OF RECEIVER

1. Authority to Repudiate Contract—In addition to any other rights it may have, the FDIC as receiver for any Covered Financial Company may disaffirm or repudiate any contract or lease

a. to which the company is a party,

b. the performance of which the FDIC determines to be burdensome, and

c. the disaffirmance or repudiation will promote the orderly administration of the company's affairs.

2. Timing of Repudiation—The FDIC as receiver appointed for any Covered Financial Company shall determine whether or not to exercise the rights of repudiation within a reasonable period following appointment as the resolution authority.

3. Claims for Damages for Repudiation—In general, the liability of the FDIC as receiver for the disaffirmance or repudiation of any contract shall be

a. limited to actual direct compensatory damages, and

b. determined as of the date of the appointment of the receiver, or for qualified financial contracts, the date of the disaffirmance or repudiation of the contract.

4. *Qualified Financial Contract*—A qualified financial contract is any securities contract, commodity contract, forward contract, repurchase agreement, swap agreement, and any similar agreement that the FDIC determines by regulation, resolution, or order to be a qualified financial contract.

5. *Certain Qualified Financial Contracts*—Subject to paragraph H(6), no person shall be stayed or prohibited from exercising any right

a. they have to cause the termination, liquidation, or acceleration of any qualified financial contract with a Covered Financial Company which arises upon the appointment of the FDIC as receiver for the company at any time after the appointment,

b. under any security agreement or arrangement or other credit enhancement related to one or more qualified financial contracts described in clause (a), or

c. to offset or net out any termination value, payment amount, or other transfer obligation arising under or in connection with one or more contracts and agreements described in clause (a), including any master agreement for such contracts or agreements.

6. *Transfer of Qualified Financial Contracts*—In making any transfer of assets or liabilities of a Covered Financial Company in default that includes any qualified financial contract, the FDIC as receiver for such covered bank holding company shall either

a. transfer to one financial institution all qualified financial contracts between any person and the company in default, all claims under the contract (other than claims subordinated to general unsecured creditors) of the person against the holding company, all claims of the company against the person, and all property securing or any other credit enhancement for these contracts and claims, or

b. transfer none of the qualified financial contracts, claims, property or other credit enhancements.

7. *Certain Transfers Not Avoidable*—The FDIC as receiver of a Covered Financial Company may not avoid any transfer of money or other property in connection with any qualified financial contract with a Covered Financial Company except for transfers in which the intent is to hinder, delay, or defraud the FDIC, company, or creditors.

I. FUNDING

1. *Establishment of Fund*—The Treasury will establish a separate fund called the Financial Company Resolution Fund (Fund), which shall be available without further appropriation for the cost of actions authorized by this legislation to the FDIC as receiver to carry out its authorities for resolving a covered financial company, including the payment of administrative expenses and principal and interest on debt obligations issued to carry out its authorities.

2. *Proceeds*—Amounts received by the FDIC to carry out its authorities under paragraph (3) and assessments received under paragraph I(4) shall be deposited into the Fund, subject to apportionment.

3. Capitalization of the Fund—When assigned as the resolution authority for a Covered Financial Company, the FDIC may issue obligations to the Secretary to capitalize the Fund.

   a. The Secretary may purchase any obligations issued by the FDIC and may use the proceeds from the sale of any securities to fund the purchase.

   b. Each purchase of obligations by the Secretary shall be upon such terms and conditions as to yield a return at a rate not less than a rate determined by the Secretary, taking into consideration the current average yield on outstanding marketable obligations of the United States of comparable maturity.

   c. The Secretary may sell any of the obligations acquired from the FDIC.

Note   The following paragraphs provide three options for funding the costs of resolving a covered financial company.

4. Funding Option 1 (ex-post assessment): Funding the Costs of Resolving a Covered Financial Company—The FDIC shall take steps to recover the amount of funds expended out of the Fund that have not been recouped.

   a. Such steps shall include one or more risk-based assessments on Tier 1 Covered Financial Companies based on their total liabilities not already assessed for deposit insurance purposes.

   b. The FDIC will determine the terms and conditions for the assessment, which by regulation, are necessary to pay in full its obligations to the Secretary within 60 months from the date it was assigned as the resolution authority of a Covered Financial Company.

c. Risk-Based Assessment Considerations—In imposing assessments, the FDIC may differentiate among Tier 1 covered companies by taking into consideration

i. different categories and concentrations of assets,

ii. different categories and concentrations of liabilities, both insured and uninsured, contingent and noncontingent,

iii. leverage,

iv. size, complexity, risk profile, and interconnectedness to the financial system,

v. the threat each poses to the stability of the financial system, and

vi. any other considerations that the FDIC deems appropriate.

d. Assessment Deduction—A Tier 1 Covered Financial Company may deduct from its assessment an amount equal to what it or any subsidiary paid to any State insurance guarantee fund association due to conservation, rehabilitation, or liquidation of a covered company or any subsidiary of the covered company.

4. Funding Option 2 (ex-ante assessment): Funding the Costs of Resolving a Covered Financial Company—The FDIC shall assess a risk-based fee on all Covered Financial Companies (Tier 1 and Tier 2) to capitalize the Fund prior to the placement of a Covered Financial Company in receivership.

a. The assessments will be based on a Covered Financial Company's total liabilities not already assessed for deposit insurance purposes.

b. Risk-Based Assessment Considerations—In imposing assessments, the FDIC may differentiate among covered companies by taking into consideration

i. different categories and concentrations of assets,

ii. different categories and concentrations of liabilities, both insured and uninsured, contingent and noncontingent,

iii. leverage,

iv. size, complexity, risk profile, and interconnectedness to the financial system,

v. the threat each poses to the stability of the financial system, and

vi. any other considerations that the FDIC deems appropriate.

c. Assessment Deduction—A covered financial company may deduct from its assessment an amount equal to what it or any subsidiary paid to any State insurance guarantee fund association due to conservation, rehabilitation, or liquidation of a covered company or any subsidiary of the covered company.

4. Funding Option 3 (no assessment): Funding the Costs of Resolving a Covered Financial Company—The Fund will be capitalized entirely by the Treasury's general fund.

Comment on Funding   Funding may be less of an issue if the proposed resolution process were to be adopted because the resolution costs are likely to be much lower than the costs of rescuing the "too big to fail" firms in the current financial crisis. In the proposed resolution process, no institution is too big to fail because all "systemic" institutions that are in default or danger of default are required to be put in receivership, with directors and senior management being replaced, shareholders losing their entire investment, and unsecured creditors losing principal on their securities based on the losses and costs of resolving failed or troubled companies. Because the largest companies typically have large amounts of unsecured debt, the creditors are likely to absorb all or most of the costs of resolving these institutions. As a result, while option 3 would not be considered in today's crisis because it imposes all of the high resolution costs on taxpayers, it is a more viable option under the current proposal because no large financial institutions are being rescued. In addition, to the extent there are some residual costs borne by taxpayers under option 3, all taxpayers and financial and nonfinancial firms benefit from the resolution process's prevention of economic and financial instability.

NOTE

1. This document does not represent the views of the Board of Governors of the Federal Reserve or the Federal Reserve System. Copyright © 2009 by the Federal Reserve Bank of Kansas City. This chapter appears here with the permission of the Federal Reserve Bank of Kansas City.

11

Chapter 11F
A Proposal for the Use
of Bankruptcy to Resolve
Financial Institutions

Thomas H. Jackson

Bankruptcy reorganization is, for the most part, an American success story. It taps into a huge body of law, provides certainty, and has shown an ability to respond to changing circumstances. It follows (for the most part) non-bankruptcy priority rules—"the absolute priority rule"—with useful predictability, sorts out financial failure (too

Many of the ideas in this chapter are a result of stimulating conversations as a part of the Resolution of Failing Tier I Financial Institutions group chaired by Kenneth Scott. I have learned an extraordinary amount from this group's inclusion of me in the process, for which I am very grateful. Errors that remain are mine.

much debt but a viable business) from underlying failure, and shifts ownership to a new group of residual claimants, through the certainty that can be provided by decades of rules and case law.

Notwithstanding its success, bankruptcy reorganization has a patchwork of exceptions, some perhaps more sensible than others.[1] Among them are depository banks (handled by the FDIC), insurance companies (handled by state insurance regulators), and stockbrokers and commodity brokers (relegated to Chapter 7 and to federal regulatory agencies).[2] In recent months, there has been a growing chorus to remove bankruptcy law, and specifically its reorganization process, from systemically important financial institutions (SIFIs), with a proposed regulatory process substituted instead, run by a designated federal agency, such as the Federal Reserve Board or the Securities and Exchange Commission.

Putting aside political considerations, behind this idea lie several perceived objections to the use of the bankruptcy process. First, it is argued, bankruptcy, because it is focused on the parties before the court, is not able to deal with the impacts of a bankruptcy on other institutions—an issue thought to be of dominant importance with respect to SIFIs, where the concern is that the fall of one will bring down others or lead to enormous problems in the nation's financial system.[3] Second, bankruptcy—indeed, *any* judicial process—is thought to be too slow[4] to deal effectively with failures that require virtually instant attention so as to minimize their consequences.[5] Third—and probably related to the first and second objections—even the best-intentioned bankruptcy process is assumed to lack sufficient expertise to deal with the complexities of a SIFI and its intersection with the broader financial market.[6]

The premise of my "Chapter 11F" proposal,[7] which I flesh out here, is that, *assuming the validity of each of these objections*, they, neither individually nor collectively, make a case for creating yet another (and very large) exception to the nation's bankruptcy laws and setting up a regulatory system, run by a designated federal agency, that operates outside of the predictability-enhancing constraints of a judicial process.[8] Rather, bankruptcy's process can be modified for SIFIs—my Chapter 11F—to introduce, and protect, systemic concerns, to provide expertise, and to provide speed where it might, in fact, be essential. Along the way, there is probably a parallel need to modify certain other existing bankruptcy exclusions, such as for insurance companies, commodity brokers, stockbrokers, and even depository banks, so that complex, multifaceted financial institutions can be fully resolved within bankruptcy.[9]

If we seek, as George Shultz has counseled us (see chap. 1), ways to make failure tolerable, we need to allow failure and to have the consequences of that failure fall on the parties who had contracted *ex ante* to bear the risks of such failure according to predictable rules. Bankruptcy, I would argue, performs precisely this function, and the objections to it that lead to another set of exceptions simply do not make the case for eliminating bankruptcy, rather than taking it and, with changes, working within its structure.[10] Can bankruptcy, even if revised along the lines I propose here, eliminate bailouts? Probably not, for the government can always intervene. But a system of established rules, judicial oversight (including appeals to Article 3 courts), and full public disclosure has a better chance of both reducing bailouts—and making the costs of them known—than does a nonbankruptcy resolution authority. The predictability of bankruptcy helps ensure, *ex post,* that risks remain where they belong, which will aid, *ex ante,* appropriate risk-taking activities as well as monitoring by those exposed to potential losses in any resulting bankruptcy.[11]

Before I set forth the proposal itself, there is one other important background question that involves the scope of any new Chapter 11F. The workshop that resulted in this book focused on systemically important financial institutions, and this chapter originally focused exclusively on that category. I am in complete agreement with John Taylor's contribution (chap. 4), which suggests that we don't have a focused or coherent definition of systemic risk, and with the observation that it is difficult, indeed imprudent, to recommend a policy change limited to SIFIs without knowing precisely what they are.

Moreover, as I thought about it—and here my views may well diverge from other contributors—the category of "systemic" is limited, unlikely to occur often outside depository bank "runs," and almost impossible to predict in advance. Let me explain by a brief detour to thinking about the issue outside of the context of financial institutions. In Chrysler—hardly the largest "American" (whatever that might mean) automobile manufacturer—much of the plan of reorganization, and the "need for speed," was premised on the repercussions that would occur to the American economy, its jobs, and its communities, if Chrysler were allowed to liquidate.[12] First, I think of these as *direct,* not *systemic,* consequences, and—even then—they would have been not consequences so much of a Chrysler bankruptcy as of an overcapacity problem in the automotive industry.

They are "direct" because they are all caused by known, contractual, linkages to Chrysler. It is known, and pre-dictable, what will happen to a dealer if Chrysler liquidates. Likewise, the effects on a Chrysler supplier are also known and predictable. The consequences might be large, but they aren't, therefore, necessarily systemic—any more than they would be if Chrysler were fully vertically integrated and thus owned both suppliers and dealers.[13] Moreover, they aren't even a consequence of a Chrysler liquidation so much as a consequence of overcapacity in the automotive industry. An industry scaled to produce seventeen million cars that needs to scale back to something smaller—whether twelve million or fourteen million or some other number doesn't really matter—has to face the wrenching consequences of that, in terms of lost jobs, shuttered plants, and effects on suppliers. In that world, Chrysler, as one of—if not the— least efficient producers *should* be the one that takes the most serious "hit" from this reality. Treating the consequences of a Chrysler liquidation as making it "too big to fail," as the government seemed to do, only implies that the effects of overcapacity will not be allowed to fall on the inefficient but will be "spread" throughout the automotive manufacturers more broadly. In other words, the efficient will be required to suffer so that jobs can be "saved." Not a very good policy, in my view.[14]

What does this have to do with financial institutions? The case for treating them as too big to fail isn't a result of the number of jobs, or suppliers, or dealers; rather, it is because of the potentially broader effects on the economy that aren't measured by the financial institution's failure itself. But I think it is still useful to consider, by analogy, a manufacturing company such as Chrysler. If the size of its operations—jobs, plants, suppliers, and so forth—aren't enough to treat its consequences as anything other than "direct," then what might "systemic" consequences be? They would be, in my view, most clearly a category of consequences visited on others not directly linked to Chrysler— John Taylor's "indirect" category (see chap. 4). As with a "run" on a bank spilling over to other banks, it would be what would happen if a Chrysler liquidation were to lead automotive buyers to decide there was something unsound about buying a car (and not just a Chrysler), and they were to stop buying GM, Ford (and Toyota and Hyundai) cars as well. *That* would be systemic—but it would also be almost impossible to predict in advance.

So, too, in the area of financial institutions. While the failure of depository banks may "spread" systemically (with the "triggering" institution, parenthetically, not necessarily "large"—thus there is an incorrect conflating of SIFI with "bigness" if one focuses on these indirect consequences),[15] it is rather hard to figure out, particularly in advance, where else such "runs" might occur. Thus, I am sympathetic to the observation Peter Wallison has made that, outside of depository banks, he is skeptical there are systemic financial institutions. Or—I might add—even if there are, we won't know them (or be able to define them) until such a "run" occurs. To be sure, financial institutions aren't manufacturing institutions, and the effects on the economy might be viewed as "systemic" without being viewed as "indirect."[16] But my sense is one of caution—which only adds to the definitional difficulty that John Taylor has so cogently pointed out.

This leads me to the notion that my proposals can—and perhaps should—be considered as proposals for *all* financial institutions, not just SIFIs.[17] Remember my premise: I'm responding to the idea that there may be "systemic" effects that others think bankruptcy cannot handle. I'm attempting to "merge" that premise with the reality that such systemic effects may be so hard to predetermine that a cogent category of predesignated SIFIs may be unwise, if not impossible. If we cannot predesignate, then I favor the consideration of the availability of Chapter 11F for all financial institutions. To be sure, if there aren't systemic consequences, then worrying about the impact of bankruptcy on parties not directly involved in the bankruptcy proceeding may be unnecessary, and some of the proposals will be superfluous. But superfluous does not mean unworkable. It would be up to the bankruptcy court (restructured as I propose) to decide when and how, within the bankruptcy process, to involve the procedures specifically focused on systemic consequences. Alternatively, if there is indeed a workable definition of what is a SIFI that emerges that permits predesignation, it could be used so as to limit my proposals to SIFIs alone. My point is only that consideration of the use of making bankruptcy *the* resolution mechanism for SIFIs does not need to await a consensus definition of a SIFI.

So, here goes. What follows is the outline of ways in which I would envision the current provisions of Chapter 11 being modified or eliminated, in order to provide a viable bankruptcy vehicle for the resolution of financial institutions (or, if we can agree on a definition to be applied in advance, predesignated SIFIs).[18]

PROPOSED MODIFICATIONS
TO CREATE A CHAPTER 11F

• Use existing Chapter 11 (or Chapter 7) procedures, modified as proposed here—probably in a new chapter or subchapter (which I will call "Chapter 11F").

Explanation: Throughout, I am attempting to capture the "good" features of the bankruptcy reorganization process, while being responsive to some of the concerns—addressing systemic concerns beyond the debtor and its immediate claimants, expertise, and speed—that have led to a resistance to consider the bankruptcy process as a viable one for the resolution of SIFIs.[19]

Perhaps here, more than anywhere, there seems to be a deep divide between those whose primary focus is bankruptcy and those whose primary focus is financial institutions or financial instruments.[20] Of course, I come at this from the bankruptcy side, but I do find, historically, claims of the necessity of an "exception" to bankruptcy to be overbroad. Oftentimes, the first reaction of people to a "new" crisis is that bankruptcy isn't up to the task or that existing nonbankruptcy agencies are better suited. Thus, we already have significant exceptions: Not just depository banks, but insurance companies, and commodity and securities brokers (at least in terms of Chapter 11). Few of these exceptions withstand detailed scrutiny.[21] The "first" Chrysler rescue from 1979 was driven, in significant part, by a fear that an automotive company could not survive bankruptcy reorganization because of loss of consumer confidence.[22] There was a large consensus around this point, and the events of the past thirty years have shown it to be completely wrong. We have reorganized dozens of large manufacturing, retail, and service businesses with almost no one not intimately involved in the proceedings even noticing. People continued to fly on United when it was in bankruptcy. People continued to shop at Kmart and eat at Ponderosa and Bonanza steakhouses when they were in bankruptcy. People continued to buy suits made by Hartmax and its subsidiaries when it was in bankruptcy. But expensive durables we were told, are different, because of warranty concerns. And then Chrysler, followed by GM, actually used bankruptcy (even though we were told that GM's board never even drafted contingency plans since bankruptcy wasn't considered a viable option) and, in terms of customer reaction, almost nothing happened.[23] Whatever defects of the recent restructuring of Chrysler and GM through bankruptcy, it is clear that the idea that filing for a bankruptcy reorganization would inevitably lead to liquidation was overstated. Similarly, the 1980s saw a concern about utility companies using bankruptcy—concerns that were also wildly off the mark.[24] Thus, I think the first reaction—bankruptcy isn't up to the task of handling large financial institutions—isn't necessarily the right reaction. I think we owe a serious look at bankruptcy's viability in terms of SIFIs before we rush to create another exception that may, later, lead to its own set of complexities, as the exceptions for commodity brokers and stockbrokers in Chapter 11 arguably did in the Lehman bankruptcy.

■ (Optional) A discrete and limited set of institutions are predesignated by appropriate government agencies/officials as SIFIs, thereby making them automatically eligible for Chapter 11F.

Explanation: As I discussed earlier, *if* we can agree on a useful definition of what makes a SIFI a SIFI (as opposed to an "ordinary" financial institution), then this Chapter 11F proposal could be limited to such institutions. The linkage between the ability to define a SIFI and implementing Chapter 11F limited to them is, in my view, tight. Without a predesignation, and if Chapter 11F were otherwise limited to SIFIs, starting an appropriate bankruptcy proceeding is made more complex, as it will not be immediately clear whether the entity is subject to Chapter 11 or to Chapter 11F. There are enough distinct features, explored later, including some that are immediately relevant, so that predesignation is superior to an early determination within bankruptcy. (While a government agency can—as I suggest—be given the power to commence a bankruptcy proceeding against a SIFI, thus giving rise to the possibility of a contemporaneous, rather than advance designation, that would work only for government-commenced bankruptcy proceedings. Traditional voluntary and involuntary proceedings would require a "sorting out" period, with its attendant complications.) Thus, my proposal is for Chapter 11F to be available to any financial institution[25] unless a satisfactory definition of a SIFI that would permit predesignation were to emerge, in which case it would be feasible, and perhaps politically more palatable, to limit its scope to SIFIs.

- The relevant government agency (e.g., FRB, FDIC, or SEC—one, not all) is given the power to file an involuntary petition with respect to a financial institution directly into Chapter 11F.

Explanation: The Bankruptcy Code depends on a debtor or its creditors to initiate bankruptcy proceedings. That's wholly appropriate for a system in which the only "relevant" interests are represented by claimants against the debtor. In the case of a SIFI, however, where there is an argument or worry about a systemic event affecting other institutions, the appropriate government agency should be able to file a bankruptcy proceeding directly in Chapter 11F. (Since I am assuming we cannot predetermine the financial institutions that are significantly important, this power would necessarily exist with respect over all financial institutions.) This is an effort to reproduce some of the "power" of the relevant government agency in proposals for giving such an agency "resolution authority" outside of bankruptcy, but requiring it to be exercised within the judicial framework of a bankruptcy proceeding.[26]

- Should the relevant government agency take specified steps that amount to a nonbankruptcy resolution of a financial institution, three or more creditors may commence a bankruptcy case under Chapter 11F for that entity, and the agency's steps will constitute grounds for an "order for relief" under § 303(h) of the Bankruptcy Code.

Explanation   In an involuntary case, the "commencement of the case" is distinct from the "order for relief," the latter being specified in § 303(h) as following from a demonstration (1) that "the debtor is generally not paying such debtor's debts as such debts become due" or (2) "a custodian . . . was appointed or took possession." This proposal would treat the efforts at a resolution by the relevant government agency as a third ground for an order for relief (perhaps comparable to the idea of the appointment of a custodian). This is an attempt, perhaps symmetrical with the prior provision, to limit end-runs around bankruptcy by a government-engineered bailout that is not subject to the rules and judicial oversight of a bankruptcy proceeding. It may not be wholly successful—one may not know (for example) if the government is engaging in such steps (indeed, it might encourage efforts at government secrecy), and it may be difficult to adequately define (and limit) the events that constitute an end-run nonbankruptcy resolution. Still, it seems to me to be a crucial feature to focus on resolution by bankruptcy rather than "bailout."

Alternative Proposals   HR 3310 provides, in proposed Section 1403, for a ten-day period (that can, on motion, be shortened, or extended for thirty additional days—although that extension is postpetition) before a bankruptcy petition may be filed in which a nonbank financial institution (the entities subject to proposed Chapter 14) must participate in "prepetition consultation in order to attempt to avoid the need for the nonbank financial institution's liquidation or reorganization in bankruptcy, to make any liquidation or reorganization of the nonbank financial institution under this title more orderly, or to aid in the nonbankruptcy resolution of any of the nonbank financial institution's components under its nonbankruptcy insolvency regime." In a similar fashion, a proposal submitted by Robert Eager would provide for a thirty-day period (extendible by the Treasury) for the appropriate federal regulatory agency to "manage the potential financial crisis," before court review would commence.[27] I am unconvinced that the idea that there should be some period of time to attempt "resolution" of a financial institution outside of the judicial framework that is, ultimately, one of the principal advantages of a bankruptcy resolution process, is a good one. Such a judicial framework has established rules, including priority rules, and has the best chance of separating out issues of resolution and responding to systemic concerns, on the one hand, and bailout, on the other hand.

- In Chapter 11F, existing bankruptcy exclusions for depository banks, insurance companies, stockbrokers, commodity brokers, and the like (see Bankruptcy Code §§ 109(b)(2), (b)(3), (d)), would not apply, so that the "entire" financial institution could be "resolved" (reorganized) within the context of a single bankruptcy proceeding.

Explanation Whatever the justifications for the current exclusions from the Bankruptcy Code (and I'm inclined to think there aren't many, except perhaps for the regime of depository banks), those exclusions create needless complexity, and interfere with successful resolution, of complex financial institutions. Because of cross-guarantees and the often vast proliferation of separate operating entities, trying to "resolve" one part of a complex financial institution, with other parts being dealt with by other regimes, is problematic at best, and likely detrimental. (Creative law-yering circumvented many of the problems of the exclusion of brokerages in the Lehman bankruptcy, and I can only imagine the complexities that would have been introduced by the exclusion of insurance companies if AIG had, in fact, been allowed to fail.[28]) The bankruptcy doctrine of "substantive consolidation" may be appropriate in cases involving significant cross-guarantees, but it only applies if all the entities are subject to bankruptcy jurisdiction. Likely the most controversial aspect would be the inclusion of depository banks, to the extent that they were a part of a broader financial institution's "empire." In this limited category of institutions, however, I think it is better to effectively duplicate the FDIC's powers and processes over the depository features of such banks within a broader bankruptcy proceeding, than to have some parts of the financial institution "resolved" within bankruptcy and other parts "resolved" by the FDIC, outside of bankruptcy. (Such would not be the case for depository institutions not themselves a part of a broader financial institution network; those institutions could continue to be resolved by the FDIC outside of bankruptcy.) Similarly, for brokerages, the appropriate Chapter 7 provisions, §§ 741–753, could be used, where appropriate, as a baseline for those parts of a complex financial institution within a Chapter 11F proceeding. Without something such as this, serious conflicts among different resolution authorities would remain not just possible, but likely.[29]

Alternative Proposals   Paul Volcker has proposed separating depository banks (i.e., deposit taking and loan making) from trading operations and other financial

services. Such a proposal would, if implemented to prohibit even parent-sub relationships, ensure that a depository bank would never be a SIFI, and thus the current
FDIC regime could continue. I view my proposal as less
radical and disruptive of existing institutions. (Although,
if it is thought that quick transfer of guaranteed deposits
to a third party is essential to preventing "runs" or other
social goals—I am not convinced it is anymore—then
some variant of Volcker's proposal may be useful to consider. Given that the FDIC transfers [naturally] assets as
well as [depository] liabilities, both a quick assessment of
assets and the quick ability to transfer them necessarily
follow. The more complex the depository bank, the more
this seems inevitably to remove this process from sal-
utary judicial oversight. Restrictions on types of risky
assets and on cross-guarantees of depository banks—even
when a part of a broader SIFI ownership structure, may
be a necessary corollary of meshing the FDIC's role over
guaranteed deposits with the bankruptcy goal of judicial
oversight and treatment predictability.) Again, the loss to
the FDIC's jurisdiction is more theoretical than real, as
many of the rights and responsibilities of the FDIC over
the depository features of such banks could be duplicated
within the bankruptcy proceeding—and depository banks
that are not part of a broader financial institution could,
without significant disruption, simply be left outside of
bankruptcy under FDIC jurisdiction.

- **Upon the commencement of a Chapter 11F case, it
  will be assigned by the chief judge of the relevant
  Court of Appeals to a member from a previously**

designated (by the relevant government agency) panel of special masters.

Explanation   The idea here is to try to get someone with relevant expertise, which a randomly assigned bankruptcy judge may very likely not have. Ideally, one could imagine specially selected experts—a preselected group of "special masters" (who have expertise both in the fields of financial institutions and bankruptcy law)—to whom these cases could be assigned. (As bankruptcy judges are not Article 3 judges, these "special masters" could presumably handle everything that a bankruptcy judge is currently able to handle without tripping into the concerns of their lack of constitutional Article 3 status. Technically, the "assignment" is through a district judge; I am ignoring this complexity for purposes of exposition.) They would be paid by the government, at prearranged rates, and, like special masters appointed by the Supreme Court, they would have authority to hire additional staff, including experts.[30] There would be an issue of the ability of these special masters to "drop everything" and take on a quick-moving SIFI bankruptcy resolution, although I think that is manageable. Indeed, both for purposes of expertise and speed, it would be possible to imagine a "panel" of special masters appointed to oversee the reorganization (or resolution) of a particularly complex financial institution.

- With respect to qualified financial contracts (QFCs), (1) there would be no automatic stay (or related call-off of bankruptcy-specific provisions) for any QFCs for which the financial institution's security was "cash" (or "cash-like"—narrowly defined) collateral, and (2) for all other QFCs of the financial institution, the traditional provisions of the Bankruptcy Code, including the automatic stay, would apply unless and until lifted by court order.

Explanation This attempts to weave a line between the current system and simply moving to a system where they, like other claims, are subject to the automatic stay (and other bankruptcy provisions) for (and before—such as in the case of preferences) the duration. The current system entails, first, set-offs pursuant to QFCs; see Bankruptcy Code §§ 362(b)(6), (7), (17), and (27). Second, the counterparties can terminate a QFC for "ipso facto" reasons of a sort described in Bankruptcy Code § 365(e)(1); see Bankruptcy Code §§ 555, 556, 559, 560, and 561. Finally, preference law (particularly) with respect to transfers to the counterparty is likewise called off; see Bankruptcy Code § 546(e), (f), (g), and (j).

It is important to note what these provisions do—and do not do—for QFCs. As has been pointed out elsewhere: "Contracts that are financial in nature are treated differently than garden variety executory contracts even if they do not qualify for the safe harbor treatment. Loans and other monetary obligations accelerate as of the date of the bankruptcy filing [Bankruptcy Code § 502(b)]. Financial accommodations contracts are not assumable and assignable by a bankrupt debtor [Bankruptcy Code § 365(c)] and bankruptcy termination clauses in these contracts are enforceable

[Bankruptcy Code § 365(e)]. In addition, while setoff generally is subject to the automatic stay, recoupment is not. Thus, other than the right to foreclose on posted collateral, which right is useful in practice only when the non-debtor counterparty has actual possession of the collateral, the special protections granted to the safe harbor contracts do not appear to be so special."[31] (I'd add to this list of "special" treatment of QFCs the ability to exempt QFC-related transfers from the trustee's avoiding powers under Bankruptcy Code § 546(e), (f), (g), and (j).)

I propose a two-part system. In the first part, for repos and other QFCs backed by "cash-like" collateral (to be predefined, in a rather limited fashion), the existing provisions—which call off the Bankruptcy Code's automatic stay as applied to setoffs, prohibition on the enforcement of ipso facto clauses, and preference provisions—would continue in force. Bankruptcy—as it does now—would relieve the financial institution from continuing obligations to post new collateral on the QFCs, as it retains the right to reject the underlying contract (even if the counterparty doesn't terminate it[32]; see Bankruptcy Code § 562). Essentially, the current Bankruptcy Code rules regarding QFCs would allow the counterparty to take steps to terminate the contracts, access existing collateral in its possession, and protect the counterparty from otherwise preference-like payments within the ninety days before bankruptcy. The rationale for this is that cash-like collateral is less likely to have a "going concern value" separate from the value of the collateral, and the important expectations of counterparties regarding access to cash collateral—at least a major part of the original rationale for excepting QFCs from the automatic stay (and related bankruptcy proceedings)—trump the costs to the financial institution by permitting the immediate termination of such cash-like collateral-backed QFCs. If there are systemic effects—beyond just allocating the significant costs of failure itself—it is most likely to be felt by the freezing in place of extremely liquid assets that, in normal times, are expected to move from entity to entity at a moment's notice.

In the second part (i.e., for all other QFCs), the existing special provisions would be rescinded, subjecting these QFCs to the ordinary provisions of the Bankruptcy Code, including the automatic stay, nonenforcement of ipso facto clauses, and applicability of preference law. Except for QFCs that might, as is the case now, be assigned by authorization of a relevant government agency to a third party in conjunction with its assigned role over deposits or other such things, these QFCs, like other financial accommodations, would be deemed "rejected" in bankruptcy, with damages fixed "as of the date of the filing of the petition" under Bankruptcy Code § 502(b), and the nondebtor counterparty would have rights in collateral posted to the QFC as of that date as well. This would help ensure, as Richard Herring notes in chapter 7, that "sophisticated counterparties" that are often in "the best position to monitor and exercise market discipline," in fact *do* that monitoring.[33] I am not denying the possibility of systemic effects as much as saying that here the first-order issue seems to me to be the allocation of losses to those, *ex ante*, who bargained for them, rather than shifting them to others. With respect to such claims, bankruptcy freezes both the value and the movement of additional collateral at the moment of bankruptcy, which appropriately signals the counterparties the extent to which they need to cope with the resulting losses. That potential, known in advance, both reduces the moral hazard (too frequent reliance on non-cash-like backed QFCs) *and* the inattention of the counterparties to worsening financial signals by the financial institution that undermines healthy monitoring.

Alternative Proposals HR 3310 is doing something with respect to QFCs and the automatic stay, but, with deference, it is almost impossible to figure out quite what. Proposed Section 1401 provides that "[e]xcept as provided in section 1408 [a provision providing for conversion to Chapter 7], sections 362(b)(6), 362(b)(7), 559, 560, and 561 do not apply in a case under this chapter." This seems designed to remove the exception from the automatic stay for QFCs in the case of Chapter 14. Unfortunately, however, by failing to call off various other Bankruptcy Code provisions, notably §§ 362(b)(17) and (27), 555, and 556, it is unclear whether this effort would fully succeed. (In addition, Section 1401 is silent about the continued effect of Bankruptcy Code § 546(e), dealing with the inability to use avoiding powers with respect to margin or settlement payments.) This could be clarified by more precise drafting, but, unfortunately, the provisions of proposed Section 1407 cast doubt on the intention of proposed Section 1401. Proposed Section 1407 provides that "upon motion of the debtor, consented to by the Market Stability and Capital Adequacy Board—(A) the debtor and the estate shall be exempt from the operation of sections 362(b)(6), 362(b)(7), 559, 560, and 561." These, however, are precisely the provisions referenced in Section 1401, which has *already*—and automatically—exempted the debtor and the estate from the operation of these provisions. In short, proposed Section 1401 seems (subject to some drafting awkwardness) to subject QFCs to the automatic stay from the get-go, while Section 1407 seems to assume that QFCs are *not* subject to the automatic stay except upon the approval of a motion. Drawing on the experience of Lehman, Harvey Miller has proposed simply eliminating the exceptions that QFCs have come to enjoy from the operation of the automatic stay.[34] David Skeel has made several proposals, including distinguishing between types of QFCs (e.g., repos would continue their exemptions but not credit default swaps—an idea comparable to my "cash collateral" distinction), but he focuses most particularly, as would be relevant to a special bankruptcy chapter for SIFIs, on removing the exemption of QFCs from the automatic stay for SIFIs.[35] My proposal is an intermediate one—to try to disentangle systemic concerns from negative consequences of having an exemption from the stay, as evidenced by Lehman. Alternatively, one could design a system in which the first part of my proposal were adopted—QFCs with "cash collateral" would not be subject to the automatic stay (and related bankruptcy provisions) and other QFCs would be subject to a very short stay (such as one business day), during which time the relevant government agency could arrange their transfer to a third party. Although closest to the existing mechanism used by the FDIC to resolve depository banks, I ultimately disfavor this as (1) too complex, (2) too difficult to accomplish without simply waiving judicial oversight, and (3) too favorable to this particular category of counterparties. Moreover, it introduces some uncertainty into the system, which is a cost over a solution that simply reverses the exemption from the automatic stay entirely in Chapter 11F.[36] *Ex ante*, there may be fewer such QFCs (and more monitoring), but I see this as a *consequence* more than a *cost*.

- **The relevant government agency is given special standing in Chapter 11F (I'm thinking here, loosely, of the idea of a U.S. Trustee or perhaps the role, amplified, of the Commodity Futures Trading Commission under § 762)—as a way of getting expertise into the system. In the case of the FDIC, its role over the resolution of the depository-specific features of banks would be embodied within the bankruptcy proceeding to the extent feasible, but they would be in coordination with, and under the ultimate control of, the bankruptcy court, rather than separate from (as is the case today).**

Explanation   As with the idea of an "expert" special master, this is a way to try to get expertise into the system, but have the expertise be subject to a neutral (albeit informed) decision maker. In a way, this tries to accomplish, wholly within bankruptcy, the idea of judicial oversight that is (in my view) introduced awkwardly in Robert Eager, where it only comes into play after "a 30-day exclusive period during which [the regulatory agency] can take actions without immediate judicial oversight."[37] The U.S. Trustee analogy is only meant to be suggestive; the actual role for the appropriate government agency should be spelled out in some detail.

- **Eliminate the exclusivity period for the filing of a plan of reorganization provided to the debtor under**

Bankruptcy Code § 1121(b) and provide that the
relevant government agency is one of the entities
permitted to file a plan of reorganization.

Explanation In the typical Chapter 11 case, the Bankruptcy Code provides that "only the debtor may file a plan
until after 120 days after the date of the order for relief
under this chapter," § 1121(b). Given both the likely need
for speed—although some of that might be accomplished by
sales under Bankruptcy Code § 363 with appropriate safe-
guards of claimants—and the concern over systemic issues
that a debtor will not internalize, it should be clear that there
is no exclusivity period and that the relevant government
agency can file its own plan, subject to meeting the substantive and procedural requirements of the Bankruptcy Code.

- **If there is a need to infuse money into the entity
  (beyond guaranteeing QFCs or otherwise buying/
  guaranteeing prepetition claims), the relevant government agency can participate by providing debtor-
  in-possession (DIP) financing, subject to the usual
  bankruptcy rules regarding priority.**

Explanation While this makes possible a government"
bailout," it would be subject to judicial oversight and bankruptcy code standards. As I note under "Alternative Proposals," it is very difficult to figure out a way to legally
constrain the government from a "bailout" that it wants;
my proposal at least has the judicial process involved, as
well as the transparency of a judicial proceeding—both significant virtues. I also want to "hedge," in case there are

some liquidity needs that would pass through the entity in bankruptcy that wouldn't fit into the ordinary DIP model (including priority).

Alternative Proposals　　HR 3310 proposes amending Bankruptcy Code § 364 to provide a new subsection (g) that provides "[n]othwithstanding any other provision of this section, the trustee may not, and the court may not, authorize the trustee to, obtain credit, if the source of that credit either directly or indirectly is the United States." (Interestingly, this provision is not limited to the proposed Chapter 14, nor is it limited to "nonbank financial institutions," which otherwise are the subject of HR 3310.) This provision seems designed to prevent "bailout" under the auspices of "bankruptcy." It is, however, both too broad and too narrow. It is too broad in that there may be cases in which financial stability can be enhanced by the government providing DIP funding, subject to the rules and processes of the Bankruptcy Code. Not all government-supplied DIP funding will necessarily function as a "bailout," in the sense of rescuing prepetition claimants (indeed, DIP funding, by its nature, does not itself go to prepetition claimants). It is too narrow in that the major way in which the government can "bail out" prepetition claimants is not affected by this provision. Whether through guarantees or purchases, the government is always able to "rescue" prepetition claimants, and then, by assignment or subrogation, assert those claims in the bankruptcy process. No bankruptcy court permission is needed to accomplish this, and a provision blocking the government's "trading in claims" would be very difficult, if not impossible, to draft without significant overbreadth concerns. Moreover—to use as an example—the Chrysler bankruptcy (to which this provision of HR 3310 would have applied)—the government provided TARP funding to the Chrysler prebankruptcy and operating funds to the "new" Chrysler formed as a result of the § 363 sale. Neither of these two provisions of government funds would have been touched by HR 3310, since neither occurred under § 364—nor, indeed, within bankruptcy. Given this, I think it is preferable not to change the current bankruptcy provisions regarding DIP funding, but subject it to bankruptcy court oversight and control.

- **Funding for sums expended by the relevant government agency on guarantees, DIP financing, special masters (and their staff), and so forth, would be developed in a manner as it would for any sort of resolution authority system.**

Explanation   The obvious analogy is the fund created for the resolution of depository banks by the FDIC. I toyed with the idea of having some of the costs imposed on the bankrupt entity's creditors—to provide an incentive, for example, for better monitoring. But I also worried that if the government is able to "shift" the cost of what it is doing to creditors, it might be too willing to guarantee, provide funding, and the like. (I think of Chrysler here.) Thus, I conclude by thinking it best to leave this to whatever system ("taxes" on relevant firms, or whatever) might be considered for a nonbankruptcy resolution system. The goal is to have the creditors (and shareholders) of the failed financial institution be neither *advantaged* (through funds "rescuing" the financial institution because of systemic concerns that improve the creditors' positions) nor *disadvantaged* (through processes—think Chrysler—designed to reorder preexisting priorities based on political considerations) by the government's concerns about systemic consequences. That should, ultimately, be the goal of any statutory changes and judicial oversight.

NOTES

1. Professor Eisenberg notes that "[h]istorically, bankruptcy law seems to have deferred to some regulatory schemes because those schemes were in place before an extensive federal bankruptcy law was available to corporations." See Theodore Eisenberg, "Bankruptcy in the Administrative State," *Law & Contemporary Problems* 50 (1987): 7–8.

2. Michael Sovern, "Section 4 of the Bankruptcy Act: The Excluded Corporations," *Minnesota Law Review* 42 (1957): 207–229, arguing there is less reason to exclude insurance companies than depository banks, and suggesting that if insured depository banks were made subject to bankruptcy, only the FDIC could invoke it and the FDIC would be appointed trustee.

3. There is disagreement about whether there is such a systemic problem. Compare Kenneth Ayotte and David Skeel Jr., "Bankruptcy or Bailouts?" *Journal of Corporation Law* (forthcoming 2010); Peter Wallison, "Memorandum for the members of the Pew Task Force on Financial Reform Project" (2009); and "Testimony of John Taylor, U.S. House of Representatives, Committee on the Judiciary, Subcommittee on Commercial and Administrative Law," October 22, 2009; with "Testimony of David Moss, U.S. House of Representatives, Committee on the Judiciary, Subcommittee on Commercial and Administrative Law," October 22, 2009, and "Statement of Michael Krimminger, U.S. House of Representatives, Committee on the Judiciary, Subcommittee on Commercial and Administrative

Law," October 22, 2009 (a serious problem). Without taking an absolute position on that disagreement—other than to note the central importance of a rigorous definition of both "systemic" and the types of institutions that might raise systemic concerns—the thrust of this chapter is to articulate a way in which bankruptcy's reorganization process might be modified so as to address systemic concerns, assuming they are valid. It is widely assumed that bankruptcy's focus on the parties before the court renders it unable to deal effectively with systemic consequences (assuming they exist). See, for example, "Statement of Ben Bernanke, U.S. House of Representatives, Committee on Financial Services," October 1, 2009, at 7 ("the bankruptcy code does not sufficiently protect the public's strong interest in ensuring the orderly resolution of a nonbank financial firm whose failure would pose substantial risks to the financial system and to the economy"); "Statement of Michael Krimminger," at 6 ("[t]he bankruptcy process focuses on resolving creditor claims and not protection of the broader public interest"); Robert Shiller, "Crisis Averted: What of the Next One?" *New York Times*, August 10, 2008.

4. This objection, in general, would have had greater saliency in the years immediately following the enactment of the Bankruptcy Code of 1978. In those years, we saw endless extensions of exclusivity periods, as well as significant judicial passivity towards the "debtor in possession" (i.e., usually prebankruptcy management, put in place by the prebankruptcy equity owners), leading to predictable delay—as those "out of the money" always have an incentive to play with other people's money. However, over time, it increasingly became the case that judges—and therefore judicial opinions—"got it," and other creative solutions, such as pre-packs and going-concern sales permitted expedition where it was appropriate, all still subject to judicial oversight and to basic rules of the bankruptcy process.

5. See, for example, "Testimony of David Moss," at 1: "Although American bankruptcy law has served us extremely well in many different contexts over the past 100-plus years, it was never designed to handle the failure of a large, systemically significant financial

institution, particularly at a moment of severe financial turmoil. For one, our bankruptcy procedure may be too slow to deal with the failure of a major financial institution in the midst of a fast moving crisis." As Ayotte and Skeel note in "Bankruptcy or Bailouts?" (at 8), this objection may be overstated: "[F]aced with extreme time pressure, buyers [for Lehman's most valuable assets] materialized, and Lehman quickly sold its viable subsidiaries, allowing them to remain in business under different ownership"—and Lehman is a case complicated in significant ways by the fact that not all of the Lehman entities (such as broker-dealers) could be brought into the reorganization process. They also take issue with the opposite concern—that bankruptcy will lead to a "fire sale," also pointing to Lehman's continuing holding of a significant portfolio of assets more than several months later. See Ayotte and Skeel, "Bankruptcy or Bailouts?" at 11. Again, I assume the truth of the objection, so as to fashion a proposal that is responsive to it.

6. See Jeffrey Golden, "The Courts, the Financial Crisis and Systemic Risk," *Capital Markets Law Journal*, June 6, 2009, and "Testimony of David Moss," at 7 ("a resolution of these financial firms requires pre-planning and cannot depend on administration by a debtor in possession, a newly appointed trustee, or a creditors' committee"). This concern isn't limited to SIFIs. See Eisenberg, "Bankruptcy in the Administrative State," at 10: "If special expertise is needed to assist troubled financial institutions, the bankruptcy court, the traditional bankruptcy forum, may be at a relative disadvantage vis-à-vis federal or state regulatory authorities." Not everyone agrees that a comparative expertise advantage would lie with an agency designated to "resolve" SIFIs. See Peter Wallison, "Pew Task Force"; Stephen Haber and F. Scott Kieff, "Wrong Incentives from Financial System Fixes," in *Reacting to the Spending Spree: Policies We Can Afford* (Stanford, CA: Hoover Institution, 2009), at http://ssrn.com.abstract=1496584. Once again, this proposal is presented *assuming* the validity of the objection, so as to fashion an appropriate response to it.

7. HR 3310 (the "Consumer Protection and Regulatory Enhancement Act"), http://thomas.loc.gov/cgi-bin/query/z?c111:H.R.3310,

would designate a new Chapter 14 to deal with "Adjustments to the Debts of a Non-Bank Financial Institution." I discuss some of the features of HR 3310 in the course of this chapter (and, no, I don't care whether the new chapter is called 11F or 14 . . .).

8. I do not mean to claim that political considerations do not enter bankruptcy, or indeed sometimes can swamp the process. I agree with Professors Roe and Skeel that the use of Section 363 (together with dramatic time constraints and constraints on competing bids) to "sell" Chrysler effectively gutted the priority rules of the reorganization process. Mark Roe and David Skeel Jr., "Assessing the Chrysler Bankruptcy," http://papers.ssrn.com/sol3/papers.cfm?abstract_id=1426530. See also Barry Adler Jr., *What's Good for General Motors*, 3 (Annex A to Congressional Oversight Panel, September 2009), at http://cop.senate.gov/documents/cop-090909-report.pdf (the Chrysler bankruptcy provisions "illegitimately distributed assets inconsistently with the priorities established under the Bankruptcy Code"). But to recognize that a judicial process is not perfect is not to say that it cannot perform better, or with greater certainty, than a nonbankruptcy "resolution" process handled by a designated government agency, where political considerations are almost certain to invade financial decisions. See Peter J. Wallison, "The Meaning of the Lehman Bankruptcy," paper presented at the American Bankruptcy Institute, November 5, 2009, http://www.aei.org/speech/100101.

9. See generally David Skeel Jr., "Bankruptcy Boundary Games," forthcoming, *Brooklyn Law Review*, draft at http://ssrn.com/abstract=1446762, at 5 ("[w]ith the benefit of twenty-twenty hindsight, we can see that the brokerage exclusion was designed with the brokerages of the 1960s particularly in view"); David Skeel Jr., "The Law and Finance of Bank and Insurance Insolvency Regulation," *Texas Law Review* 76 (1998): 723 (banks, probably no; insurance companies, probably yes); and Kimberly Summe, chapter 5 of this volume ("True progress will be made when our bankruptcy regime reflects the diverse nature of contemporary financial groups. In order to ensure that future failures of systemically important entities are

tolerable for the financial system, a unified bankruptcy approach must be adopted.").

10. See, for example, "Testimony of Harvey Miller, US House of Representatives, Committee on the Judiciary, Subcommittee on Commercial and Administrative Law," October 22, 2009, at 3: "No rationale is given for why the existing bankruptcy law and bankruptcy courts could not deal with the resolution of such financial crises, provided that the bankruptcy code is amended to restore the applicability of the bankruptcy code's automatic stay to derivatives, swaps and other securities transactions."

11. This point is made very nicely in chapter 7 by Richard Herring.

12. Declaration of Thomas J. LaSorda, April 30, 2009, at 3–4 (Docket # 51, linked to through www.chryslerrestructuring.com):

> Should Chrysler liquidate, the reverberations throughout the American economy (and NAFTA economies generally) will be severe in both breadth and depth. A Chrysler bankruptcy would mean the immediate loss of 38,500 Chrysler jobs in the United States—including 27,600 union members—and 55,000 Chrysler jobs worldwide. Chrysler's workers and retirees and their surviving spouses will lose over $9.8 billion in health care and other benefits as well as $2 billion in annual pension payments. Chrysler's annual cash payments of nearly one billion dollars per year to over 106,000 retirees will disappear. Twenty-three Chrysler manufacturing facilities and 20 parts depots in the United States will close immediately. Chrysler's $35 billion in annual automotive supplier payments will evaporate, bankrupting many of these suppliers. Indeed, over $5.3 billion currently owed to automotive suppliers will go unpaid. The effects on dealers will be similarly far-reaching—over 3,200 dealers would close, taking with them 140,000 jobs—and the dealers' local communities will likely lose $100 billion in annual sales. Moreover, the 31 million owners of Chrysler automobiles will see their vehicles lose their warranties, and

their ability to get parts and service for the cars, which will translate to a significant loss in their value.

These ideas were repeated throughout the Chrysler papers and proceedings.

13. I leave open the question as to whether such a firm might ever be "so large," in terms of its own size and direct consequences, to be considered "systemic." My intuition is "no," because in a world in which *no* entity should be "too big to fail," the players to this failed enterprise can all be dealt with in an existing bankruptcy proceeding. The government might want to deal with the consequences of the failure, such as in job retraining programs, but it does not need to be "represented" in the proceedings of the failed company so as to "represent" interests not otherwise adequately represented. Bankruptcy's structure was up to the task of reorganizing (or liquidating) Chrysler and GM; the abuse of the process in order to achieve government bailout goals will, I think (or hope), come to be recognized as a sad failure of bankruptcy's rules and the judicial oversight process. See Roe and Skeel, "Assessing the Chrysler Bankruptcy"; Adler, *What's Good for General Motors*.

14. This is one of the general problems with "bailouts"; they not only distort *ex ante* bargains (and attendant monitoring) but also interfere with natural readjustment processes. Responding to an overcapacity problem by trying to "save jobs," is tantamount to a decision to save inefficient players, rather than deal directly— through retraining and other possible interventions on those who lose jobs—with the consequences.

15. Perhaps the catch phrase should be "too systemic to fail" rather than "too big to fail."

16. For example, vertical integration wouldn't necessarily encompass counterparties and their dealings with a financial institution. Even so, these *are* contractual relations, whose risks are known in advance. And, as a note of factual caution, Lehman's failure did not result in the failure of any of Lehman's counterparties. (Peter Wallison pointed this out in commenting on this chapter.) But if it had,

would those results be "systemic"? I remain skeptical, but there are perhaps reasons to treat them as "systemic" when we might not treat the failure of a supplier to Chrysler in a similar fashion.

17. To be sure, we have definitional ambiguity over what is a "financial institution" just as we have over what is "systemically important." But I will assume that the difficult issues are not those of what are "financial institutions" but what are "systemically important." To eliminate manufacturing concerns with a financing arm, perhaps there will need to be some clear guidelines of "predominance," or some such thing, of financial services over, say, manufacturing. As I will discuss later, the current FDIC regime for depository banks could be left in place for depository banks that are not a part of (i.e., a subsidiary of) a larger financial institution.

18. My bankruptcy proposal is easily seen as in parallel, rather than in conflict, with proposals such as Darrell Duffie's (see chap. 6), as there will still potentially be cases where the contractual methods don't work, and bankruptcy (or insolvency) results. Similarly, Richard Herring's contribution in chapter 7 involving the mandatory adoption of wind-down plans, would, I would think, facilitate a bankruptcy resolution such as I am proposing here.

19. Certain concerns—most particularly, speed—could be significantly aided by a proposal such as Richard Herring's; see chapter 7. Even if not able to forecast every detail in advance, as Joseph Grundfest cautions in chapter 8, they would almost certainly provide a wealth of information and background thinking that would be extraordinarily useful in a bankruptcy proceeding.

20. Compare "Testimony of Harvey Miller" and Ayotte and Skeel, "Bankruptcy or Bailouts?" with "Testimony of David Moss" and "Remarks by FDIC Chairman Sheila Bair to the Exchequer Club of Washington D.C.," June 18, 2008 ("I believe that we need a special receivership process for investment banks that is outside the bankruptcy process, just as it is for commercial banks and thrifts. The reason goes back to the public versus private interest. The bankruptcy process focuses on protecting creditors. When the public interest is

at stake, as it would be here, we need a process to protect it."). See also Peter Wallison, "Pew Task Force," arguing for the preferability of bankruptcy over a government resolution process.

21. Sovern, "Section 4 of the Bankruptcy Act"; Skeel, "The Law and Finance of Bank and Insurance Insolvency Regulation."

22. See R. Reich and J. Donahue, *New Deals: The Chrysler Revival and the American System* (New York: Times Books, 1985), 102–112.

23. Albeit, warranties were assumed, as they almost surely needed to be; Chrysler, however, did *not* assume nonwarranty products liability claims.

24. See Eisenberg, "Bankruptcy in the Administrative State."

25. Apart from, perhaps, depository banks not themselves a part of a larger financial organization, which might continue to be resolved under existing FDIC procedures.

26. A similar provision is in Barney Frank's "Discussion Draft" of October 27, 2009 (Section 1105 "Authority to File Involuntary Petition for Bankruptcy").

27. Robert Eager, "Recommendation Regarding Resolution Authority for Systemically Significant Financial Institutions," October 5, 2009.

28. As of 2007, AIG "was ranked the largest life insurer and the second largest property/casualty insurer by premiums written in the United States," and "is supervised in the United States by a host of state insurance regulators"; see "Report of Neil Barofsky: Factors Affecting Efforts to Limit Payments to AIG Counterparties," SIG-TARP Report 10-003 (November 17, 2009), at 2–3 and n. 7.

29. See, for example, chapter 5 of this volume by Kimberly Summe: "There are no systemically important entities . . . that conduct the significant majority of their derivative business out of an identified financial holding company," and thus "the Obama administration has missed a unique opportunity to address the economic and procedural inefficiencies produced by our fragmented bankruptcy regime. . . . True progress will be made when our bankruptcy regime reflects the diverse nature of contemporary financial groups."

Also from Summe's chapter: "The three largest derivatives portfolios are now held by the United States' three largest bank holding companies."

30. I don't see these as full-time judges, as we hope there wouldn't be sufficient work—which is also a defect of any proposal to create (by analogy to the federal court of appeals for patents) a special "court" for financial institutions; the judges (hopefully) would spend much of their time with nothing to do. This might be somewhat less the case if Chapter 11F applied to all financial institutions, rather than just SIFIs, and might justify a single court staffed with several "experts" as judges. Even there, the advantage of the special master system may be in allowing a level of pay to actually bring forth individuals with the necessary expertise, who may not be willing to toil, full-time, at a bankruptcy judge's salary.

31. Shmuel Vasser and Matthew Kerfoot, "Preferential Treatment of Derivative Contracts—Savior or Scourge?" paper presented at the American Bankruptcy Institute's 2009 Legislative Symposium, November 16–17, 2009, at 5–6.

32. Indeed, there is a strong argument—by analogy to financial accommodation contracts—to treat QFCs as terminated upon bankruptcy, so that rights and liabilities are fixed as of that time, and also neither assumable nor assignable by the debtor (with perhaps an exception for those involved with FDIC-controlled depository banks that might be assigned as a part of the depository bank resolution process within Chapter 11F). Cf. Kimberly Summe's discussion in chapter 5, of *In re Lehman Brothers Holdings Inc.*, Case 08-13555 (Bankr. SDNY Sept. 15, 2009) ("Metavante") ("The congressional history behind the safe harbor provisions indicated to Judge Peck that it was the intent that swap market participants would immediately, or at least 'fairly contemporaneously,' terminate qualified financial contracts").

33. See chapter 7 by Richard Herring.

34. "Testimony of Harvey Miller": "This caused a massive destruction of value for Lehman. As of September 15, 2008, the bankruptcy

date, Lehman's derivative counterparties number approximately 930,000, of which approximately 733,000 sought to terminate their contracts."

35. Skeel, "Bankruptcy Boundary Games," at 24 and 28. That assumes, of course, that we can effectively predesignate SIFIs.

36. Cf. Edward Morrison and Joerg Riegel, "Financial Contracts and the New Bankruptcy Code: Insulating Markets from Bankruptcy Debtors and Bankruptcy Judges," *American Bankruptcy Institute Law Review* 13 (2005): 641.

37. Eager, "Recommendation Regarding Resolution Authority."

12

Evaluating Failure Resolution Plans

KENNETH E. SCOTT

QUITE A FEW PLANS ARE BEING proposed for better ways to resolve the failure of systemically important financial institutions (or SIFIs), in order that no longer may one be "too big to fail" and we can depart from an era of widespread bailouts at taxpayer expense. The goal is generally agreed on, perhaps because it is also generally poorly defined. The key concepts in the discussions are "failure," "systemic risk," and "bailout," and usually little attention is devoted to defining them.

I want to attempt to identify the central elements of such plans and to clarify the differences among which we must choose. My focus, therefore, is not on measures that hope to prevent failure, through regulation or operating requirements or better management, but on what is the best course to follow when they do not succeed. So I shall review what I think are the main questions raised at the conference that led to this volume, and then at the end some of the answers that seem to me to be indicated.

To begin with, what do we mean by the "failure" or insolvency of a "financial institution"?

There are two concepts in common use: equity insolvency—inability to meet obligations as they come due, which is a liquidity standard—and economic insolvency—assets are less than liabilities, which is a balance sheet standard. Banking law includes both: assets less than obligations, and inability to pay obligations in the normal course of business (12 USC §1821(c)(5)). For a nonbank financial institution to be forced into bankruptcy, however, there is only the liquidity standard of not paying obligations when due. If one wishes to minimize the amount of losses from a failure, is that the appropriate criterion? But to go to the economic standard, one immediately confronts all the valuation problems for the holdings of large and complex firms. The dilemma is posed by the controversy over "fair value" accounting; to the extent that the opponents of marking assets to market have their way, economic insolvency is further obscured.

What firms are we talking about? With Goldman Sachs and Morgan Stanley now bank holding companies, need we go beyond that category? Of course, at some point they may attempt to exit from that status, and the proposals, hardly uncontroversial, by Paul Volcker, George Shultz, and Nicholas Brady (chaps. 1–3), among others, to separate banking from proprietary trading could lead to new large and complex firms.

If our concerns were limited to banks and bank holding companies, which ones? Different proposals refer to them as Tier 1 financial holding companies, large interconnected financial companies, and so on, but with definitions to follow. Should the definition be in the statute or left to administrative discretion? Should they be designated in advance, with periodic updatings, or determined at the time of failure? Or should all financial institutions be covered in bankruptcy by a new Chapter 11F such as Tom Jackson advocates (see chap. 11)?

Even if limited to bank holding companies, there is an issue over the scope of coverage. At present, failed banks are resolved by the FDIC, while holding companies and subsidiaries fall under Chapter 11 of the Bankruptcy Code, and brokerages go into Chapter 7 for liquidation or to the SIPC. Whatever the plan, should at least this fragmentation be ended?

Who is in charge of the resolution process? At present, it is the FDIC for banks and a "debtor-in-possession" (or trustee) for most corporations. Should there be some form of consolidation here, too? For example, could the FDIC continue to administer the assets/liabilities of failed banks, but under the overall supervision of a bankruptcy court when it is part of a larger organization? Or should the FDIC be given jurisdiction that extends beyond insured banks to cover all SIFIs, as William Kroener argues (see chap. 9)? Instead, should a new breed of "special masters" with expertise in large complex financial institutions be developed to administer SIFIs in bankruptcy?

Related to this, who can commence a resolution proceeding? A banking supervisor or the FDIC can do so; if the Comptroller of the Currency, for example, determines that a national bank is insolvent (or merely in an unsafe or unsound condition to transact business), it may without notice or hearing appoint the FDIC as its receiver. For a nonbank institution, three creditors may file an involuntary petition that the court may grant (after a hearing, if needed) and issue an order for relief. In the case of a SIFI, who should have this power? Should "failure" be determined by the exercise of regulatory agency discretion, or should private creditors also have authority to trigger a failure? Government agencies are subject to political pressure to "forbear" from forcing a closure, as banking history demonstrates only too clearly, while private parties have grounds to petition only when a financial institution is not paying its current bills. If the power is concurrent, either could be the first to move, a possibility to which Tom Jackson refers.

Given a failure proceeding, how are losses to claimants to be determined? By administrative agency judgment, as in the power of a bank receiver to choose which assets and liabilities are to be assumed by a purchaser or transferred to a bridge bank (12 USC §1821(n)(1)(B))? Or by the outcome of market measures in a potentially more transparent judicial proceeding? This is a central element in the contrasting analyses of William Kroener and Tom Jackson.

The judicial process is likely to have certain advantages over an administrative process. The value of assets can be first determined in auctions or sales under Code §363 (assuming the sale is not rigged as it was in Chrysler).[1] Failing that, there is provision for hearings on valuations. And the whole proceeding is open to the safeguard of judicial review. All of these consume time.

The administrative process has the advantages of dedi-cated expertise and greater speed, as the 140 bank failures so far demonstrate. Part of that speed comes from the capacity of the Insurance Fund to take losses and issue guarantees upfront (but that has its moral hazard downside as well). And part of the speed comes from the absence of hearings and effective judicial review—should that be viewed as a net plus or minus?

The speed disadvantage of the judicial process might be lessened if the current proposals, which Richard Her-ring describes in some detail in chapter 7, for "living wills" (wind-down or failure plans) for financial institutions become reality, and especially if the result is simplification of the complex corporate structures of hundreds of subsid-iaries and affiliates exemplified by Lehman that Kimberly Summe recounts in chapter 5. Of course, if the failure plan is to be enforced by a regulator with near-limitless power to order changes in business activities and capital structure, as well as corporate simplification, a host of additional consid-erations are raised.

Turning from process to more substantive matters, how are failure losses (however determined) to be allocated—to various firm "stakeholders" (shareholders and creditors) or to taxpayers? No aspect of the current financial crisis has created more public anger than the use of public money to rescue failed firms by loans and capital assistance so that creditors would be "bailed out."

There seems to be a near-universal desire to devise an approach to failure resolution that does not depend on pub-lic funds, and that goal will be explored next. An insurance fund, such as the one the FDIC administers for banks, can put some of the costs on covered firms (e.g., predesignated SIFIs) and (hopefully) not on taxpayers. The just-passed House bill (HR 4173) would create a $150 billion fund for this purpose, by assessments on all financial institutions with more than $50 billion in assets (most of which are unlikely to be of systemic importance).

But a caveat is in order. The government will always have the capability of bailing out favored claimants on an ad hoc basis, whether for reasons assertedly economic or actually political. The best that can be done is to try to design a resolution process that makes it somewhat less justifiable economically and less attractive politically. If such bailouts have to take the form of explicit budget expenditures that are highly visible and cannot be disguised as part of the resolution process (as appears currently to be the case with Fannie and Freddie), that might help.

Do the loss allocations follow priority rules set and known in advance, or are they to some degree established ad hoc in individual cases? Put another way, to what extent is the private ordering of seniority and subordination of claims, voluntarily entered into, honored in the resolution process? Consistency and predictability are vital to efficient private finance—and especially for troubled companies.

In theory this is the major advantage of resolution and reorganization under the Bankruptcy Code, with a well-developed set of rules and long history of interpretation. The theory was tested, and found vulnerable, in the Chrysler Chapter 11 reorganization, in part because judicial oversight in that case was defective or perfunctory. The essence of a "bailout" is that certain creditors are given more (or others less) than what their claims are entitled to under settled bankruptcy law. As noted, there will inevitably be ways for the government to prefer favored claims, but it should be the role of the judiciary to force them to take place outside the bankruptcy proceeding and its structure of priority rules (Bankruptcy Code §1129) on which credit markets depend.

Finally, and most importantly, are there any ways by which direct spillover costs can be reduced with minimal damage to the preceding considerations? There are always losses to third parties from the failure of almost any firm, large or small. But here we are concerned with a small subset of giant firms that occupy central positions in our system of financial intermediation and the flow of credit.

The fear is that a failure or small set of failures might lead to the systemic risk of widespread collapse of the whole system. It would help greatly if we had a comprehensive and tested model of exactly how that might occur, but none exists. Work on developing one should have high priority. In its absence, there is plenty of talk about systemic risk and a paucity of clarity about its genesis, as John Taylor makes abundantly clear in chapter 4.

The main suggestions from the conference, particularly by Kimberly Summe and William Kroener, are that we focus on the role and position of those qualified financial contracts (QFCs)—repos and derivatives in particular—that are transacted daily in huge volume and key to the functioning of credit markets. The law, for both banks and other institutions, exempts them from some of the key provisions of the Bankruptcy Code, including the automatic stay and preference sections. The result is that the risks of counterparties to a failed institution are greatly reduced: they can terminate their contracts, net their positions, seize their collateral (if any and they are in the money), and sell it immediately.

Does that reduce risks to the financial system as a whole, or increase them because going-concern value in the insolvent firm is destroyed and counterparties have weaker incentives to monitor the information and police the exposures of firms whose survival is becoming more problematical? Would it better preserve value to transfer in bulk all of a given counterparty's positions to an acquirer, as was the prior rule for FDIC? Subjecting QFCs to standard bankruptcy rules would prevent abrupt termination and sales of collateral and the resulting impact on both the failing firm and the market generally, but it would increase the risk of declining collateral value—which is the greater cost? Should such a change apply only to SIFIs?

Those are fundamentally empirical questions, and ones to which we have no reliable answer. Perhaps we can, appropriately enough in this discussion, hedge our position. We could continue the exemption but only for QFCs with cash collateral: repos and some OTC derivatives. This would view the automatic stay as intended mainly to protect the business from the forced sale by secured creditors of firm-specific assets, in order to preserve going-concern value in firms that can still achieve operating profits. Cash is not a firm-specific asset.

My own conclusions? I have identified a lot more questions than I have answers, and my answers can only be tentative. I think we are missing a lot of both the facts and theory necessary for any answer in which we can have much confidence.

That, of course, is no impediment to congressional action. So let me indicate, as I have already intimated here, where I for one would be inclined to come out on these key elements. They can also provide a sort of checklist from which to construct the plan that we all might favor.

I think we should want both an equity and an economic standard for failure of a SIFI. Most of the time, as a practical matter, financial institutions are brought down by the flight of their short-term creditors, as we saw for Bear Stearns and Lehman. But ample liquidity can be used to prolong and deepen economic insolvency, the problem the Fed always faces in its discount window and other liquidity facilities. To the extent that we can get better *current* asset values, market discipline on the management of financial institutions is enhanced, to the benefit of both counterparties and taxpayers.

Which firms are SIFIs, and who should be in charge of their resolution? At this time, they are all bank holding companies, and thus it might make sense to have them all designated and administered in failure by the FDIC on a consolidated basis. (There are, of course, other firms that play an essential service role in the financial system—such as custodians or exchanges—but I would put them in a different category.) However, that was not true in the past and may not be true in the future. It therefore makes sense to me that there also be a provision in the Bankruptcy Code for their reorganization, perhaps (to offer another option) with retention of the FDIC for the insured bank part of the firm. That would permit proceedings to be instituted by either an agency determination or private creditor or voluntary filings—concurrent jurisdiction.

I would regard the judicial procedure as much to be preferred over agency discretion in disposing of assets and determining losses, and in allocating those losses to claimants in a predetermined and predictable order of priority. Bankruptcy courts should be charged with ensuring that any government intervention to protect certain creditors is not achieved in the bankruptcy proceeding but outside it, openly and with appropriated funds.

Finally, to reduce the likelihood of a systemic risk collapse of other institutions producing a government bailout, I share Tom Jackson's position that the automatic stay exemption for QFCs (in either FDIC or judicial proceedings) should be retained only in the situations involving cash collateral—most repos and many derivatives. Other derivatives should be subject to the usual bankruptcy constraints, which would cause counterparties to exert greater vigilance over the financial risk taking of financial firms.

NOTE

1. Mark Roe and David Skeel Jr., "Assessing the Chrysler Bankruptcy," http://papers.ssrn.com/sol3/papers.cfm?abstract_id=1426530.

A Summary of the Commentary*

JOHANNES STROEBEL

DISCUSSANTS AND MEMBERS OF THE audience offered much useful commentary at the conference where the chapters in this book were first presented. Here is a brief summary of the commentary organized into three sections corresponding to Parts II, III, and IV of the book.

SYSTEMIC RISK IN THEORY AND IN PRACTICE

In commenting on John Taylor's paper, **Monika Piazzesi** reiterated the need for a clear definition of systemic risk before any reform proposals were enacted. She agreed that in the meantime a pragmatic solution to the failure of financial institutions involved using Chapter 11 bankruptcy. This would make policy more transparent and accountable. Piazzesi argued that all types of bailouts had unacceptable negative consequences.

---

*A list of commentators other than chapter authors is provided at the end of this summary.

If individual banks were bailed out, this would provide payoffs to equity holders and creditors in the case of default, lowering the cost of capital for banks. This would consequently lead to excessive risk taking and capital misallocation. Limiting bailouts to banks that are considered too big to fail would furthermore only create incentives for banks to become too big.

Alternatively, a system in which banks are jointly bailed out only if a certain proportion of them are in trouble (e.g., by lowering interest rates) has its own problems. As before, this would lower the cost of capital and encourage risk taking. In addition, such a system would create an incentive for banks to coordinate their risky strategies, increasing systemic risk in the process. If a bank were alone in pursuing a risky strategy, no bailout would occur. If, however, banks coordinated in taking large risks, the probability of a bailout in bad states would increase. Currency mismatches and maturity mismatches are examples of such risks that are correlated across banks. Furthermore, bailouts focused on financial institutions that are "interlinked" (e.g., AIG) would generate incentives for banks to create more linkages (e.g., through credit default swaps) and to hide those linkages from the regulators.

Consequently, Piazzesi concluded that a policy focused on bailing out banks that were systemically important or interlinked would create more risk taking and more interlinkages. Instead, she proposed, it was better to focus on Chapter 11 alternatives of dealing with failing banks.

Ronald McKinnon suggested that to the extent that the definition of systemic risk was hindered by a lack of transparency in the interbank market, one solution could be to require that banks publish their interbank order book electronically. John Taylor commented that for the overnight interbank market, such a procedure was already operational and could be adopted by the Fed.

Kimberly Summe asked about the precise channels through which a bank was incentivized to take certain actions as a result of an expectation to be bailed out. Monika Piazzesi responded that if a failing institution survived following a bailout, agents would not fully internalize the risk of failure. This would lead to a mispricing of risk and excessive risk taking.

Jonathan Berk suggested that since systemic risk was endogenous, it may be an impossible endeavor to search for a precise definition. Taylor, however, disagreed with this assessment. There exist data—used, for example, by Craig Furfine and Darrell Duffie—that allow the estimation of bank reaction functions at any point in time.

Robert Hall argued that credit spreads, implied default probabilities, and stock prices already provide a good measure of financial vulnerability. This measure of financial vulnerability is important to take into account when deciding on policy. The LTCM and Russia crises, for example, occurred during times of low financial vulnerability. Consequently, the knock-on effects were limited. During the recent financial crisis, however, Baa corporate over Treasury spreads were 400 bps higher than normal, signaling extreme vulnerability. Hall concluded that given this environment of high vulnerability, he was more sympathetic to the bailout decisions that were made.

Paul Kupiec commented that some countries, including Austria and Mexico, had very good overnight bank lending data and models. These are network models and are used to determine banks' exposures. Kupiec argued that without considering the reaction functions of banks, just by looking at the spot function of interconnectedness, the risk of default will be underestimated.

James McAndrews mentioned that the New York Fed regularly works with Federal Funds data to analyze financial vulnerability. Recent research by Afonso et al. and others has shown that following the Lehman bankruptcy, there was little reaction in the Federal Funds market. McAndrews argued that a bank's reaction function is something that is very hard to predict. This is epitomized by the fact that none of the thirty top creditors of Lehman failed while the Reserve Primary Fund, with only $700 million of Lehman papers, broke the buck. John Taylor commented that he believed there to be a potential to model and estimate bank reaction functions, by making models such as those considered by Ashcraft and Duffie operational.

In commenting on Kimberly Summe's paper, **Gary Stern** began by outlining two key policy objectives for regulating the financial services industry. First, customers of financial services firms should be well served in terms of product choice, pricing, and product availability. Second, adequate protection of the taxpayer should be guaranteed. Stern commented that in recent years, policy has been more successful at achieving the former of the two objectives.

Stern agreed with Summe on the value of real-time analysis of the health of financial institutions as an input into regulation and supervision. In particular, he argued that this was possible since regulators were already on the premises of important financial institutions on a full-time basis. Furthermore, Stern agreed with Summe on the importance of focusing regulatory resources on systemically important institutions, shifting them away from institutions such as community banks.

Stern then discussed the issue of publicly identifying systemically important, too big to fail institutions. He argued against the constructive ambiguity approach advocated by people such as Paul Volcker and Jerry Corrigan. In particular, Stern voiced his concerns about the possibility of ever credibly developing and communicating constructive ambiguity. However, he also pointed out that clearly designating institutions as too big too fail would, *ceteris paribus*, lead to increased moral hazard and mispricing of risk. This mispricing of risk would cause significant resource misallocation.

Stern proposed that one way of addressing the problems of too big to fail was to shift supervisory efforts from prevention to preparation. More resources should be focused on thinking about how to limit the spillovers associated with failure in order to provide policy makers with a viable alternative to bailouts. Only when policy makers can credibly identify the potential systemic consequences of a failure can they confidently make a decision not to intervene.

Such preparation would involve a real-time analysis of all potentially systemic financial institutions. Regulators would identify each institution's major counterparties, exposures, and financing sources. Stern suggested that such an analysis would show that a number of the institutions considered do not currently represent a systemic risk. He recommended publicizing in real time which institutions were not considered systemically important, allowing policy makers to rule out any possible intervention. For those institutions for which the analysis would suggest a serious, systemic risk, Stern advocated the use of supervisory authority to reduce exposure to levels that policy makers can be comfortable with.

Finally, Stern addressed the importance of ensuring that creditors were aware of such a regime shift aimed at significantly reducing the likelihood of future bailouts. To the extent that this change can be credibly communicated, uninsured creditors will have an incentive to better understand and monitor the risk taking of financial institutions. This can reduce the mispricing of risk in the market, decrease resource misallocation, and consequently lower the likelihood of financial crises going forward.

David Skeel asked Summe whether she thought that the movement of Lehman CDS spreads leading up to Lehman's failure was driven by expectations of a bailout. Summe responded that in her view, CDS spreads were impacted by the fact that market participants were expecting a bailout or a possible merger with Bank of America or Barclays. She argued that such misperceptions by the market were further evidence for the need to publicly declare those institutions deemed systemically important.

Skeel also wanted to know whether Summe was sympathetic to insuring repos in a way similar to deposit insurance. Summe argued that for those institutions that relied on repos for financing on an overnight basis, repos were very different from a customer's deposit in a commercial bank. Rather than insuring repos, she suggested imposing penalties for settlement failures and tightening up some contractual problems that allowed institutions to walk away from repo relationships.

Franklin Edwards asked Stern which body or institution he envisioned to make the decision of classifying institutions as systemically important, especially given the political ramifications of such a decision. Furthermore, he questioned whether predesignating institutions as systemic would not also require systemic prudential regulation, since taxpayers needed to be protected from any losses involved in bailouts. Stern agreed that inclusion in the "systemically important" bucket was ambiguous. However, he argued that the market had already developed some way of addressing this issue, pointing to Moody's ratings that adjust for the probability of government protection. Furthermore, Stern agreed that his plan would not replace safety and soundness regulation, but argued that while necessary, such regulation was insufficient. Stern argued that a regulatory system that was pervasive enough to solve the problem of moral hazard would be extremely inefficient and undesirable.

Tom Jackson commented that there was a potentially unwarranted confluence between systemically important financial institutions and institutions that were too big to fail. The consequence of designating an institution as systemically important need not be to make them too big to fail and thus create a moral hazard problem. Instead, it could be to deal with the systemic consequences directly, without having to bail out creditors and owners. Stern agreed but argued that without further action, the threat to impose losses on the creditors was not credible.

Patrick Grady asked about the details of the rapid downsizing of the Lehman derivatives portfolio described by Summe. He wanted to know whether the drawdown was linear, and whether the thirty thousand remaining outstanding derivative contracts represented a disproportionately large fraction of the initial total derivative value. He also inquired about who the counterparties to the remaining outstanding contracts were. Summe stated that all her data were publicly available and came from Alvarez & Marsal, who were in the process of preparing a report to be submitted to the bankruptcy court. She was not aware of a precise estimate of the fraction of the initial $35 trillion of derivatives value that had been terminated, but she estimated it to be at least half, if not greater. Summe also explained that the remaining counterparties had most likely come to the conclusion that the ISDA Master Agreement did not require them to terminate their trades. Some of them were so far out of the money because of low interest rates that they did not want to terminate the trade. These usually were smaller counterparties, not other big Wall Street firms.

WHAT FINANCIAL FIRMS CAN DO

In commenting on Darrell Duffie's paper, **David Skeel** divided policies for dealing with failed financial institutions into two categories: (1) to restructure regulation in order to induce an earlier intervention and (2) to prevent institutions from becoming insolvent in the first place. The solution to the S&L crisis was in the former category, with regulators stepping in and shutting down troubled financial institutions. Skeel argued that while the Obama administration views its own proposals as addressing both (1) and (2), they really just institutionalized bailouts and thus should be considered as a member of category (2). Skeel argued that

Duffie's proposal also attempts to prevent failure rather than to force early failure.

Skeel then raised some questions about Duffie's proposal for distress-contingent convertible debt. He pointed out the similarities between the idea of distress-contingent debt and the early twentieth-century "income bonds," which had payments of interest dependent on the income level of the issuer. Skeel voiced his concerns about the application of automatic triggers for contingent debt. There were problems of strategic invocation if the triggers were manipulable or executable by a third party. In recent years, hedge funds have started to invoke the triggers of other bonds, holding up companies for a good return to the bondholders. While this may not be a major concern with Duffie's particular proposal, it is important to keep in mind. There are also uncertainties about the accuracy of the measure, and the possibility of managers of financial institutions manipulating the triggers in a way similar to their current manipulation of capital. More generally, Skeel pointed out that following the introduction of contingent debt, players higher up the capital structure may have less incentive to monitor.

Skeel also addressed the proposal for mandatory rights offerings. In addition to the concerns mentioned by Duffie, he highlighted another roadblock to such rights offerings. Skeel reviewed the government's handling of the Bear Stearns failure, in which equity holders but not debt holders took a hit. This made it very difficult for any firm to raise money through issuing equity.

Skeel was also concerned whether the current proposals would be effective in a systemic crisis, since they did not address issues such as possible runs on the repo market.

Consequently, he argued, the resolution decision remains crucial—even if the proposals did work in most instances, there will always be situations in which institutions fail. Skeel emphasized that in these situations bankruptcy was superior to a new resolution process.

An important issue with the bankruptcy process is whether to preserve the current special treatment of derivatives and QFCs. Skeel argued that in his view there was a need for a stay on derivatives, at least in some circumstances. One approach could be to have a stay on derivatives in bankruptcy for SIFIs, but not for other institutions. While this would create a disincentive to conduct derivatives business with SIFIs, the resulting deconcentration of the derivatives market is desirable.

Jonathan Berk cautioned against putting certain ideas in place to solve a particular moral hazard problem, while assuming that moral hazard did not apply to the idea we put in place. In Duffie's proposal, everything depends on when the conversion will be triggered. Consequently institutions will do anything to avoid hitting the trigger. Berk argued that it was crucial to structure proposals to avoid this type of moral hazard. Duffie conceded that some concerns about moral hazard were warranted. Nevertheless he maintained that the current reliance on capital requirements already involved moral hazard on the decision to pull triggers for intervention with troubled financial institutions. However, while competing ideas often propose to change the level of the currently employed triggers (e.g., by increasing regulatory capital), his proposal would not involve increasing capital per se but would instead ensure that capital is available when most needed.

Vineer Bhansali argued that while very elegant, Duffie's proposal was similar to asking banks to buy CDSs on themselves. He asked how Duffie envisioned the pricing of these contingent bonds to proceed. Duffie responded that if enough such bonds became available, supply and demand would manage to price them correctly. He argued that pricing contingent debt should not per se be more complicated than pricing equity.

Paul Kupiec suggested that one of the key relevant issues not discussed so far related to tax policy, which encourages leverage through the interest tax shield. He suggested that maybe we needed to change the rules of the game with respect to taxation, rather than tampering with the already complicated rules relating to capital requirements. Duffie responded that research about why firms issue debt was not at all conclusive. Adverse selection may still encourage the issuance of debt, even without the tax incentive. However, he agreed that policy should not encourage firms to issue more debt than they otherwise would.

In commenting on Dick Herring's presentation, **Joe Grundfest** started by cautioning against overly optimistic expectations about the efficacy of even the most carefully drafted wind-down plans. He used an analogy (developed more fully in his chapter in this book) with prenuptial agreements to outline his concerns. As a practical matter, he argued that it was impossible to anticipate all the problems that may arise and that may require the implementation of a wind-down plan. To the degree that financial crises are almost by definition caused by unexpected problems, such "incomplete contracting problems" will prevail.

Furthermore, Grundfest argued, if unexpected circumstances arose, it was not unlikely that parties would like to change preexisting agreements.

Grundfest also argued that the preferred solution should always be to avoid litigation. Problems with the predictability of litigation outcomes further strengthened the case for structuring the financial system such that the risk of financial crises can be minimized. This could involve adjusting capital requirements, making organizations smaller so that they are not too big to fail, and having more rational portfolio diversification so that exposure to single sectors of the economy can be reduced. Herring agreed with this, but he responded that formulating wind-down plans should be considered as one way of restructuring businesses. Meeting the hurdles for a wind-down plan that the regulators and boards should impose would involve very substantial restructuring. Creating wind-down plans thus provides a way to rationalize the industrial structure.

Robert Hall argued that Herring's wind-down proposal gave too little attention to the correlation of risk taking across financial institutions. While the system can usually tolerate the failure of a single institution, recent bailouts were driven by a fear that all institutions were at risk, such that a single failure could precipitate the failure of many. Hall identified the trade in highly leveraged, highly volatile securities related to real estate as the primary cause of correlation among U.S. financial institutions. Herring argued in response that Continental Illinois was an example of a large bailout that was unrelated to real estate. He argued that what was needed was a tool that allowed policy makers not to engage in bailouts in response to the inevitable claims about spillover costs.

Michael Boskin commented on the problems arising from involving judges in the process of dealing with failing institutions. He argued that there was a generic risk of judges deciding to ignore important issues due to their view of the stakeholders involved or their political persuasion. He concluded that it was very important to ensure that the process of dealing with failure did not depend on the reliability of inherently unreliable institutions.

BANKRUPTCY VERSUS RESOLUTION AUTHORITY

In commenting on Bill Kroener's paper, **Chuck Morris** argued that how a failing firm should be resolved depends on whether its failure poses a systemic risk. In the absence of systemic risk, Morris argued, bankruptcy is a great process for handling failure. If systemic risk is present, however, we need to consider alternatives that explicitly target financial stability as a goal, as we do for banks and other depositories. Morris agreed with Kroener that the advantages of a resolution process are its speed, preservation of franchise value, and lower administrative costs, while a disadvantage is that it has less clear and predictable rules on creditor priorities. He noted that another important weakness of the current resolution approach mentioned by Kroener is that the process for making a systemic risk exception is essentially a political decision that is biased toward finding too much systemic risk and thus results in too many bailouts.

Morris concluded that the question is whether it would be best to refine the Bankruptcy Code to deal with systemic issues or to refine the resolution process so that it does not result in too many bailouts and overprotection of creditors. He argued that it would be best to refine the resolution process and then introduced the plan proposed by the Kansas City Fed. This plan, which is outlined in detail in chapter 10 of this book, aims to put together a realistic resolution process for dealing with the failure of systemic nonbank institutions.

Robert Hall commented that both the Kroener and the Morris proposals preserved a feature of the FDIC resolution process that was fundamentally broken, which is that it occurs too late. He argued that when reorganizing a bank while capital was still positive, there should always be some payout to shareholders. Action should be taken when banks are in danger of failing, not when they have already failed. Every time uninsured creditors take a haircut or the FDIC has to pay off on deposit insurance, something in the monitoring process has gone wrong. Morris agreed with Hall that banks are being closed too late. He asserted that there was a problem with the current way of using regulatory capital measures to determine when to close an institution. In particular, these capital ratios are only a lagging indicator of a bank's true capital position. Morris also mentioned that the current rules make it difficult to require banks to raise more capital when they are meeting the regulatory requirements.

James VanHorne remarked that giving short-term claims higher priority would discourage the stretching out of the maturity structure, increasing the risk of a crisis at maturity. In addition, placing a judicial review process in place is bound to delay the resolution process, since agents would want to preserve their option value by delaying the process as much as possible. Morris agreed that the judicial review process could cause delays, but he argued that when you are taking someone's property, you have to have some process for judicial recourse.

Paul Kupiec mentioned that the regulatory capital of many closed banks was positive, yet the loss rates were substantial. Consequently, accounting rules do not provide reasonable fair values for institutions. In terms of prompt corrective action, it is hard to argue that it is working very well at the moment; but during the 1990s, there were examples of prompt corrective actions that seemed to have worked well. Hence, Kupiec concluded that the process can work well during normal times when banks have valuable franchises and there are profitable banks around to buy up other banks without direct regulatory intervention.

Frank Edwards recalled that John Taylor and Monika Piazzesi, on the one hand, had argued that it was extremely difficult to define systemically important institutions. Bill Kroener and Chuck Morris, on the other hand, seem to propose a special resolution procedure for systemically important institutions, despite not knowing who will be subject to it. He suggested that we should focus our energy on making the bankruptcy process more effective, rather than relying on a resolution process that applies to not yet specified institutions. Morris agreed that it is hard but noted that the bankruptcy process proposed in Tom Jackson's session also relied on defining systemically important institutions.

Kimberly Summe asked a question relating to the Obama administration's proposal to migrate OTC derivatives to exchanges. She wondered whether the proposed resolution authority would also address entities such as a poorly capitalized central clearinghouse. Morris responded that many of those institutions operated under bank charters (e.g., the

ICE Trust has a state member bank charter out of New York) and thus would be covered.

Michael Boskin commented that he considered it unwise to codify a consultation with the president in a resolution process.

In commenting on Tom Jackson's Chapter 11F proposal, **Peter Wallison** agreed on the superiority of the bankruptcy system over a resolution authority in dealing with failed institutions. He also supported the proposal to allow all financial institutions, not just predefined SIFIs, to use the proposed new Chapter 11F bankruptcy process.

Wallison questioned whether it was at all possible for failing nonbank financial institutions to cause systemic breakdown. In particular, he argued that he did not think the Lehman failure caused a systemic breakdown; as Summe had shown, none of the major counterparties of Lehman declared bankruptcy following Lehman's failure. Instead, Wallison suggested that Lehman was an example of a failing nonbank financial institution that did *not* cause systemic collapse. To the extent that the creation of a resolution authority for nonbank financial institutions was justified by possible systemic consequences of a collapse, there is little evidence for the need to create such an authority.

However, in Wallison's view, the collapse of Lehman *does* provide a prominent example of moral hazard generated by pervasive bailouts. After Bear Stearns was saved, it was rational for market participants to expect that all institutions larger than Bear would also be bailed out—such expectations were reflected in the low levels of Lehman CDS spreads in the months preceding its failure. This meant that creditors were taking too little precaution against the possibility that Lehman might fail, and they became complacent about monitoring their counterparty risk to Lehman.

Wallison was convinced that there was no possible way to know in advance when an institution is a SIFI; he argued that at best one can identify SIFIs when the context arises. Hence, it becomes unclear to the market which institutions would be taken over by the government under a new resolution authority and which would be allowed to fail. This would create pressure on the government to resolve any big or politically well-connected institutions that might fail. Such pressures would not be limited to financial institutions but could also include pressure to bail out institutions such as Chrysler and GM. The perception of likely bailouts will give large institutions a significant competitive advantage over small firms. In particular, the reduced default probability will lower the cost of capital for those institutions deemed too big to fail.

Wallison concluded by reviewing a set of recommendations agreed to by eleven of the fifteen members of the Pew Task Force of which he is a cochair. One of the recommendations was that it would be a bad idea to designate SIFIs in advance. Furthermore, the Task Force agreed that in the case of the failure of an institution, the default procedure should be bankruptcy. The group also agreed that the government should have the ability to take failed institutions out of the bankruptcy process and resolve them in an administrative way, but they could not reach consensus on the hurdles for such a procedure. Wallison preferred to require Congress to approve the funds necessary for an administrative resolution within ten business days, with the Fed providing financing in the meantime. Other members of the group preferred to call for a consultation between the president and the Treasury secretary before resolving institutions administratively.

Michael Wiseman agreed with Tom Jackson on the importance of having a single regime. The current system is too complicated with fifty states regulating insurance companies, the FDIC supervising banks, and bankruptcy procedures applying to bank holding companies. He emphasized the importance of ensuring that whatever regime was decided on would be adopted for all institutions, whether systemically important or not. Having a single regulator would also help enormously with coordinating policy internationally. Currently someone in another country looking at an insolvency of a U.S. firm has a hard time figuring out whom to deal with. Jackson agreed with this sentiment. He argued that the current system was fundamentally broken due to the large number of exceptions. Jackson also warned against a split system, in which some institutions would be resolved administratively and some through the bankruptcy process.

Ernest Patrikis added that holding companies are often little more than shells. Typically, they do not engage in business. They issue securities and perhaps, like AIG, guarantee subsidiaries. Patrikis argued that he thus regarded bank holding companies as universal banks with incorporated departments. The main activity of a holding company was to manage its subsidiaries. Hence, a holding company will have financial problems when its subsidiaries are not upstreaming sufficient dividends. It is necessary, therefore, to treat the holding company and its subsidiaries as a group under a single regime. Indeed, the Fed already supervises bank holding companies on a consolidated basis. Patrikis argued that the one issue that needed more attention was handling the failure of a global organization.

Following Kenneth Scott's remarks on criteria for evaluating failure resolution proposals (chap. 12), **John Taylor** asked Scott why he did not comment on the proposals of George Shultz, Paul Volcker, and Nick Brady to constrain financial institutions to some extent in order to prevent bailouts. Scott responded that his criteria were primarily intended as input into an evaluation of alternative resolution criteria. The proposals to constrain institutions, in contrast, are mainly focused on reducing the likelihood of failure (and potentially on simplifying the resolution procedure in the case of failure). Scott argued that although he could not foresee all the possible ramifications of such a change to the financial system, it was worth taking these ideas seriously.

Michael Boskin asked how it was possible to generalize our thinking about a resolution process from looking at individual failing institutions to considering a situation in which there is widespread insolvency. He also wanted to know how such a generalization was in tune with our current approach to the problem, which involves keeping interest rates low while hoping that the resulting profitability will help to restore the balance sheets of financial institutions. Scott commented that these were issues broad enough to merit another conference. He suggested, however, that one could distinguish between systemic risk as a contagion event (i.e., the domino knock-on story) and a more common situation in which a large external event impacts several institutions simultaneously. Scott suggested that when dealing with the former, the problem was a little more straightforward than when dealing with the latter. In addition, he argued that the analysis of the Lehman failure as a systemic contagion event was probably incorrect. Rather, it was a situation in which the boom and subsequent bust of house prices affected a large number of institutions.

COMMENTATORS

Jonathan B. Berk	A. P. Giannini Professor of Finance, Graduate School of Business, Stanford University
Vineer Bhansali	Managing Director and Head of Analytics for Portfolio Management, Newport Beach office, PIMCO
Michael J. Boskin	Senior fellow at the Hoover Institution and T. M. Friedman Professor of Economics, Stanford University
Franklin R. Edwards	Professor of Finance and Economics, Graduate School of Business and Arthur F. Burns Chair in Free and Competitive Enterprise, Columbia University
Patrick W. Grady	Founder, CEO and chairman, Rearden Commerce
Robert E. Hall	Robert and Carole McNeil Hoover Senior Fellow and Professor of Economics, Stanford University

Paul H. Kupiec — Associate Director of the Division of Insurance and Research, FDIC

James J. McAndrews — Senior Vice President, Money and Payments Studies Function, New York Federal Reserve Bank

Ronald I. McKinnon — William D. Eberle Professor of International Economics, Emeritus, Stanford University

Monika Piazzesi — Professor of Economics, Stanford University

Ernest T. Patrikis — Partner, White & Case, LLP

David Arthur Skeel — S. Samuel Arsht Professor of Corporate Law, University of Pennsylvania

Gary H. Stern — Former president, Federal Reserve Bank of Minneapolis and coauthor of Too Big to Fail: The Hazards of Bank Bailouts, Brookings Institution Press, 2004.

James C. VanHorne — A. P. Giannini Professor of Banking and Finance, Emeritus, Graduate School of Business, Stanford University

Peter J. Wallison — Arthur F. Burns Fellow in Financial Policy Studies, American Enterprise Institute

Michael M. Wiseman — Partner, Sullivan & Cromwell, LLP

A Conversation about Key Conclusions

GEORGE P. SHULTZ AND JOHN B. TAYLOR

WHAT ARE THE MAIN CONCLUSIONS and policy recommendations that emerge from this book? During the final session of the conference at which the chapters were presented, we discussed this question.

GPS: So, John, what would you say is the main conclusion from all this interesting analysis and discussion?

JBT: I am struck that so many issues raised here are not being addressed in the financial reform legislation now being considered by Congress. To put it bluntly, the legislation does not deal with the underlying causes of the financial crisis. So my top recommendation, based on what we learned here, would be for the Congress to return to the strategy it set out when it established the Financial Crisis Inquiry Commission (FCIC). *Let the FCIC complete its congressional mandate to investigate the causes of the financial crisis, explain the causes clearly to the American people, and then, only then, pass a reform plan designed to address these* causes. Nick Brady put it well: "You can't fix what you can't explain"; as did Kimberly Summe: "Let us hope that our policy makers choose not to legislate based on the caprice of public sentiment" but rather based on a sound assessment of the problem. I know that some say the crisis was too complex to explain in simple understandable terms, but the short background essay distributed by Ken Scott (which is the appendix to this book) suggests otherwise. What would be your main takeaway, George?

GPS: I am more convinced than ever that we have to *define and measure systemic risk operationally* if we are going to make any progress. Without an operational definition the bailout mentality will continue. I said this at the opening of the conference, and your essay and Monika Piazzesi's discussion of it confirmed this. I heard no one disagree. It's clear that we do not have a workable definition yet, despite much discussion and research over the past year. As Paul Volcker says, it is "a fuzzy concept." There is even disagreement about whether systemic risk in the recent crisis was due to government or the private sector. Defining and measuring systemic risk is a very big project and will require a concentrated effort by economists, lawyers, and financial market participants using data on loans and counterparty relationships and experience. That should be the priority now.

JBT: I agree, and my next point follows directly. Once systemic risk has been defined and measured clearly enough that it can be applied to a particular situation or firm, we should *develop a framework to deal with the systemic risk in ways other than bailout*. The framework should be highly credible, accountable, and transparent. The goal of the framework would be to determine whether a failing firm creates a systemic risk and, if so, what can be done about it. The framework would include the "preparation" proposal stressed by Gary Stern in his commentary. After a decision is made about how to deal with the situation, a detailed report should be published and released publicly. The report would explain why the decision was made, what alternatives to bailout were considered, and why they would or would not work. Such a framework will help government officials avoid the bailout.

GPS: I think the essays and the discussions represent substantial progress on finding a credible alternative to bailouts. The hours of work and frequent Saturday meetings of Ken Scott's Resolution Project have really paid off. Tom Jackson's Chapter 11F bankruptcy proposal shows us how to deal with many of the criticisms that skeptics had made about the slowness of bankruptcy or about the lack of financial expertise in the bankruptcy courts. In addition, Darrell Duffie explained how new types of contingent convertible debt and mandatory rights offerings can be deployed without "relying on the backstop of a government bailout." Peter Wallison and David Skeel were in agreement with Tom on bankruptcy, as were most who commented from the floor. So I say let's *write Chapter 11F into the law so that we have a credible alternative to bailouts in practice.* We can then be ready to use a rules-based bankruptcy process to allow financial firms to fail without causing financial disruption.

JBT: A recurring message here is that government should do no harm. This is the message of Paul Volcker when he warns that "[z]ero interest rates may be necessary at the moment, but they themselves lead to some dangerous possibilities in terms of breeding more speculative excesses." The reason that Tom Hoenig, Chuck Morris, and Ken Spong place so much emphasis on rules-based process in their Kansas City resolution plan is that they want to limit discretion and avoid the harm that can come from government interventions. As Bill Kroener has stressed, any new resolution process must prevent government agencies from interventions that could cause further panic. Let us not forget also that the sequence of events in the fall of 2008 suggests that government statements and interventions may well cause or exacerbate panics. My conclusion from all this is that we *recognize that government actions can cause panics, and set a high priority on preventing such action in financial reform legislation.*

GPS: Paul Volcker and Nick Brady argued strongly that we *constrain financial institutions that have access to Federal Reserve loans and federal guarantees more than other financial service organizations.* I agree. To be clear, we should not prevent innovative financial products, but neither should we allow financial structures to put taxpayer funds at risk because of such products. Separating proprietary trading from banking is one means of prevention, and this does not mean going back to Glass-Steagall and taking underwriting out of banks. Other financial institutions can establish separate "mutual funds" if they want to engage in such activity, and make clear that the funds are not guaranteed by the parent organization. As Nick Brady told us, "Safety and soundness is a categorical imperative.

If we don't start there, we'll find ourselves back in the same situation."

JBT: Various people mentioned how we need to improve regulation. We heard that regulators and supervisors can't keep up with rapid financial innovation or that they need more access to data. Dick Herring explained the complexity that arises in the international context as different countries have different regulations, which causes firms to change their behavior in ways that increase risk. Joe Grundfest points to the ways that government agencies can change laws and regulations retroactively, and how skilled lawyers can assist in creating this unpredictability. Conflicts of interest may also arise as people move in and out of government. In my view, the most important lesson is that we should *make regulations simpler and easier to administer*. A regulatory system cannot be based on complicated formulas. International cooperation is essential for reducing complexity, as Dick Herring has shown, and can be encouraged through the sharing of wind-down plans for firms operating across national regulatory agencies. As Nick Brady tells us, "Either the investment bankers will outwit the regulators, or the regulators will overreact."

GPS: *Remember that markets work.*

There is a narrative about the financial crisis that states the problem was a failure of the market system. That narrative is wrong. A long period of easy money led to excessive risk taking, and government pressure to make questionable loans triggered a housing bubble.

Yes, many financial institutions went wild, so let's fix the problem of financial institutions and hope that government will behave better in the future. Government should set the rules of the game, implement them credibly, and then get out of the way. The rules should be clearly stated and stable over time so that people understand them and make decisions based on them. Then we can let markets work.

JBT: Well, that's a good note to end on. So we have eight main concluding recommendations:

- Let the Financial Crisis Inquiry Commission complete its congressional mandate to investigate the causes of the financial crisis, explain the causes clearly to the American people, and then, only then, pass a reform plan.
- Define and measure systemic risk operationally.
- Develop a framework to deal with the systemic risk in ways other than bailout.
- Write Chapter 11F into the law so that we have a credible alternative to bailouts in practice.
- Recognize that government actions can cause panics, and set a high priority on preventing such actions in financial reform legislation.
- Constrain financial institutions that have access to Federal Reserve loans and federal guarantees more than other financial service organizations.
- Make regulations simpler and easier to administer.
- Remember that markets work.

APPENDIX

The Financial Crisis:
Causes and Lessons

KENNETH E. SCOTT

PART 1: THE CRISIS

The policy workshop that resulted in this book was preceded quite obviously by the events of the last several years and the enormous expenditures that resulted, as losses cascaded through the financial system (and beyond) and governments shifted those losses to taxpayers in an effort to combat a severe recession or worse. There is now agreement by all that this experience should not be repeated, but the first step is to understand how such huge losses were created. Can we institute some regulatory reforms that give us confidence that it will be prevented from happening again? Are there better ways to deal with the problem of financial institutions that are "too big to fail"?

A lot happened even before the perceived beginning of this crisis in 2007, so although the events are recent, I will review the period from 2001 to date, as part of our inquiry into the lessons to be learned. Much of it is probably familiar but worth revisiting.[1]

This necessarily simplified account is divided into three stages: first, a look at the key factors that led to the increasing riskiness of U.S. home mortgages; second, how those risks were transmitted as securities from U.S. housing lenders to institutional investors around the globe; and third, how those risks led to huge losses and created a credit crunch that moved the impact from the financial economy to the real economy. The goal is to lay a factual foundation for deriving the lessons that ought to be taken away from this very expensive experience.

Causation

Starting points in a historical account are somewhat arbitrary, but I will begin with the monetary policy followed by the Fed after the dot-com bust of 2000. Concerned about deflation and the Japanese stagnation of the 1990s, the Fed in 2001 abruptly lowered its target rate from 6.5 percent to under 2 percent, and then kept it at 1 percent until July 2004. The inflation rate over this period was around 2 percent, so the real rate of interest was negative. Needless to say, borrowing by both businesses and households was greatly stimulated.

For most households, the largest and most heavily debt-financed purchase they will ever make is to buy a house, so housing demand in particular is rate sensitive and responded strongly to the monetary stimulus. With plentiful and cheap liquidity, some of it also coming from the trade surplus investments of the Asian export economies, a sharp and steady house price appreciation (HPA) was the result. From the first quarter of 2001 to the first quarter of 2006, house prices increased on average 7.7 percent per year.

U.S. housing policy for some time has been to encourage home ownership, and a number of government agencies were formed to support housing finance. Government-sponsored enterprises, or GSEs (Fannie and Freddie), would insure residential mortgages that met their standards, for a fee. They would also buy the loans and put them into a pool, which could then be sold to private investors, thereby providing funds for additional purchases from banks and mortgage originators. The GSEs thus led the way for the development of a securitization market for conventional mortgages.

Congress from about 1977 on embarked on a program to expand mortgage lending to minorities and low and moderate income groups (LMIs). It began modestly with the Community Reinvestment Act, to prevent "redlining" of certain urban areas in which a bank was allegedly refusing to lend at all, but shifted in 1995 to measuring the volume of loans to LMI borrowers by banks and to establishing ever-growing "targets" (beginning at 30 percent and ultimately reaching 55 percent) for the percentage of "affordable housing" loans in all those bought or guaranteed by the GSEs. The goal was to push homeownership rates ever higher, and it involved pushing credit standards ever lower.

The process reached its zenith with the creation and promotion of "subprime" loans—loans to borrowers with poor credit scores (<660), multiple recent mortgage delinquencies or foreclosures, debt-service–to–income ratios (DSIs) of more than 50 percent, and the like. With a somewhat better credit score, the loans were called "Alt-A." Conventional down payment requirements of 20 percent dropped to as low as 3.5 percent for the GSEs (and to zero for some private originators), because significant down payments were viewed as "barriers" for low-income families.

New products were invented, to make mortgages more "affordable" for buyers with very limited income or resources, and for owners drawing out their equity in refinancing. Adjustable rate mortgages (ARMs) evolved into "hybrid" ARMs with low initial rates that would reset to market rates after two or three years, or "option" ARMs in which the buyer could chose the monthly payment. Interest-only (IO) loans involved no amortization of principal for a period of ten or fifteen years. Down payments could be borrowed through a second mortgage. Approval processes were automated; income statements were not verified, and such "no-doc" loans became commonplace.

The private sector entered subprime lending in a large way, selling the mortgages not only to the GSEs but into a burgeoning private securitization market. Private (non-GSE-backed) issuance of subprime and Alt-A securities amounted to around $560 billion in 2004, $830 billion in 2005, $840 billion in 2006, and $470 billion in 2007 (with only $4 billion in 2008), for a total of about $2.7 trillion.

Was all of this based on "predatory lending" or borrower fraud? No doubt one can find cases of misrepresentation on both sides, but that is not really the story. Both borrowers and lenders were expecting HPA to create some equity and enable a sale or refinance of the property when the resets hit, and under those circumstances they were both acting quite rationally without any need for deception. Borrowers, with little or no down payments (or remaining equity), had nothing much to lose financially. (Indeed, in about half the states, mortgage loans are legally nonrecourse; the buyer can walk away without any personal liability.) In effect, buyers were renting at the low initial rates, with an option to purchase at the reset date. Mortgage originators or lenders were not keeping the credit risk but selling it into investor pools, which I examine next.

Transmission

Mortgage securitization had begun simply, with bundling of conventional mortgages insured by a GSE into a pool, shares in which could be sold to investors as reasonably safe securities with the borrowers diversified across geographic regions and economies. But with the advent of an increasing volume of subprime mortgages, it became more complicated. Investors wanted higher returns, but they also wanted safety. (A first principle of finance theory is that they move in opposite directions, but put that point aside.) So, to simplify, claims on the cash flow of the residential mortgage-backed security pools (RMBS) were divided into "tranches" or levels of seniority, with those at the bottom first to take losses or shortfalls in payments and those at the top holding first claims viewed as quite secure, with relatively low contractual return entitlements and AAA ratings.

It was not difficult to sell the AAA tranches, but there was less demand for lower ratings. The solution: put the lower tranches into a new pool combined with the tranches of a hundred other pools, and create a new hierarchy of claims in a collateralized mortgage obligations (CMO) pool. Then repeat the process, and add in some other kinds of consumer debt (auto loans, credit card loans, student loans, etc.) and perhaps some commercial loans, and form a collateralized debt obligations (CDO) pool. The process of creating asset-backed securities (ABS) need not, and did not, stop there. It continued into CDO^2 pools (as illustrated in figure A.1) and structured investment vehicles (SIVs).

As you went down this securitization chain, the actual original loans underlying it all were becoming further and further removed from the securities held by investors. So to provide some reassurance and maintain the AAA ratings, various forms of "credit enhancement" were used. Municipal bond insurers ventured into insuring these new kinds of bonds; credit default swaps (CDS) were purchased to shift some credit risk off investors. Reliable estimates are hard to come by, but aggregate issuances (2004–2008) of mortgage-backed securitizations (MBSs), agency and private, may have amounted to something on the order of $9 trillion, bought up by institutional investors, to their current regret, all around the globe.

Losses

Six years or so of constantly accelerating HPA could not go on forever, as is true of any exponential function. The exact moment when a bubble will burst seems impossible to predict, but burst it did toward the end of 2006.

With house prices now falling and resets coming on line, subprime delinquencies began rising steeply, and the whole structure simply crumbled.

FIGURE A.1 Subprime Mortgage into AAA Credits

Matryoshka—Russian Doll: Multi-Layered Structured Credit Products

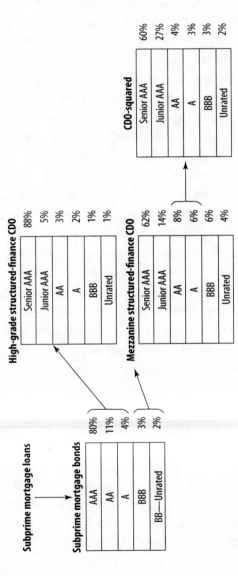

Note: CDO = collateralized debt obligation.
Sources: IMF staff estimates and IMF Global Financial Stability Report (IMFGFSR), April 2006, box 2.2., p. 60.

House values quickly fell below the amount of the mortgage debt (since there was no significant down payment cushion), and the embedded option was clearly out of the money. These "underwater" loans went into default and foreclosure, and the lower tranches of MBS pools incurred losses, while the upper tranches were obviously becoming more risky and hence declining in value.

This process inevitably affected subsequent pools down the chain, but by how much? In a given MBS pool, one could observe the defaults and at least in theory use the information on thousands of borrowers to try to model future performance. But for subsequent pools, the information on the underlying original loans was lacking, and the complexity made credible estimates of risks and losses nearly impossible.[2] The rating agencies knew trouble was coming and in 2007 started downgrading more and more ABS issues. Their value became indeterminate, and trading in them dried up, which eliminated external market prices, while their acceptability as collateral diminished accordingly.

What made the situation even worse was that there was poor disclosure of the positions held by the various investors in subprime loans and securities based on them—in particular, by commercial banks and investment banks, and some hedge funds. Those who had created these securities were among the largest holders. They were at the heart of the credit markets in the financial system, and they were with great reluctance announcing write-downs in their positions. The common belief was that both agency downgrades and bank write-downs were significantly lagging the actual loss of economic value, and hence there was a spreading concern with the solvency of counterparties among participants in the interbank and prime brokerage markets.

The growing appreciation of the seriousness of the problem throughout 2007 was followed by the dramatic failures of 2008, culminating in September: the GSEs (Fannie and Freddie), which owned or guaranteed $5.4 trillion of mortgage debt, were taken over and put into conservatorships on the 7th; Merrill Lynch was forced into acquisition by Bank of America on the 14th; Lehman filed for bankruptcy on the 15th; and the Fed made an $85 billion bailout loan to AIG on the 16th. On the 19th the Treasury Secretary announced a "bold approach" to "remove these illiquid assets that are . . . threatening our economy" and requested a massive appropriation to forestall a complete collapse; the effect on the market was immediate. Contrary to popular lore, the Lehman failure and refusal to bail it out was not a fatal trigger but only one in a series of signals of the mounting magnitude of losses. In the four weeks from Friday, September 12, 2008, just before the Lehman bankruptcy, through Friday, October 10, the S&P 500 fell by a huge 28 percent. But there was no decline in the first week of that period, from September 12 to September 19. The 28 percent decline occurred from September 19 to October 10.[3]

On October 1, the $700 billion TARP bill was signed into law. The initial interpretation of increasing credit stringency throughout 2007 and 2008 was that MBSs weren't trading because of a liquidity problem. The Fed constantly lowered its federal funds target rate (it is now close to 0), opened the discount window wide, and came up with a host of new lending facilities—but they still didn't trade. TARP was first conceived as a program to purchase MBSs off bank balance sheets, but it immediately ran into the valuation problem. So on October 14 the Treasury converted it into a program to inject $250 billion into bank equity, in an effort to address concerns among banks over counterparty solvency.

Not surprisingly, credit cutoffs and insolvency fears spread from the financial sector into the real economy around the world, financing for business and international trade plummeted, and a severe recession was well underway. But it is not the purpose of this appendix to examine the measures taken by various governments to deal with the consequences of the financial market crisis, and the effectiveness of the different remedies attempted. My focus is on the primary causes and the ideas of how to prevent its recurrence, not on all the devastating secondary effects.

PART 2: LESSONS

What were the critical mistakes and deficiencies in the account we have just reviewed? The media, participants, and politicians have put forth a host of favorite culprits, usually shifting blame to someone else: MBSs, rating agencies, excessively compensated CEOs, CDSs, deregulation, greed, mark-to-market accounting, predatory lenders, repeal of Glass-Steagall, hybrid ARMs, short selling of bank stocks, borrower fraud, dishonest mortgage brokers, inadequate consumer protection for financial products, and so on. It would take a lot more time than I have to try to deal with each of them, and it's probably unnecessary. Some are minor factors or even irrelevant to the cause of the crisis, whatever their independent merits, but I will try to take up the more salient in three broad categories: defects in financial products, defects in risk management, and defects in government policy.

Financial Products

CDSs, or derivatives in general, have received a lot of the blame for the crisis. But CDSs created none of the losses borne by subprime lenders or mortgage investors. They are an instrument for transferring, and thereby spreading, some of the risk, and they worked as designed. The CDSs in the Lehman failure, and in the GSEs and others, were all settled and paid promptly. (In addition, they served as a good measure of changing risk perceptions.) Of course, AIG wrote far too many customized CDSs on MBSs for too low a price, but that was a defect in risk judgment, not in the derivative instrument.

Subprime lending often took the form of hybrid loans, with low initial rates and resets after two or three years to market rates, and borrower income was ignored or not checked. In effect, mortgage lending became collateral based rather than borrower based. There is nothing intrinsically unsound about lending on collateral, but lending on collateral appreciation was the real problem. The Fed in 2008 reacted by prohibiting subprime loans without regard to ability to repay from income or net worth. Data show that the best predictors of default are the size of the down payment and credit history—factors that are politically sensitive and not addressed by the new rule.

The subprime loan problem was magnified by the securitization process, so should securitization be banned—for example, by permitting banks to issue covered bonds but not form ABS pools? Pools offer wide diversification across localities and borrower characteristics, raise capital and shift risk from the banking system to other institutional investors (as do CDSs). But in a recession, the correlation between mortgage loans and other forms of consumer credit proved much higher than anticipated, so the diversification benefit was modest.

The greater difficulty, as already noted, was that the complexity, created as tranches went down the line from the original RMBS pool into additional layers of pools, rendered the securities "toxic"—incapable of being reliably valued or sold. In my view, the remedy for that is clear, if challenging. It is not clear that such a degree of complexity is economically warranted or will revive. But to whatever extent securitization does revive, one change seems essential.

The SEC could by rule mandate detailed disclosure of the characteristics and performance of all loans in original pools and all tranches in subsequent ones, which would then be aggregated in a central data repository available to all. This would enable rating agencies (and others) to model the initial risk and adjust to monthly performance information. It would also facilitate evaluation of rating agency performance and the entry of new competitors who believed they had superior models. Various detailed proposals along these lines exist, but they are yet to be implemented.

Firm Risk Management

It is obvious that there was almost universal underestimation of the risks being incurred. Some of it seems related to agency costs and incentive problems, but it goes beyond that. Does the answer lie in regulation, or corporate governance changes, or in a learning process that has already occurred?

Mortgage originators (brokers or bank affiliates) retained very little credit risk on the loans they made; they just took in fees and sold on the loans. The agency problem is evident, and contractual arrangements tried to bound it with representations and warranties, holding periods, and put-back clauses. They didn't work very well, because they were poorly drafted and many of the brokers had very thin capital in relation to their loan volume. The GSEs automated their acceptance process to meet their constantly rising "targets," and they lost the ability to monitor underwriting effectively, while the banks formed pools in "bankruptcy-remote" entities and sold on the ownership of credit risk. Or so they believed, until they found themselves with large holdings on their own balance sheets, and, for reputational concerns, having to take back responsibility for some of their special purpose entities (SPEs).

The SPE accounting rules are now changed, acceptable mortgage originators now have to hold loans for longer periods and have higher capital margins, and the CEOs who oversaw these operations have now mostly lost their jobs and a great deal of their net worth. So some lessons have in fact already been learned, but why were they needed? There are several different theories.

One is that the top management in these giant financial institutions didn't understand what their underlings were doing. If that was the case, the compensation incentives to look at are not just those of the CEOs but those of the traders and lenders making the actual decisions. Their payouts should reflect the maturity or duration of their decisions' risk. To some extent that is already happening. But to focus attention on the level of compensation of top management (as opposed to the design of the incentive structure) panders to public anger while misidentifying the important issues.

Another is that deposit insurance and other features of the government safety net for banks (including bailouts), as well as the tax code, make debt cheaper and thereby subsidized leverage and led bank management to take excessive risk quite rationally, regardless of its compensation structure. To offset this, supervisors rely on prudential regulation and capital requirements, but both have significant limitations (to be explored later).

Still another is that neither the top management nor those below understood that there was a bubble rising, though the HPA information was there for all to see, nor did they appreciate its implications. If that was the case, measures such as requiring the board to oversee a chief risk officer, as has been suggested, may be of little help. It is hard to mandate foresight. Some urge that the solution is to have a government systemic risk regulator (SRR), and we'll turn to that idea later, too.

Government Policy and Regulation

What role did government regulation and policies play in this sorry tale? There is a lot of media talk of deregulation, or regulatory gaps or loopholes, being the cause. What were they, exactly? It is necessary to distinguish between regulatory authority and regulatory performance, and I will begin with regulatory authority. My contention is that in most instances there was ample existing authority for U.S. regulators to have addressed these issues, if they had perceived the need and acted on it.

Some point to the fact that derivatives were largely unregulated. Which ones, and what was the critical missing requirement? There are only two prospects that figured in my prior tale:

- MBSs/ABSs? They were not derivatives but securities, and always subject to regulation as such. I believe disclosure was inadequate in critical ways, but it was not because authority was lacking.
- CDSs? As noted, they were not a cause of losses in subprime mortgages or securities, but a mechanism to spread that risk. In doing so, they did create a potential for spillovers that sellers and buyers may have underestimated and inadequately hedged, but again, those are among the secondary effects that are beyond the scope of this chapter.

Some find a case for a new consolidated consumer financial protection agency, since that function is now divided in the United States among a number of agencies. If by consumer we mean household investors, MBSs/ABSs were bought almost entirely by large institutions, not retail investors. If we mean borrowers, the Fed and other banking agencies had extensive regulations already on the books—so extensive that probably no one would argue that they could not be made more comprehensible. But again, a lack of authority is not the issue.

Was there insufficient authority to regulate the issuers of all those subprime mortgages and securities? Almost all of them were made or funded by banks that were heavily regulated by the Fed or Office of the Comptroller of the Currency or FDIC—it is hard to find an absence of authority to have imposed higher credit standards there. The question is why the legal authority wasn't used more effectively.

Some believe the capital requirements for banks were too low, so they should be increased, perhaps on a progressive scale for larger institutions. Of course, *ex post* it is clear that capital was too low in any insolvent institution, by definition. But *ex ante*, how does one determine the proper amount to require? Under the Basel rules, a bank is "adequately capitalized" if it has a total risk-based capital ratio of at least 8 percent. The 8 percent number has no analytic foundation; it was simply the average ratio prevailing in the banking industry at the time. Banks are not "significantly undercapitalized" unless the ratio is below 6 percent, and not unless the ratio of tangible equity to total assets is below 2 percent are they viewed as "critically undercapitalized" in the United States (and subject to imminent closure if more capital is not immediately raised).

When assets are "risk adjusted" (downward) according to an elaborate schedule to determine a ratio denominator, it opens up opportunities for regulatory arbitrage. Of especial relevance to this analysis is the fact that residential mortgages under the Basel rules were awarded a risk weight of only 50 percent, thus lowering the capital charge. But if a bank sold a portfolio of its mortgages to an MBS pool and then acquired an equivalent amount of AAA securities, the risk weight dropped to 20 percent. For a bank "adequately capitalized" at 8 percent, that meant the bank was required to carry only 1.6 percent of capital against the credit risk. That would not sustain much of a market downturn.

Of course, one could institute different risk weights or larger capitalization numbers, and that is being pursued. But whatever the number, it rests ultimately on the value of the assets, and this crisis has shown how questionable some of those values can be. Banks have strong incentives to overstate asset values and understate losses. Capital requirements are dependent on the reliability of measurements of asset values, and banks (aided by politicians in both the United States and the European Union) have pushed successfully against the accounting rules that would require marking assets to current values and for accounting rules that would enable certain assets to be carried at historical cost despite subsequent adverse economic developments.

That renders reported capital ratios a very flawed indicator of economic risk and potential insolvency. A study of the 123 U.S. banks that failed in 2008 and the first three quarters of 2009 found that, two quarters before the takeover, they had a median total risk-based capital ratio of 7 percent (and an average of 9.4 percent), and that there was no statistically significant relationship between reported capital ratios and the losses to the Insurance Fund that the FDIC estimated at the time of closure. Increased capital requirements and leverage limits might serve to reduce failures to some degree, but no one should underestimate the ability of banks to determine their own risk levels whatever the regulations say.

That leads us back to government policy and regulatory performance. This entire process began with very loose monetary policy, maintained for several years as the economy recovered from the dot-com bust, which created the foundation for a housing boom. It was fed by a government housing policy that continually pushed for lower lending standards to turn renters into homeowners, even those whose marginal financial condition meant they could safely afford only rentals. This was, in my view, probably the most important single factor in the whole debacle. It came about because Congress desired to subsidize particular groups without direct on-budget expenditures but indirectly through regulation and guarantees, thereby denying the existence of any subsidization—until the whole scheme collapsed. And the benefit, to be compared to the enormous cost? The household homeownership percentage rose from 67.5 percent at the beginning of 2001 to 68.4 percent at the beginning of 2007; it is now back down to 67.6 percent.

Systemic Risk Regulation

Why did bank regulators and monetary policy makers and the congressional housing committees get it so disastrously wrong? The currently popular answer is that what we needed was a Systemic Risk Regulator (SRR and "macro-prudential" regulation. The SRR would collect vast amounts of information—rather unspecified—from very many quite large, "systemically important" firms—also unspecified. The SRR might issue advice or warnings about perceived developing risks or concentrations to financial firms and their regulators, which seems to be the EU approach. But in the Obama administration's version, it would have sweeping powers to force those firms to alter their operations in some way, to prevent the occurrence of an event that might lead to systemic collapse. So there are two separate, and separable, parts of the concept, which we should examine. The U.S. debate often seems to be about who or what would be the SRR, but that is probably not of great interest outside the Beltway, and I will put that question aside. How would it work?

It is certainly feasible to impose extensive reporting requirements, if you know what you want and are indifferent to costs, on firms that you have somehow picked out as the ones that are "systemically important." And I agree with the proposition that the individual participants in this meltdown did not have sufficient information across various products about the holdings of others to help them assess the correlations and risk of their own positions and those of potential counterparties, assuming they were given access to such detail. But there are two reservations:

- I know of no macromodels of systemic risk that incorporate financial intermediaries. When the SRR gets all that required information, how can it reliably analyze it? How can it know that it has even gotten the right information?
- Without a tested model and a fair degree of certitude, how does the SRR (in the strong version) successfully order those large systemically important firms to change their business operations or their financial structure? It is safe to predict that they would exert political counterpressure. Regulatory agencies in the past (and present) in the United States have not been particularly bold in going counter to congressional desires.

At a more basic level, is the real problem just one of information? What was the essential information that was not available to the Fed and bank regulators that would have led them to have forestalled the present crisis? The fundamental information about HPA, declining lending standards, and the growth of opaque MBS-based securitization was no secret. In hindsight, of course, it all becomes clear. But at the time, with a very few exceptions, it was disregarded by everyone—GSEs, Wall Street CEOs, bank regulators, members of Congress.

To my mind, lack of power and authority to regulate has not been the heart of the problem; lack of foresight and judgment about the unexpected is. Regulators, even an SRR, are no more endowed with superior foresight on taking office than others. And that is not intended as a criticism of individuals. The state of economic theory and knowledge about the occurrence of systemic risk does not match the lofty goal of saying we are going to prevent it from happening.

Twenty years ago, to deal with the U.S. S&L collapse, the administration put through legislation to pay the bill (a mere $150 billion) and, of course, provide new regulation. The then Treasury secretary testified that "[t]wo watchwords guided us as we prepared a plan to solve the problem—*never again.*" And naturally politicians are saying the same thing again today, while repeating some of the same errors in their control of the FHA and its exploding volume of government guarantees for mortgage loans. (Its capital is now down to 0.53 percent, which would be terminally undercapitalized for a private bank.)

I would suggest that we not count entirely on preventing major financial failures from happening again, in a manner no one now foresees. A good part of our thinking and efforts should be directed toward better methods of resolving such failures when they do occur. The whole exercise is how to allocate the losses, not to taxpayers but to private participants in the failed firm, in a way consistent with maintaining incentives for market discipline while minimizing to the extent possible spillover costs. That is the topic, and the reason, for this book and its preceding workshop.

Notes

1. This essay is adapted from the opening address at a conference on "The Financial Market Crisis: Causes, Remedies, and Prevention" held by the Institute for Monetary and Financial Stability, Goethe University Frankfurt, under the auspices of the Federal Minister of Finance and Deutsche Bundesbank, October 22–23, 2009.

2. See K. Scott and J. Taylor, "Why Toxic Assets Are So Hard to Clean Up," *Wall Street Journal*, July 20, 2009, p. A13.

3. See John B. Taylor and Akila Weerapana, *Principles of Economics*, 6th ed. (Boston: Houghton Mifflin, 2009), 486.

About the Authors

Nicholas F. Brady, former U.S. Treasury secretary, is currently chairman of Darby Overseas Investments Ltd. and a partner in Holowesko Partners Ltd. He was senior partner at the Wall Street investment banking firm Dillon, Read & Co. Inc. for nearly two decades and also served as chairman of Purolator Inc., a Fortune 500 company. At the Treasury, Brady designed and implemented a successful strategy (which came to be known as the Brady Plan) to resolve the Latin American debt crisis. He has served on the boards of a number of companies and is currently chairman of Franklin Templeton Investment Funds and director of Hess Corporation and Weatherford International Ltd. He received his BA from Yale University (1952) and his MBA from Harvard University (1954).

Darrell Duffie is the Dean Witter Distinguished Professor in Finance at the Graduate School of Business, Stanford University, where he has been a member of the faculty since receiving his PhD at Stanford in 1984. His recent research focuses on asset pricing, credit risk, capital markets, and over-the-counter markets. Among other positions, he is president of the American Finance Association, a fellow and member of the Council of the Econometric Society, a research associate of the National Bureau of Economic Research, and a fellow of the American Academy of Arts and Sciences. He

313

is currently on the editorial boards of *Econometrica* and the *Journal of Financial Economics*, among other journals.

Joseph A. Grundfest is the W. A. Franke Professor of Law and Business at the Stanford Law School and a nationally prominent expert on capital markets, corporate governance, and securities litigation. He founded the award-winning Stanford Securities Class Action Clearinghouse, which provides detailed, online information about the prosecution, defense, and settlement of federal class action securities fraud litigation. He also launched Stanford Law School's executive education programs and continues to codirect Directors' College, the nation's leading venue for the continuing professional education of directors of publicly traded corporations. He also codirects the Rock Center for Corporate Governance, as well as the Stanford Program in Law, Economics, and Business. Before joining the Stanford Law School faculty in 1990, he was a commissioner of the Securities and Exchange Commission and served on the staff of the President's Council of Economic Advisers as counsel and senior economist for legal and regulatory matters.

Richard J. Herring is the Jacob Safra Professor of International Banking and a professor of finance at the Wharton School, University of Pennsylvania, and founding director of the Wharton Financial Institutions Center. From 2000 to 2006, he served as the director of the Lauder Institute of International Management Studies; from 1995 to 2000, he served as vice dean and director of Wharton's undergraduate division. During 2006, he was a Professorial Fellow at the Reserve Bank of New Zealand and Victoria

University; during 2009, he was the Metzler Bank Fellow at Johann Goethe University in Frankfurt. He is cochair of the Shadow Financial Regulatory Committee and executive director of the Financial Economists Roundtable, the Advisory Board of the European Banking Report in Rome, and the Institute for Financial Studies in Frankfurt. He previously served as cochair of the Multinational Banking seminar and was a fellow of the World Economic Forum in Davos and a member of the Group of 30 task force on the reinsurance industry. He received his undergraduate degree from Oberlin College in 1968 and his PhD from Princeton University in 1973.

Thomas M. Hoenig is president and chief executive officer of the Federal Reserve Bank of Kansas City. He assumed the role of president on October 1, 1991. He is the longest serving of the twelve current regional Federal Reserve Bank presidents and is also the longest-tenured member of the System's Federal Open Market Committee. He joined the bank in 1973 and was its senior officer in banking supervision during one of the most tumultuous periods in the history of the region's financial institutions, the banking crisis of the 1980s. At that time, he was involved with nearly 350 banks that either failed or received assistance. During the recent financial crisis, he has been especially vocal about the regulation of the financial industry, the need for addressing so-called "too big to fail" institutions, and the role of monetary policy. He speaks often on banking and monetary policy issues as well as on the structure, history, and role of the Federal Reserve System. He received his doctorate in economics from Iowa State University.

Thomas H. Jackson, Distinguished University Professor at the University of Rochester, served as president of the university from 1994 to 2005. Before he became Rochester's ninth president, Jackson was vice president and provost of the University of Virginia, which he first joined in 1988 as dean of Virginia's School of Law. He had been professor of law at Harvard from 1986 to 1988 and served on the Stanford University faculty from 1977 to 1986. A 1972 graduate of Williams College, Jackson earned his law degree from Yale in 1975. He first clerked for U.S. District Court judge Marvin E. Frankel in New York in 1975–76 and then for Supreme Court justice (later chief justice) William H. Rehnquist in 1976–77. The author of bankruptcy and commercial law texts used in law schools across the country, he served as Special Master for the U.S. Supreme Court in a dispute involving every state in the country over the disposition of unclaimed dividends held by brokerage houses.

William F. Kroener III is counsel at Sullivan & Cromwell LLP. He served as general counsel of the Federal Deposit Insurance Corporation from 1995 to 2006. His law practice focuses on the supervision and regulation of banks and other regulated financial institutions and their advisers. He currently serves as cochair of the American Bar Association Task Force on Financial Markets Regulatory Reform, vice chair of the Banking Law Committee of the American Bar Association Business Law Section, a member of the Executive Council of the Banking Law Committee of the Federal Bar Association, an advisory member of the Financial Institutions Committee of the Business Law Section of the State Bar of California, and a member of the Regulatory Appeals

Committee of the Dubai Financial Services Authority. He speaks and writes regularly on financial regulatory topics and has taught as an adjunct professor at Stanford, George Washington, and American University law schools. He has served on the Stanford Law School Board of Visitors and as national chair of the Stanford Law Fund. He is a graduate of Yale and Stanford law and business schools.

Charles S. Morris is vice president and economist in the Supervision and Risk Management Division's Banking Research Department at the Federal Reserve Bank of Kansas City. He conducts research on banking and financial markets with an emphasis on regulatory and policy issues. He also supports the bank's senior management by preparing analyses, briefings, and recommendations on regulatory and policy issues. He has conducted research in a variety of areas, including banking, financial instruments, general finance, rural finance, and macroeconomics. He joined the bank as an economist in the Economic Research Department in 1983. He was promoted to assistant vice president and economist in 1992 and to vice president and economist in 1997. In 1999, he left the research area and led several business areas of the bank before returning to a research role in 2008 as head of the Banking Research Department. He holds a BA, an MA, and a PhD in economics from the University of California, Los Angeles.

Kenneth E. Scott, the Parsons Professor Emeritus of Law and Business at Stanford Law School and a Hoover Institution senior research fellow, is a leading scholar in the fields of corporate finance reform and corporate governance who has written extensively on federal banking regulation. His current research concentrates on legislative and policy developments related to the current financial crisis, comparative corporate governance, and financial regulation. He has extensive consulting experience, including work for the World Bank, the Federal Deposit Insurance Corporation, the Resolution Trust Corporation, and, most recently, the National Association of Securities Dealers. He is also a member of the Shadow Financial Regulatory Committee, the Financial Economists Roundtable, and the State Bar of California's Financial Institutions Committee. Before joining the Stanford Law School faculty in 1968, he served as general counsel to the Federal Home Loan Bank Board and as chief deputy savings and loan commissioner of California and worked in private practice in New York with Sullivan & Cromwell.

George P. Shultz is the Thomas W. and Susan B. Ford Distinguished Fellow at the Hoover Institution. Among many other senior government and private sector roles, he served as secretary of labor in 1969 and 1970, as director of the Office of Management and Budget from 1970 to 1972, and as secretary of the Treasury from 1972 to 1974. He was sworn in on July 16, 1982, as the sixtieth U.S. secretary of state and served until January 20, 1989. In January 1989, he was awarded the Medal of Freedom, the nation's highest civilian honor. Shultz rejoined Stanford University in 1989 as the Jack Steel Parker Professor of International Economics at the Graduate School of Business and as a distinguished fellow at the Hoover Institution. He is the Advisory Council chair of the Precourt Institute for Energy Efficiency at Stanford and chair of the

Energy Initiative External Advisory Board at the Massachusetts Institute of Technology. He is the chairman of Governor Schwarzenegger's Council of Economic Advisers and a distinguished fellow of the American Economic Association.

Kenneth Spong is a Senior Economist in the Banking Research Department at the Federal Reserve Bank of Kansas City. He has been with the Federal Reserve since 1973 and is engaged in research on a variety of topics related to the regulation, supervision, and performance of banks and other financial institutions. This research includes corporate governance and the ownership and management structure of banks, large banks and too-big-to-fail concerns, small business lending, interstate banking, and home financing and homeownership issues among low-income households. In addition, he has written a book on bank regulation, *Banking Regulation: Its Purposes, Implementation, and Effects,* which is now in its fifth edition. He has an MA in economics from the University of Chicago and a BA in mathematics and economics from the University of Kansas.

Johannes Stroebel is a PhD student in economics at Stanford University, where he is the Dr. Carl M. and Carolyn C. Franklin fellow. He is a member of the Working Group on National and Global Economic Markets at the Hoover Institution. His research focuses on the U.S. housing market and on analyzing government responses to the recent financial crisis. His recent paper "Foreclosure and Bankruptcy: Policy Conclusions from the Current Crisis" with Theresa Kuchler analyzes the interaction between household decisions to declare Chapter 7 bankruptcy and to enter into foreclosure using individual state data in the United States. He holds a BA in philosophy, politics, and economics from Merton College, Oxford.

Kimberly Anne Summe is the general counsel of Partner Fund Management, a San Francisco–based investment adviser. She is also an adjunct professor at the Stanford Law School. Summe was previously a managing director in prime brokerage at Lehman Brothers; prior to that she served as general counsel of the International Swaps and Derivatives Association. In the latter capacity, Summe was responsible for developing industry standard contracts for the over-the-counter derivatives industry, as well as addressing regulatory issues in dozens of jurisdictions. She was a banking associate at Pillsbury Winthrop and at Sullivan & Cromwell and has published more than a dozen articles on various banking and securities law topics. Summe's interest in the capital markets has led her to establish a nonprofit organization, Paladin Connect, that offers the pro bono services of leading global law firms to microfinance institutions. Summe received her law degrees from the University of Chicago and Cambridge University and a postgraduate degree from the London School of Economics.

John B. Taylor is the Bowen H. and Janice Arthur McCoy Senior Fellow at the Hoover Institution and the Mary and Robert Raymond Professor of Economics at Stanford University. Among other roles in public service, he served as a member of the President's Council of Economic Advisers from 1989 to 1991 and as undersecretary of the Treasury for international affairs from 2001 to 2005. He is currently a member of the California Governor's Council of Economic Advisers. His new book *Getting Off Track: How Government Actions and Interventions Caused, Prolonged, and Worsened the Financial Crisis* is an empirical analysis of the recent financial crisis. He also recently coedited *The Road Ahead for the Fed* in which twelve leading experts, himself included, examine and debate proposals for financial reform and exit strategies from the financial crisis. Before joining the Stanford faculty in 1984, Taylor held positions as a professor of economics at Princeton University and Columbia University. He received a BS in economics summa cum laude from Princeton and a PhD in economics from Stanford University in 1973.

Paul Volcker worked in the United States federal government for almost thirty years and served two terms as chairman of the Board of Governors of the Federal Reserve System from 1979 to 1987. He divided the earlier stages of his career between the Federal Reserve Bank of New York, the Treasury Department, and the Chase Manhattan Bank. He retired as chairman of Wolfensohn & Co. when it merged with Bankers Trust. From 1996 to1999, he headed a committee that determined existing dormant accounts and other assets in Swiss banks of victims of Nazi persecution. From 2000 to 2005, he served as chairman of the Board of Trustees of the International Accounting Standards Committee and headed a private Commission on the Public Service in 2003. He chaired the Independent Inquiry into the United Nations Oil-for-Food Program in 2004 and a panel of experts to review the operations of the Department of Institutional Integrity at the World Bank in 2005. In November 2008, President-elect Obama chose him to head the President's Economic Recovery Advisory Board. Educated at Princeton, Harvard, and the London School of Economics, he is a professor emeritus of international economic policy at Princeton University.

INDEX

LaVergne, TN USA
08 February 2010
172353LV00002B/2/P